W9-DHT-416

Alternative Approaches

to Capital Gains

Taxation

Studies of Government Finance
TITLES PUBLISHED

Alternative Approaches to Capital Gains Taxation

MARTIN DAVID

A background paper prepared for a conference
of experts at the Brookings Institution together
with a summary of the conference discussion

Studies of Government Finance

THE BROOKINGS INSTITUTION

WASHINGTON, D.C.

THE BROOKINGS INSTITUTION is an independent organization devoted to nonpartisan research, education, and publication in economics, government, foreign policy, and the social sciences generally. Its principal purposes are to aid in the development of sound public policies and to promote public understanding of issues of national importance.

The Institution was founded December 8, 1927, to merge the activities of the Institute for Government Research, founded in 1916, the Institute of Economics, founded in 1922, and the Robert Brookings Graduate School of Economics and Government, founded in 1924.

The general administration of the Institution is the responsibility of a self-perpetuating Board of Trustees. The trustees are likewise charged with maintaining the independence of the staff and fostering the most favorable conditions for creative research and education. The immediate direction of the policies, program, and staff of the Institution is vested in the President, assisted by an advisory council chosen from the staff of the Institution.

In publishing a study, the Institution presents it as a competent treatment of a subject worthy of public consideration. The interpretations and conclusions in such publications are those of the author or authors and do not purport to represent the views of the other staff members, officers, or trustees of the Brookings Institution.

BOARD OF TRUSTEES

Foreword

THE FEDERAL CAPITAL GAINS tax structure has remained virtually unchanged since 1942, when the present six-month holding period and 25 percent alternative tax rate on long-term gains were adopted. For many years, tax experts have argued the merits of the capital gains tax. To help clarify the issues in this important area of tax policy, a conference of experts was held at the Brookings Institution on May 17 and 18, 1966, to review the present tax treatment of capital gains and losses, and to evaluate the major alternatives. This volume contains the background study and a summary of the conference, both prepared by Martin David of the University of Wisconsin.

The reader should be reminded that capital gains taxation is highly controversial. The purpose of this volume is to explain the major issues so that proposals for revision may be better understood. However, it is very difficult to present conflicting points of view in a manner that will be satisfactory to all; thus, the author's presentation may not represent an interpretation and evaluation as it might have been prepared by others. For different points of view, the reader should refer to Chapter X, which summarizes the discussion at the experts' conference and to the extensive literature cited in the bibliography at the end of the volume.

The author is indebted to Roger F. Miller and Harold M. Groves, and members of the reading committee—Harvey E. Brazer, John Brittain, Dan Throop Smith, and Richard E. Slitor—for valuable comments and suggestions on earlier drafts of the manuscript. Mr. Smith wishes to be recorded as dissenting from the basic viewpoint of the author (particularly with regard to the definition of income for tax purposes) and from many of the conclusions in the study.

The author gratefully acknowledges the assistance of Toshiuko Otsuki and Jane Hornaday in the preparation of Chapter IV and of Joan Gamble for her aid in the typing of the manuscript. Mrs. Evelyn P. Fisher also assisted in the preparation of the statistical data and in checking the manuscript. Virginia C. Haaga edited the study and prepared the index.

This volume and the experts' conference were part of a special program of research and education on taxation and public expenditures, supervised by the National Committee on Government Finance and financed by a special grant from the Ford Foundation.

The views expressed here are those of the author and are not presented as the views of the National Committee on Government Finance or its Advisory Committee, or the staff members, officers, or trustees of the Brookings Institution or the Ford Foundation.

Kermit Gordon
President

April 1968
Washington, D.C.

Studies of Government Finance

Studies of Government Finance is a special program of research and education in taxation and government expenditures at the federal, state, and local levels. This program, which is supported by a special grant from the Ford Foundation, was undertaken and supervised by the National Committee on Government Finance appointed by the trustees of the Brookings Institution.

MEMBERS OF THE ADVISORY COMMITTEE

Contents

Text Tables

Text Figures

Appendix Tables

Appendix Figure

CHAPTER I

Introduction

THE TAX TREATMENT OF CAPITAL GAINS has been the subject of continuing controversy ever since income taxation was first introduced in the United States more than fifty years ago. This book undertakes to examine the arguments for and against preferential treatment of income received in this form, as well as to weigh the many, widely varying proposals for reform of the present tax. It also seeks to analyze the major issues that arise in connection with the taxation of capital gains and to provide some guidance to those who are interested in reform of the present tax system.

Major Elements in the Capital Gains Tax Formula

The tax law singles out a select group of transactions for special treatment,[1] the tax rate on gains from these transactions being only a fraction of that applicable to ordinary income. While the reduction in tax liability due to losses incurred in such transactions is generally limited, the reduction per dollar of loss may exceed the tax increment per dollar of gain.[2] Generally, losses incurred must be de-

---

[1] The structure of the law is discussed in Chap. II.

[2] This is because net long-term losses are sometimes deductible in full from other income items, while net long-term gains in excess of short-term losses augment taxable income by a fraction of the gain.

1

ducted from the gains before the capital gains tax is applied.[3]

The determination of the capital gains tax thus rests on (1) the definition of the favored transactions, (2) the definition of the offsetting transactions, and (3) the appropriate rate formula. For convenience, these elements are designated the capital gains tax base, the capital loss offset, and the capital gains tax rate, respectively. Clearly, the value of the tax saving to any taxpayer depends on both the extent to which his transactions fall within the area that receives favorable treatment and the nature of the rate formula. It is relatively easy to define a rate formula. But because a viable definition of transactions is far more difficult to achieve, litigation, legislative change, and the efficiency of auditing techniques have been continually modifying the status of those transactions that are not expressly defined in the law.[4]

Economic Impact of Capital Gains Taxation

In general, a different allocation of resources and a different institutional framework evolve in response to alternative tax structures. The present tax formula for capital gains leads to different allocations in labor, asset, and product markets than would one in which all transactions were taxed alike. To cite a rather obvious difference, the demand for the services of lawyers rises as taxpayers try to minimize their taxes by taking capital gains.

The effects of the capital gains tax on economic growth, efficient use of economic resources, and stabilization of the economy at full employment are of major importance for public policy.

Growth Effects

Capital gains taxation affects the rate of economic growth because it affects the level of real investment. It influences the demand for investment as well as the supply of financial securities.

On the demand side, the present capital gains tax increases the return on appreciating assets relative to that under a uniform tax sys-

---

[3] This is the case with transactions in capital assets. Other rules apply to business property.

[4] Stanley S. Surrey, "Definitional Problems in Capital Gains Taxation," in House Committee on Ways and Means, *Tax Revision Compendium* (1959), Vol. 2, pp. 1203-32

tem. The individual is offered an additional return for postponing consumption. Saving by households is higher in the aggregate because appreciation is taxed at preferential rates. Whether the resulting higher level of real investment is significant for the growth of the economy depends on the extent to which a lower level of saving by households would be a limiting factor in business real capital investment.

On the supply side, businesses respond to the higher demand for appreciating securities by increasing their rates of saving. Dividend payouts are lower, corporate retained earnings are higher, and real investment is financed more by internal corporate savings and less by new issues of stock. The value of the retained earnings of a corporation is reflected in the value of its securities on the market. The lower dividend payout caters to the preference of households for appreciating securities. Whether the resulting equilibrium is more favorable to real investment than is the equilibrium that would be established under a uniform tax system depends on the extent to which the smaller volume of new issues means higher costs of financing new ventures, and on the number of business investors who find their sources of funds rationed by an imperfect market for funds.

Since the present tax treatment of appreciating assets affects both the supply of and the demand for such assets, it affects the turnover of asset stocks as well as their price levels. Because the present system is likely to mean a higher rate of household saving relative to that under a uniform tax on income, it is also likely to mean a higher level of security prices. At the same time the "lock-in" effect associated with appreciated securities may amplify the fluctuation in stock prices. It has been hypothesized that the volume of securities offered for sale on the market during periods of generally rising prices will fall below what it would be under a tax system in which the timing of tax payment is not determined by the taxpayer. Thus an initial increase in prices due to strong demand could be magnified by a reduction in the supply of securities coming on the market. The importance of this effect of capital gains taxation has not been quantitatively determined.[5]

[5] See Harold M. Somers, "Reconsideration of the Capital Gains Tax," *National Tax Journal*, Vol. 13 (December 1960), pp. 304-09, and Raymond L. Richman, "A Comment," *National Tax Journal*, Vol. 14 (December 1961), pp. 402-04.

Efficiency Effects

The efficiency effects of capital gains taxation derive from tax-induced changes in the relative yields of alternative investments. Changes in yields influence the private allocation of resources among available opportunities. Investments resulting in capital gains have relatively higher after-tax yields than do those that pay current income. The capital assets definition under the present law thus induces shifts in the allocation of investment that may divert significant amounts of risk capital away from optimum uses. Investment is attracted to timber, real estate, iron and coal mining, and corporations that retain their earnings, at the expense of manufacturing and dividend-paying corporations.

In addition to its effect on the level of saving by businesses and households and on the allocation of investment among industries, the capital gains tax can affect the supply of labor and the real cost of the tax system. These two effects, however, are less important than the investment effects of the tax. The labor supply is affected, since the total tax burden and the marginal rates on additional hours of work are changed because of the special tax treatment of capital gains. It is not clear whether more or less labor resources are devoted to leisure activity under the present tax system than would be under a uniform system of income taxation, but the evidence seems to indicate that work incentive effects are not substantial.[6]

The cost of tax compliance is significantly greater under the capital gains tax system, since the taxpayer may buy additional after-tax income by purchasing legal and accounting services in order to minimize taxes. While the additional costs may not be large relative to the gross national product, they do represent the time and effort of able managerial and professional talent that could otherwise be used to enhance the productivity of the economy.

Stabilization Effects

The effect of the capital gains tax on efforts to stabilize the economy is two-fold:

[6] See George F. Break, "Income Taxes and Incentives to Work: An Empirical Study," *American Economic Review*, Vol. 47 (September 1957), pp. 529-49, and Robin Barlow, Harvey E. Brazer, and James N. Morgan, *Economic Behavior of the Affluent* (Brookings Institution, 1966).

1. It alters the dynamic response of the economy to exogenous changes in the level of demand. If dynamic behavior responses induce increased tax yields in time of inflationary pressures and reduced yields during periods of deflation, the nondiscretionary effects of the tax are beneficial. They are undesirable if the reverse is true.

2. In addition, the tax may inhibit appropriate discretionary responses by making it more difficult to forecast the behavior of the economy. Variability in the timing of asset sales under the present capital gains tax may lead sometimes to stabilizing responses in tax yields and sometimes to unstabilizing responses. If so, discretionary stabilization policy will be less effective than under a system where the taxpayer has less latitude in timing his tax payment. This may be termed the discretionary effect on stabilization.

There is little evidence concerning the direction and importance of these economic effects. The discussion that follows indicates areas where more evidence is needed, as well as the relationship between equity arguments for capital gains tax reform and the probable economic effects of the present tax system.

Major Issues

Throughout the history of the capital gains tax many arguments for and against the preferential treatment accorded capital gains in the Internal Revenue Code[7] have been advanced. The scope of the problems with which this study must deal is indicated by a quick survey of questions that have been raised.

Are capital gains income?

One of the major arguments against taxing capital gains is that they cannot properly be considered a part of taxable income. According to this view, taxes on capital gains are in the nature of a levy on capital that can be dissociated from the current income stream of the taxpayer. This theory suggests the analogy of a tree and its fruit. The fruit represents the annual income or proceeds and should be subject to tax; the tree cannot be pruned through taxation, for it will then ultimately yield smaller annual returns.

Others argue that gains should not be taxed because they are the

[7] Internal Revenue Code of 1954, as amended (Title 26 of the U.S. Code), referred to hereinafter as Internal Revenue Code.

result of nominal money increases in the value of property rights rather than real increases in those rights. Alternatively, gains may arise from fluctuations in the interest rate that cause fixed-payment contracts to be valued at a premium or at a discount. In this case, it is argued, gains should not be taxed, since they prevent the investor in a fixed-income contract from exchanging one contract for another and maintaining his former flow of income.[8]

While such arguments for excluding capital gains from the concept of taxable income are appealing, they cannot be reconciled with a widely accepted economic definition of income as the algebraic sum of an individual's consumption expenditures and the change in his net worth. Under such an accretion concept of income, capital gains appear to be essentially similar to any other form of receipt that may be disposed of by consumption expenditures or by increments to wealth. The only valid alternative would be to define taxable income in real terms and exempt from tax that portion of capital gains that is not associated with a change in the real purchasing power of the taxpayer.

Should capital gains be taxed currently, at realization, or at another time?

Even those who concede that capital gains are legitimately a part of income disagree about the appropriate timing of the tax payment. Unlike most other major forms of income, which are taxed on an accrual basis, capital gains are taxed only when they are realized through sale or other disposition of an investment. Accrual taxation, it is argued, would lead to inopportune liquidation of property rights as well as extremely difficult problems of tax accounting and valuation. Even taxation upon realization is opposed on the grounds that it locks in investment into particular stocks, bonds, and other types of property. Some have suggested that the lock-in effect could be eliminated by postponing tax payment until funds are removed from investment assets and are actually consumed. Those who favor taxing gains at accrual counter such arguments by stressing the inequity of such "roll-over," the cost to the government of deferred

[8] For an especially good discussion of the price and interest arguments for exempting gains from tax, see George F. Break, "On the Deductibility of Capital Losses Under the Income Tax," *Journal of Finance*, Vol. 7 (1952), pp. 214-29.

taxes, and instances where income is already taxed on accrual rather than on actual receipt or realization.

Should capital gains be subjected to progression?

Progression of tax rates creates a third and vexing problem for the taxation of capital gains. A large income in one year is taxed at higher rates than is an equal total of smaller incomes distributed over a longer period. The taxpayer who realizes gains on just a few sales in odd years is likely to pay higher taxes on those gains than is a taxpayer engaged in frequent transactions producing capital gains that can be spread over a longer period of time. The extent of this inequity is limited, however, by the 25 percent maximum rate applicable to capital gains. High-income taxpayers whose ordinary income is taxable at rates of 50 percent or more at the margin will not face increased progressivity from irregular realizations of capital gains. The problem of undue progression is not unique to capital gains taxation but arises with all types of income fluctuation. It can be argued, however, that capital gains and losses are among the most volatile elements of income and offer an extreme example of the need for income averaging.

Whether gains should be subjected to full progression or to some lesser tax increment is a question of the philosophy underlying rate progression. Progression could apply to short-term (annual) income, including transitory elements, or, alternatively, it could be applied to average income over a longer period. It is even possible that rates should be graduated according to the cumulative stream of income over a lifetime.

Should capital gains escape tax through gift or bequest at death?

Capital gains are taxed only when assets are sold or exchanged. Capital gains become exempt from tax if the appreciated asset is transferred after the taxpayer's death.[9] The effective zero tax rate on appreciation on property disposed of in this manner provides a tre-

---

[9] See Office of the Federal Register, National Archives and Records Service, General Services Administration, *Code of Federal Regulations: Title 26* (1967), Section 1.170-1 (c). Since the appreciated value of the property was never realized through sale or exchange, no taxable income accrues. (However, the full value of the asset is available for deduction as a charitable contribution.)

mendous incentive for the holding of property by persons with a short life expectancy.[10]

Should capital losses be fully or partially offset against ordinary income?

The timing of capital gains taxation permits the taxpayer to search the properties in his portfolio for those on which he wishes to realize gains or losses for tax accounting purposes in a particular tax year. If he selects only properties involving capital losses, the unlimited deduction of losses from income would permit him to offset tax liabilities on income from other sources. If he had unlimited opportunities to deduct losses from other income, the taxpayer could either average his income over a series of tax years or defer tax liability by consigning losses to early years and gains to later ones. It is argued that the resulting erosion of the tax base might mean serious revenue losses for the government. In addition, the deferral would result in inequity for those who did not hold appreciated assets. There has been a continuing controversy over the appropriate treatment of capital losses in a system that taxes capital gains at preferential rates.

How does capital gains taxation affect risk incentives and liquidity in capital markets?

Opponents of capital gains taxation suggest that it reduces the incentive to accept risk. They also contend that the liquidity of assets is reduced, since potential capital gains taxes create large transaction costs. The investor responds to these costs by reducing the turnover of his portfolio. A counter-argument stresses the relatively small role of tax considerations in the investment decision and the overriding importance of informed management in an uncertain market.

Organization of the Study

This book is the third major survey of problems in the taxation of capital gains in the United States since 1951.[11] While duplication

---

[10] See Charles C. Holt and John P. Shelton, "The Lock-In Effect of the Capital Gains Tax," *National Tax Journal*, Vol. 15 (December 1962), pp. 337-52.

[11] See Lawrence H. Seltzer, *The Nature and Tax Treatment of Capital Gains and Losses* (National Bureau of Economic Research, 1951), and U.S. Treasury Department, Tax Advisory Staff of the Secretary, *Federal Income Tax Treatment of Capital Gains and Losses* (1951).

cannot be avoided, I have tried to make this survey a complement to the earlier studies. Seltzer's monograph remains a monument of pertinent data that has no peers, while the Tax Advisory Staff study summarizes legislative history and reform proposals in a more succinct and comprehensive form than is attempted here.

In the chapters that follow, alternative approaches to capital gains taxation will be examined to determine what treatment is most desirable, considering both the equity of the tax structure and its effect on allocation, growth, and output. The provisions of the tax law are set forth in Chapter II, and examples of definitional problems and capricious treatment are given. The conceptual basis for a measure of taxable income is developed in Chapter III.

Chapter IV presents some basic statistical data on the capital gains tax in recent years and material for evaluating alternative amendments to the present capital gains tax.

In Chapter V, a general outline of reform proposals is presented. Limited amendments to the present structure are discussed in Chapter VI. Certain arbitrary aspects of the present law, which could be eliminated through a narrowing of the area eligible for capital gains, minor changes in the holding period, and changes in the treatment of capital losses, are also discussed in Chapter VI.

Proposals for taxing gains that are transferred by gift or bequest are presented in Chapter VII. Extension of the capital gains tax base to such transactions appears desirable from almost any point of view.

In Chapter VIII, proposals for eliminating preferential capital gains rates are discussed, together with schemes to minimize the tendency for higher rates to decrease the number of asset transactions via a lock-in effect.

Chapter IX analyzes roll-over and a reduction of capital gains tax rates as alternative devices for minimizing lock-in effects.

Chapter X summarizes the views expressed at a conference of experts held in May 1966 to discuss the issues in capital gains taxation and alternative methods of taxing capital gains. The conference revealed a continuing diversity of opinions on major issues.

CHAPTER II

The Law and Equity

THE UNITED STATES TAX LAW distinguishes three broad categories of receipts in excess of costs: exclusions, capital gains, and ordinary income. Exclusions are omitted entirely from the personal income tax base; capital gains are partially included in the tax base; and ordinary income is taxed in full at the statutory graduated rates, after exemptions and deductions.[1] Depending on his sources of income, any particular taxpayer may be taxed at the full rates implied by the legal schedules of rates or at some fraction thereof. The arguments for and against the particular exclusions in the present law cannot be discussed in detail here, but it is enough to note that there are such exclusions and that the present capital gains treatment of income is half way between that accorded to wages and salaries and that accorded to such income as unemployment compensation or interest on municipal bonds.

A wide variety of objectives may be imputed to the special treatment of gains and losses on capital assets available under Subchapter P of the Internal Revenue Code. Averaging income from volatile sources, stimulating real investment, encouraging risk-taking, stabilizing the capital markets, and encouraging the formation of new

[1] For information on other aspects of the tax structure and major issues in tax reform, see Harvey Brazer, *A Program for Federal Tax Revision,* Michigan Pamphlets, No. 28 (University of Michigan, Institute of Public Administration, 1960); Richard Goode, *The Individual Income Tax* (Brookings Institution, 1964); and Joseph A. Pechman, *Federal Tax Policy* (Brookings Institution, 1966).

10

enterprises have all been cited as potential benefits of the special treatment. The fact is, however, that the provisions in the law are blunt tools for shaping policy to meet these objectives. The definition of capital assets, the provisions for special tax rate treatment, and the enumeration of situations in which gains (or losses) on the exchange or sale of capital assets are to be recognized as income all fall far short of promoting the alleged objectives of capital gains taxation.

With certain exceptions, the law seems to make a purely semantic distinction. It distinguishes receipts resulting from transactions that involve the final disposition of an investment asset from recurrent profits earned from services, from trading, or from the use of capital. The former type of receipts is given special treatment; the latter is not. Key concepts developed in the law and the courts attempt to define "investment asset" and "final disposition." The period over which the asset has been held, the nature of the asset, and the occupation of the taxpayer have all been used in arriving at a definition of capital assets.

Even after a category of disposition of assets that should receive special treatment has been defined, there are practical problems because of difficulties in evaluating the amount of gain or loss, or a lack of cash to meet the tax liability, or involuntary dispositions of property, or situations in which the form of the law has been manipulated to produce results that controvert the spirit of the underlying distinction.

The legal fabric that distinguishes the tax treatment of gains and losses on capital assets from gains and losses on other assets is described below. Five areas of law are explained:

1. The capital assets definition
2. Exceptions to, and extensions of, that definition
3. The concepts surrounding final disposition and the recognition of gain
4. The basis for measuring gain or loss
5. Areas in which practical difficulties inhibit application of uniform rules or constructs

The third and fourth areas deal with problems that are not unique either to the taxation of capital gains or to the gain from investment.

Principles for measuring gain or loss and recognizing that gain or loss at final disposition would be required even if special tax treatment for capital gains were eliminated. These provisions must be carefully explicated, despite the seeming independence of the capital gains problem. Taxation of capital gains only when *legally recognized* creates the channel through which a large part of the appreciation on investment assets escapes taxation at death. Moreover, appending provisions for the special tax treatment of capital assets to principles for measuring and recognizing gains and losses produces some idiosyncrasies that must be considered in formulating an alternative tax treatment of capital assets. For these reasons, the following discussion begins by describing legal provisions affecting the recognition and measurement of gain. The dimensions of the capital gains tax provisions are outlined on pages 19-20. On pages 20-29 the general definitions of transactions eligible for special tax treatment are discussed, together with exceptions and extensions and other dimensions of the law; and rules for accounting categories of gain and loss are given on pages 29-33.

This chapter concludes with a discussion of the legislative intent of these various provisions and of the concepts of equity that will be used in evaluating the law in the subsequent analysis.

The Basis for Taxation of Property Transfers

Gains or losses on the sale or exchange of certain classes of property (specified in Subchapter P of the Internal Revenue Code) receive special tax treatment. The provisions for special capital gains taxation thus are part of a larger category that defines (1) types of property transfers, (2) when transfer is recognized for tax purposes, and (3) the consequences of any transfer for future tax computations. These concepts are pertinent to some of the major problems in capital gains taxation, such as the collapsible corporation, taxation of appreciation implicit in a decedent's estate, and deductibility of capital losses.

Gain on the sale or other disposition of an asset is generally recognized as income to the taxpayer. A few transactions are explicitly exempted from this general rule (for example, the exchange of property for property of like kind and the transfer of assets for shares of a corporation owned or controlled by the taxpayer).

The amount of gain or loss is determined by the difference in the value of money and property received and the adjusted basis of the property disposed of. Adjusted basis is a legal term that defines an origin or benchmark from which gain or loss can be measured. For many assets the adjusted basis is cost less depreciation taken. However, special rules establish the basis of assets that were not acquired in an arm's-length transaction. In one instance, a portion of recognized gain is exempt from inclusion in income; in many instances, losses may not be deducted from other income or gains.[2] The net effect of these rules for recognizing and determining the amount of gain and loss is that each transfer of property has two tax implications: gain or loss may be added algebraically to the adjusted gross income of the transferor, and a basis is established from which the transferee computes a subsequent gain or loss at the time he sells or disposes of the property.

Recognition of Gain or Loss

Figure 2-1 shows how various transfers of property affect the transferor and the transferee under the present law. Most transactions follow the left-most path: an arm's-length sale results in a recognized gain. The alternatives include some in which the tax liability can be deferred or avoided, particularly when the transferor is a corporation controlled by another taxpayer.

Nonrecognition of gain or loss occurs in four general situations:[3]

1. No gain or loss is recognized if there is no change in the economic circumstances of a taxpayer, but only a change in the form in which property is held (for example, an exchange of property for property of a like kind under the Internal Revenue Code, Section 1031; exchange of assets for shares in a newly formed corporation under Section 351; spin-offs, split-ups, or split-offs under Section 355).

2. No gain or loss to the transferor is recognized in the final disposition of assets by donation or bequest or by terminal liquidation of a corporation (under Sections 336 and 1002).[4]

3. No gain or loss is recognized when assets are exchanged for

---

[2] Gain on the sale of a residence by a person aged 65 or over is partially exempt. Losses on household goods are generally not deductible.

[3] A host of special rules and definitions describe exceptions, extensions, and qualifications to these general rules. References are to the Internal Revenue Code.

[4] Section 1002 specifies that gain or loss is to be recognized on sale or exchange. Dispositions by bequest are not mentioned.

FIGURE 2-1. Recognition of Gain or Loss on the Disposition of Assets, and Related Consequences

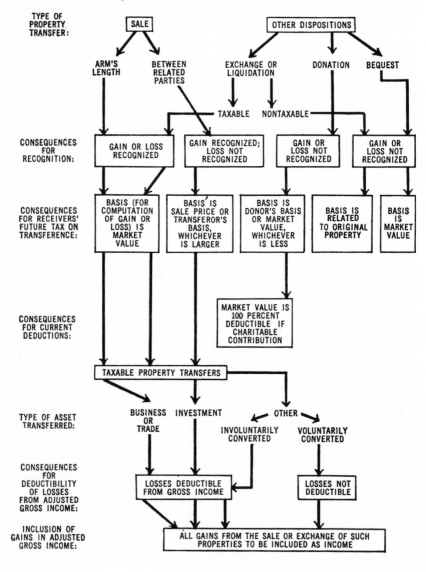

stock in certain types of corporate reorganization and expansion (Sections 354 and 1032).

4. Even when the payment reflects a disinterested valuation, losses on sales or exchanges of assets between closely related persons are not recognized (Section 267).

While the law is generally consistent with these principles, nonrecognition extends to other transfers. Moreover, the intent of the law is obscured by exceptions and additions to the Internal Revenue Code sections cited above.

Nonrecognition of gains on the exchange of like properties may have been motivated originally by a desire to refrain from applying the tax to gains or losses whose exact value could not readily be ascertained. Nonrecognition on exchanges also means that the tax is not assessed when the taxpayer has not increased his liquidity (as he does in a cash sale). The provision enables the taxpayer to "roll-over" his investments in any properties that are "held for productive use in trade or business or for investment . . ." (Section 1031). Securities and stock in trade are excluded. The provision thus permits the investor to exchange specific properties within a class, such as rental real estate, without recognizing gain or loss. However, investors who wish to liquidate properties of a certain class—those held for business or investment, such as an owner-managed enterprise—must recognize gain whether disposition is in the form of an outright sale or taxable exchange. In the latter situation, taxes are assessed despite valuation and liquidity problems. It is not altogether clear why nonrecognition should have been extended to exchange of like properties. Illiquidity or lack of market valuation does not usually obstruct the application of a tax. Perhaps Congress considered these investments sufficiently desirable that the owner's ability to hold them should not be impaired by payment of the tax. (It should be noted that Section 1033 of the Internal Revenue Code limits nonrecognition to those situations where the replacement property is "similar or related in service or use." That category has been more narrowly construed than the "like kind" stipulation of Section 1031).

Section 1034 specifies that a gain from the sale of a personal residence is not recognized when the proceeds of the sale are reinvested in another residence within one year, if the cost of the new home equals or exceeds the sale price of the old.[5] Similar provisions under Section 1033 extend roll-over to gains realized when property has been disposed of under circumstances over which the owner had no control (seizure, requisition, condemnation, or whole or partial destruction).

Nonrecognition has also been established to facilitate the creation of corporate entities. Nonrecognition of gain or loss on the exchange of assets for securities or on the division of assets in a given corporation among newly formed corporate entities appears quite appropriate. The consolidated balance sheets of the parties to the transaction look identical before and after the event. Casting existing economic interests into a new legal mold facilitates conduct of the business, yet does not constitute a final disposition of assets.

Once the corporate entity has been established, it is taxed independently of the individuals (or corporations) that are its stockholders. When assets are sold or disposed of, gain or loss is recognized as in the case of any other taxpayer so long as the corporation continues to exist. When the corporation is liquidated and its assets disposed of, gains are not recognized to the corporation, under the second rule given on page 13, above. Why the gains of a dissolving corporate entity should be favored relative to those of a continuing one is not clear. A tax on gains realized in liquidation could be treated as part of the income reported in the terminal tax return of the liquidating entity.

It is even less clear why in a similar situation the individual taxpayer should be exempt from income tax. Gain or loss on assets disposed of by bequest upon the taxpayer's death are not recognized, under Section 1002, which recognizes only gain on sale or exchange. Failure to recognize such gains, combined with a step-up of the basis of the asset to the heir, means that gains passing into the estate are never taxed as income.

The third general area of nonrecognition applies to the myriad sit-

---

[5] The gain is also not recognized if a taxpayer begins construction of a new home within a 12-month period and uses that home as his principal residence. The home must have been the principal residence of the owner for at least 12 months (a period longer than the holding period defining long-term capital assets). Persons aged 65 or older are partially exempted from including a gain on the sale of their principal residence as that from the sale of a capital asset. Any gain on a residence sold for less than $20,000 is entirely exempt. Gain on a residence sold for more than $20,000 is excluded from income in proportion to the ratio of $20,000 to the sales price. A taxpayer and his spouse may elect to make this exclusion only once.

uations in which corporations reorganize and merge through the exchange of stock (Section 354). While the creation of new corporate entities leaves the economic interests of the stockholders unchanged, the reorganization of corporate entities by mergers or the exchange of assets for stock generally alters these interests. Thus nonrecognition of gains in these transactions constitutes a roll-over. It is unlike the roll-over permitted the individual homeowner under Section 1034 or that allowed the businessman under Sections 1031 and 1033. Application of the tax in this situation may involve valuation and liquidity difficulties similar to those encountered in the exchange of properties; however, the nonrecognition is in no way restricted to reorganizations that preserve a continuity of economic interests and risks in a given enterprise. Thus nonrecognition of corporate gains and losses under Section 354 is the broadest and most flexible provision under which a taxpayer may alter his economic interests without recognition of any accrued gain or loss.[6]

Amount of Recognized Gain or Loss

When it has been determined that the transfer of property constitutes an appropriately taxed sale or exchange, the extent of taxable gain or the amount of deductible loss must be defined. (See Figure 2-1.) Generally all gains and all losses must be added algebraically to adjusted gross income. (The amount may subsequently be modified by applying the capital gains provisions.) However, opportunities for manipulating recognition of losses are circumscribed:

1. Section 165 of the Internal Revenue Code limits losses of individuals to those incurred in a trade or business, those incurred in a transaction entered into for profit, and those in excess of $100 associated with fire, theft, or other casualty. Losses resulting from the sale of assets associated with personal use and consumption are not deductible.

2. Losses on sales between related taxpayers (Section 267) or between a taxpayer and a corporation that he controls (Sections 165 [g] and 1239) may not be deducted from income, since such sales may not reflect a fair market price. Understatement of the value might afford the seller a reduction in tax at a high marginal rate, while the

---

[6] Since an individual may always form a corporation that he controls, the advantages of Section 354 accrue to individual taxpayers as well as to large corporate entities.

buyer ultimately would be taxed at a low rate, thereby avoiding a part of the taxes that would otherwise be due from the related taxpayers.

3. Losses are also not recognized when early recognition of loss would interact with capital gains provisions to allow 100 percent deductibility of current losses and limited taxation of associated gains at some future time. This avenue of manipulation is closed by Section 1091(a) of the Internal Revenue Code, which prohibits wash sales.

Basis

Nonrecognition means that the transferor pays no current tax. This fact may be recorded for future tax computations in one of two ways: (1) the unrecognized gain may be deducted from the market value of other property owned by the transferor to establish his basis, or (2) the basis of the property transferred may be carried over to the transferee. The first method is applied in the roll-over of properties under Sections 1031, 1033, 1034. The second is applied when property is donated.[7] Neither method is applied to bequests; appreciation of property held by the decedent does not affect the transferee, whose basis is the market value of the asset at the time of the transferor's death.

While this sketch of the rules governing the taxation of property transfers is incomplete, it shows that the transfer of property has a variety of tax consequences. To the extent that the taxpayer has discretion over the form of property transfers and may endow particular transactions with certain legally prescribed characteristics, he may manipulate the tax liabilities incurred. The change in tax liability reflects, to some extent, differences in the economic value to the transferor of alternative modes of transfer. However, the correlation between economic events and the tax imposed is far from perfect. Both individuals and corporations may avoid taxation of gains on investment property by appropriate exchanges or gifts. Only when the interactions between such transfers and preferential capital gains taxation are considered can the true scope of the tax avoidance possible under the present law be determined.

---

[7] Carry-over is also used to reduce recognized gain on property for which losses were disallowed to the previous owner under the Internal Revenue Code, Section 267. However, the basis for a loss remains the taxpayer's cost, despite earlier unrecognized losses to the previous owner.

Dimensions of the Capital Gains Tax Provisions

Capital gains acquire special tax status through a complex of legal provisions that not only differentiate transactions accorded capital gains treatment from ordinary income transactions or receipts but also differentiate among different types of transactions that may receive capital gains treatment. The capital gains provisions modify and augment the rules for measuring gain and loss set forth above. However, the capital gains provisions do not alter the rules affecting recognition of gain.

The provisions of the law will be considered under the following categories:

1. Eligibility criteria
   a. Capital assets—general rule
   b. Property used in a business or trade
   c. Other eligible transactions
2. Holding period criteria
3. Netting gains and losses and the capital gains deduction
4. Timing of the tax payment
5. Rate schedules applicable to gains
6. Rate schedules applicable to losses[8]

The first two define the extent of eligible transactions; eligibility generally requires sale or exchange. The remaining dimensions de-

---

[8] A parallel, but less detailed, classification may be found in Richard E. Slitor, "Problems of Definition Under the Capital Gains Tax," *National Tax Journal*, Vol. 10 (March 1957), pp. 26-37.

The following definitions of tax accounting terms are used here:

Adjusted gross income is gross receipts less excluded items of income (*exclusions*) and most business expenses (deductions for adjusted gross incomes).

Taxable income is adjusted gross income less *personal deductions* (nonbusiness deductions) and *exemptions* (for dependents, age, and blindness).

Ordinary income treatment of incremental items of income means that the tax on the increment is computed according to the appropriate rate established in the Internal Revenue Code schedules for single, married, and head-of-household taxpayers. Alternatively, the term may be used to indicate that the full amount of the incremental item is added to taxable income.

Capital gains treatment of incremental items of income cannot be readily summarized, but it may result either in a partial inclusion of the item in taxable income or in computation of the tax on the increment according to a fixed alternative rate of 25 percent rather than the rate specified in the Internal Revenue Code schedules.

fine the rate (or credit) that will be permitted in computing the tax liability. Each of them will be discussed below.

Eligible Assets

Asset transactions entitled to capital gains treatment are a subset of the taxable property transfers shown in Figure 2-1. Sale or exchange of investment assets or property that is held for use in the taxpayer's trade or business is generally eligible.[9] Eligible assets are defined by two general rules (Internal Revenue Code, Sections 1221 and 1231) and a variety of special rules. The logical structure of these distinctions is shown in Figure 2-2.

Capital Assets (Section 1221)

Property held by the taxpayer is a capital asset unless it is explicitly excluded. Thus:

... "capital assets" means property (whether or not connected with a trade or business), *but does not include the following:*

(1) inventoriable assets;
(2) property held for sale to customers in the ordinary course of the taxpayer's trade or business;
(3) notes and accounts receivable acquired in the ordinary course of trade or business ... ;
(4) depreciable business property;
(5) real property used in taxpayer's trade or business;
(6) a copyright, a literary, musical or artistic composition or similar property (but not a patent or invention) held by the taxpayer who created it, or by one whose basis in the property is determined by reference to the basis of the one who created it;
(7) short-term (maturing not more than one year from date of issue) noninterest-bearing Government obligations (State or Federal) issued on or after March 1, 1941, on a discount basis (Internal Revenue Code, Section 1221, Regulations 1.1221-1).[10]

[9] Sale or exchange does not include other dispositions. Thus, redemption of bonds, cutting of timber, and mining must be separately enumerated in the law if they are to bring about recognition of gain or loss (Internal Revenue Code, Sections 631 and 1232).

[10] *U.S. Master Tax Guide, 1964* (Commerce Clearing House, Inc., 1963), Para. 636, pp. 303-4.

FIG URE 2-2. Delineation of Transfers Eligible for Capital Gains Treatmen

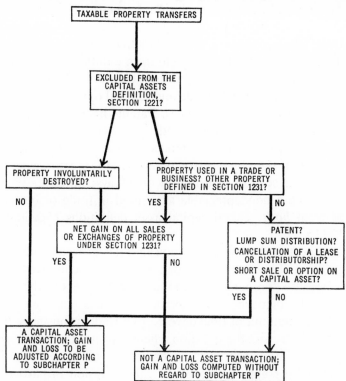

These seven categories are general statutory exclusions that limit the scope of the basic capital assets definition. Judicial interpretation and specific statutory exceptions substantially modify the structure suggested by this general class of excepted assets. Securities, land, leases, residences, or personal property could all be capital assets in the hands of particular taxpayers. At the same time, there are situations in which none of these is a capital asset. The distinctions can best be seen by discussing the positive intent of the capital asset definition.

Three features stand out in the exclusions mentioned above. Assets acquired and traded as a routine transaction in a business are excluded (items 1, 2, and 3). Assets reflecting value created by the holder are excluded, presumably since such value is considered to be a return to personal services (item 6).[11] Trading of assets to realize

[11] The reasons for the exclusion of real and depreciable business property (items 4 and 5) are historic and will be discussed in connection with Section 1231 property below.

the return customarily considered to be interest is excluded (item 7 plus Section 1232). These exclusions suggest that the intent of the law is to restrict capital gains treatment to a class of transactions on which the holder realizes a gain or loss that does not represent a recurrent and normally expected yield from wealth or a return to management or labor services in a business enterprise. In fact, however, both the Internal Revenue Code and judicial opinion contradict this general intent in several instances. Patents held by the creator are reincluded among capital assets under a special rule (Section 1235). In addition, the courts have extended capital gains treatment to the sale of a patent right by a person other than the creator, even though rights are often sold for recurrent income flows; moreover, the patent appears to be a nondepreciable asset used in trade or business excluded from *both* general capital asset definitions (Sections 1221 and 1231).

One aspect of the basic definition that has proved troublesome is the exclusion of inventory and stock in trade. Difficult problems have arisen because "property held for sale to customers in the ordinary course of the taxpayer's trade or business" has not been precisely defined. The amount of time devoted to a trade or business, the frequency of sales, and the question whether or not the business is the taxpayer's primary source of income have all been discarded as measures of the appropriateness of this exclusion in particular instances.[12] The difficulties inherent in distinguishing investments from stock in trade[13] have led to special rules for dealers in securities, for taxpayers who subdivide real estate for sale, and for taxpayers who receive payments on the cancellation of a lease or distributor's agreement.[14] As a result, a stockbroker may designate personal investment holdings and treat them as capital assets, while a real estate dealer may not. Indeed, the casual investor in real estate may find

[12] See Peter Miller, "The 'Capital Asset' Concept: a Critique of Capital Gains Taxation: I," *Yale Law Journal,* Vol. 59 (April 1950), pp. 860-67. In *Corn Products v. Commissioner* (350 US 46, 47, 50-53) it was held that a corn oil producer trading in corn futures was not trading in capital assets. Such trading, albeit of financial securities, is intimately tied to the conduct of the underlying business and hence does not involve a capital asset under a broad interpretation of this exclusion.

[13] *Van Suetendoel v. Commissioner* (T.C., 1944) and *Mauldin v. Commissioner* (U.S. Ct. of Appeals T.C. 1952, 19S F. 2d 714).

[14] When the distributor has a substantial capital investment in the distributorship. See Internal Revenue Code, Sections 1236, 1237, and 1241.

that he is considered to be conducting a trade, with property for sale to customers. Real estate investments involving the subdivision of unimproved property are thereby largely excluded from the class of capital assets.[15]

Property Used in a Trade or Business

Section 1231 of the Internal Revenue Code entitles the taxpayer to treat a net gain on all sales and exchanges of property used in a trade or business as a gain on a capital asset. Net losses are treated as ordinary losses on the sale of assets that are not capital assets.[16] This treatment of gains and losses creates a "quasi-capital assets" category, which may qualify for capital gains treatment. Depreciable property and real property used in a trade or business excluded from the basic capital asset definition set forth in Section 1221 (items 4 and 5 above) receive the benefits of this quasi-capital asset status.

Under earlier versions of the capital asset definition, a machine or building used in a business, but not for sale to customers, would have been considered a capital asset. Limitations on the extent to which losses on sales of capital assets could be deducted from other income meant that substantial corporate losses incurred from 1934 to 1938 could not be used to reduce tax liability. This led to the exclusion of depreciable property from the capital asset definition in 1938. By 1942, profits on the sale of assets for conversion to the war effort led to the reverse problem—gains on depreciable property not held for sale to customers could no longer be preferentially taxed. The Revenue Act of 1942 provided the present asymmetric treatment of quasi-capital assets. The Revenue Acts of 1962 and 1964 subsequently provided that part or all of the gain associated with the reduction of basis through depreciation should be treated as ordinary income. The asymmetric tax treatment remains in effect for any gains in excess of that amount.[17]

The basic capital asset definition and Section 1231 in combination deny capital gains treatment to the kinds of property listed below.

[15] Joyce Stanley and Richard Kilcullen, *The Federal Income Tax: A Guide to the Law* (The Tax Club Press, 1955), pp. 328-31.
[16] Such assets must have been held for more than six months.
[17] See Anita Wells, "Legislative History of Treatment of Capital Gains under the Federal Income Tax, 1913-1948," *National Tax Journal*, Vol. 2 (March 1949), pp. 27-31. The 1962 and 1964 provisions have been aptly termed "recapture" provisions (see Internal Revenue Code, Sections 1245 and 1250).

Stock in trade or other property of a kind that would properly be included in the inventory and property held primarily for sale to customers in the ordinary course of the taxpayer's trade or business; gain or loss is ordinary gain or loss. Section 1231 does not apply. . . . A copyright or other artistic property held by the artist or by someone in whose hands it has the same basis that it had in the hands of the artist, certain trade notes and accounts receivable, and certain short-term government obligations issued on or after March 1, 1941 on a discount basis: gain or loss is ordinary gain or loss. Section 1231 does not apply.[18]

Assets that are entitled to Section 1231 treatment include livestock used for draft, dairying, or breeding; real estate used in a trade or business; and items of depreciable property (subject to depreciation allowances under Section 167 of the Internal Revenue Code).[19] Unharvested crops and royalties from sales of timber, iron ore, and coal are included as well. The latter group of transactions, which receive capital gains treatment, actually appear closely akin to current, income-producing sales, which are generally excluded by the capital asset definition in Section 1221.

But under the basic definition, crops are excluded from capital assets, as they are inventory held for sale to customers. Royalties from the sale of timber, coal, or iron ore are not proceeds of a sale or exchange; hence they too are excluded under the basic definition. But Section 631 (b) and (c) treats these categories as if they were

[18] Stanley and Kilcullen, *op. cit.*, pp. 327-28.

In addition, certain transactions are specifically excluded from both capital asset and Section 1231 asset categories under special rules: (1) sales of assets to relatives or controlled corporations (Section 1238); and (2) sales of certain domestically controlled foreign corporations and similar transactions (Sections 1246-49). The first exclusion relates to the general principle that gain or loss must reflect market valuations. The second is associated with the problem of excess accumulations under the Internal Revenue Code, Subchapter G, Sections 531 ff.

[19] Casualty losses and involuntary conversions must also be included in the computation of net gain or loss on Section 1231 property. This provision may affect the amount of tax liability by specifying which gains and which losses must be added to determine the net gain or loss that is eligible for capital gains treatment. Many properties subjected to casualty losses or involuntary conversions would be capital assets under the basic rule in any case. Inclusion of such properties among Section 1231 quasi-capital assets assures that losses on involuntary conversions of capital assets are fully deductible. Losses on assets other than capital assets would be fully deductible in any case (except for the first $100 of personal casualty losses); inclusion of such losses here assures that other quasi-capital assets sold during a particular year do not qualify for special treatment as a net gain at the same time that these losses are fully deducted from income.

proceeds of the sale of a capital asset. The income received resembles rent, dividends, and other recurrent flows derived from a property right. Such income has clearly been excluded from treatment as gains on the sale of a capital asset.[20] The sale of timber is readily regarded as a capital asset transaction under the basic rule (Section 1221) when it results from occasional cuttings of woodlots by farmers and other small investors. They may see the growth of a stand once in a lifetime and may be engaged primarily in other businesses. The corporation that harvests trees regularly and continues to hold the land on which they grow appears to be selling an item of stock in trade or a crop. Yet the corporation also receives statutory capital gains treatment on its cuttings under Sections 631 and 1231.

Clearly these contradictory provisions create a "gray area" of definitional problems that may produce sizable inequities among taxpayers, and the resulting confusion is fundamental. So long as a gain or loss on the sale or exchange of a capital asset is entitled to preferential tax treatment, it is essential to define the concept "sale or exchange" in order to distinguish the resulting "gain or loss" from interest, rent, and other forms of ordinary income. Furthermore, when the asset is sold and payment is received immediately, no problem arises. But when payment is deferred, contingent, or distributed over several future tax years, gain or loss must be distinguished from the interest payments implicit in the sale. And this creates more complexities.[21] When only a part of the rights to an asset are sold and some interests are retained, the distinction between return to capital (gain or loss) and ordinary income becomes even more complex. A long-term lease results in ordinary income, while an installment sale results in gain or loss.[22]

---

[20] See Boris L. Bittker, *Federal Income, Estate, and Gift Taxation* (3rd ed.; Little, Brown, and Co., 1964), pp. 552-66. In the case of *Rhodes' Estate v. Commissioner* (U.S. Ct. of Appeals, Sixth Cir., 1942, 131 F.2d 50), the purchase of dividend rights and subsequent dividend payments resulted in ordinary income, not capital gains. (Bittker, *op. cit.*, pp. 66 and 525.)

[21] The Internal Revenue Code attempts this distinction in Section 483, imputing interest to installment sales contracts.

[22] *A rents* property to *B* for fifty years. The rents received are income. *A sells* property to *B* on an installment basis over a fifty-year period; a part of each installment payment must now be allocated to return on capital (gain or loss) and interest on the unpaid balance. The gain or loss included in the installment payment is taxable at capital gains rates. But in the first case, the corresponding rental is fully taxed. (Tax-free recovery of capital is permitted by depreciation if the property is leased.)

Sale or Exchange Distinguished from Recurrent Receipts

When a property interest is divided and part of it is retained by the seller, it may be extremely difficult to distinguish income from gain or loss in the proceeds. The practice of dividing a property in such a way as to create a terminable interest separate from the residual rights of ownership has been particularly suspect.

The courts have tried to define the boundary between income and the proceeds from transfers of property rights.[23] In *Commissioner v. P. G. Lake*[24] it was held that the assignment of a retained interest in an oil payment could not be considered a gain on the sale of a capital asset, since the proceeds of the assignment were "essentially a substitute for what would otherwise be received at a future time as ordinary income."[25] This distinction between the anticipation of future income and the sale of a capital asset has been made in other instances. In *Arnfeld v. United States*[26] it was decided that the taxpayer could not declare the proceeds from the assignment of an annuity contract as the proceeds of a sale of a capital asset on the grounds that the sale was a mere assignment of the right to income.

It is clear from these cases that the sale of a future stream of income may not always be considered to be a sale of a capital asset. Conversely, the sale of a property right (namely a patent right) in return for periodic payments may not always produce ordinary income. The distinction between these situations and several others is unclear. Proceeds from the sale of patent rights and the lump-sum termination of an employee pension trust anticipate future income or involve extended periodic payments. Both are favored by statutory treatment as gains from sales of capital assets.[27] Capital gains treat-

---

[23] The problem encountered is substantially broader than the question of the tax treatment of capital assets. However, because of preferential capital gains taxation, the number of situations in which the distinction can lead to differential tax liabilities is greatly increased. (See J. S. Eustace and C. S. Lyon, "Assignment of Income: Fruit and Tree as Irrigated by the P. G. Lake Case," *Tax Law Review,* Vol. 17 [1962], pp. 293-430.)

[24] U.S. Supreme Court, 1958; 356 U.S. 260.

[25] Opinion of the court, cited in E. N. Griswold, *Cases and Materials on Federal Taxation* (The Foundation Press, 1960), p. 574.

[26] 163 F. Supp. 865 Ct. Cl. 1958.

[27] Internal Revenue Code, Sections 1235, 402, 403, and 1240.

ment is denied to the extent of the original issue discount of a bond.[28] Here the intent of the Internal Revenue Code appears to be to deny capital gains treatment to sales and exchanges if the gain is essentially like ordinary income. For similar reasons, a gain on the sale or exchange of stock in a collapsible corporation is taxable as an ordinary gain.[29] The resulting contradiction makes it impossible to ascertain a clear intent underlying tax treatment of assignment of future income.

Thus, the identification of a class of transactions in property as capital asset transactions is obviously difficult. The purpose for which it is held becomes a pivotal question in determining whether a particular asset is eligible on the basis of its business uses or its personal investment value. The basic capital gains definition has been difficult to interpret, since under it, all assets are included unless they are specifically excluded. Arbitrary rules have distinguished the quasi-capital asset treatment given to business-related assets under Section 1231 from the preferential treatment of other capital assets.

Whether a transaction is appropriately deemed a sale or an exchange becomes important when the property consists primarily of rights to future income. The opinions of the courts appear to be contradictory to statutory provisions that deal with patents and certain forms of royalty income. An equally delicate distinction arises when the transaction defers the transfer of ownership or divides ownership interests.[30] In Section 631, Congress has extended capital gains treat-

[28] Section 1232. A gain on the sale of bonds, up to the amount of any issue discount (or a pro rata share of that discount based on the period over which the bonds have been held) is not considered to be a gain on the exchange of a capital asset.
[29] Section 341. A "collapsible corporation" is defined as one formed or used principally to manufacture, construct, or buy property that is not a capital asset, Section 1231 property held for more than three years, or unrealized receivables. Further, the corporation must have been formed with a view to having the shareholders sell or exchange the stock or to having a large distribution made to the shareholders before the corporation realizes a substantial share of the taxable income to be derived from the property, and to having the taxpayers realize gains attributable to the property. This provision is necessary to limit the conversion of ordinary income into capital gains. However, the exact application of the law and exceptions to this general definition are too complicated for presentation here.
[30] For a more detailed discussion of the case law and distinctions involved, see Stanley S. Surrey, "Definitional Problems in Capital Gains Taxation," in House Committee on Ways and Means, *Tax Revision Compendium* (1959), Vol. 2, pp. 1203-32.

ment to profits received recurrently. The courts have moved in a similar direction in their treatment of patent royalties.

Distinguishing recurrent profits from a trade or business from gains resulting from the final disposition of an investment has clearly proved troublesome. The tax treatment of gains from the cutting of timber, patent royalties, and deferred sales contracts illustrates the difficulty of drawing a clear distinction between the two forms of receipt that is universally acceptable for granting capital gains treatment.

The Holding Period Criteria

Generally, capital gains taxes apply only to gains resulting from transactions in which the property transferred has been held for some minimum period. For capital assets and Section 1231 property (with the exception of livestock), the holding period is six months. Livestock must be held for twelve months; no minimum holding period applies to patents. Transactions in capital assets held beyond the six-month holding period result in long-term capital gains or losses. Transactions in capital assets held for six months or less result in short-term capital gains and losses. Transactions in Section 1231 property are considered as sales of ordinary noncapital assets if the property has been held for six months or less.

The holding period has been an important aspect of the tax formula for capital gains since passage of the Revenue Act of 1921. At that time, short-term and long-term capital transactions were distinguished by a holding period of two years. Later, in 1934, the length of the holding period controlled the percentage of gain included in income according to five classes of assets.[31] The present holding period for capital assets dates from 1942. Six months was considered a suitable length of time for distinguishing speculative activity from investment.[32]

The appropriateness of an arbitrary period, particularly a period of less than one year, for differentiating speculative from investment

---

[31] The classes and percentage inclusions were: Less than one year, 100 percent; one year, not over two years, 80 percent; two, not over five years, 60 percent; five, not over 10 years, 40 percent; and over ten years, 30 percent.

[32] The same six-month limitation applied to company officers and principal stockholders in defining a "speculative turn" under the Securities and Exchange Act. See Wells, op. cit., p. 28.

activities has been questioned.[33] Clearly, both professional traders and amateurs may try to gain from short-term price fluctuations through transactions that require holding for more than six months. At the same time an investor with long-term portfolio objectives may find a new investment opportunity, or early failure of a past investment, that demands trading in less than the holding period of six months.

While the specified six-month period has arbitrary elements, it has been supported on tax grounds. Eliminating the minimum holding period would lead to undue revenue losses. Speculative traders do conduct a large part of their business in assets held for less than six months and are taxed at ordinary rates. However, if the holding period were lengthened to one year, it could be argued with more convincing logic that special treatment ought to be given to transactions that reflect a return in more than one tax year.

To limit the circumvention of the holding period requirements, the purchase or sale of property in connection with short sales and options are treated in Sections 1233 and 1234 of the Internal Revenue Code. The intent of those sections is to prevent a taxpayer from hedging a transaction with appropriate corollary options so as to obtain a minimum tax liability. In the absence of these provisions a taxpayer could insure a certain long-term gain on property by selling short for delivery after the minimum holding period. He could also purchase a put option for the same purpose.[34]

Netting Gains and Losses and the Capital Gains Deduction

The logic of the holding period and eligibility requirement establishes four classes of property:

1. Long-term capital assets (property not excluded by the exceptions listed in Section 1221, plus property specifically reincluded that has been held more than six months)
2. Short-term capital assets (property not excluded by the excep-

---

[33] Surrey, *op. cit.,* pp. 1215-16; Miller, *op. cit.,* pp. 840-48.

[34] That is, the owner of the property sells it *within* the six-month period but stipulates delivery *after* six months. When the sale is closed, the property has been held for more than six months and qualifies for long-term treatment. Alternatively, the owner may buy a put option under which he is guaranteed a purchaser at the current price at the end of the six-month holding period.

tions enumerated in Section 1221, plus property specifically reincluded that has been held six months or less)
3. Quasi-capital assets (property defined by Section 1231 that must have been held more than six months)
4. Noncapital assets (the residuum)

Gain or loss on the sale of any item of property in one of these classes is computed as the difference between sale proceeds and the adjusted basis. Within each class all gains and losses that must be recognized may be added algebraically to give a corresponding total of current gain or loss.

Special tax treatment is accorded net long-term capital gains in category 1 and net gains (not recaptured) on quasi-capital assets in category 3. A capital gains deduction is permitted for both of these. However, if the deduction were permitted on the total net gain under category 1, an anomalous situation would arise. Equal net long-term gains and short-term losses, less the capital gains deduction, would add algebraically to an amount less than zero. The resulting amount could be deducted from gains on noncapital assets or ordinary income from other sources. Since similar property is involved in both the short-term and the long-term capital asset categories, this result seems unreasonable. Losses on capital assets should be permitted to cancel out gains without reducing ordinary income. Hence it is clear that rules must be established for the order in which net gains and losses in these four categories must be added to arrive at an appropriate capital gains deduction. (This has been termed the "hotchpotch" problem.)

A related problem occurs because net long-term capital gains are reduced by the capital gains deduction prior to inclusion with other income, while net long-term capital losses are not adjusted symmetrically. Thus equal net gains and net losses in two tax years, less the capital gains deduction, would effectively produce a deduction from other income received during those tax years. This is the same problem that was encountered above with short-term losses and long-term gains, except that two tax years are involved rather than one.

These two problems in aggregating gains and losses are treated in different ways under the Internal Revenue Code: (1) Section 1202 provides that 50 percent of the excess of net long-term capital gains over net short-term capital losses may be deducted from the gross income of individual taxpayers, and (2) Section 1211 limits the extent to which capital losses may be deducted from income. In effect, short-term losses offset long-term gains, dollar for dollar, in determining the capital gains deduction. Net losses on capital assets are not offset by gains in other years, nor are they reduced prior to being deducted from income by a provision symmetric to the net capital gains deduction. Instead, the absolute amount of net losses on capital assets that may be used to offset income from other sources is limited. Any losses that are not considered in computing the current year's tax may be carried forward and included in the calculation of capital gains and losses in subsequent years.[35]

The derivation of the capital gains deduction and the amount of gain or loss included in income can now be clearly stated. (See Figure 2-3.) Recognized gains and losses can be categorized in the four groups specified above.

Gains on quasi-capital assets corresponding to depreciation taken must be treated as ordinary income. Gains on depreciable machinery and equipment (Section 1245 property) and on real estate held less than twelve months must be treated as ordinary income to the extent of depreciation already deducted from the taxpayer's cost or basis.[36] A part of the gain on the sale of real estate (Section 1250 property) held for more than twelve months is also considered to be ordinary income. The portion of gain to be treated as ordinary income is determined by depreciation claimed in excess of straight-line depreciation and a percentage based on the length of time that the property has been held. The percentage is 100 for sales made within twelve to twenty months following acquisition and declines 1 percentage point a month thereafter.

Once depreciation has been recaptured under these provisions, any remaining net gain on quasi-capital assets may be added to the amount of gain or loss on long-term capital assets. Capital losses carried forward from past years must be appropriately subtracted. The capital gains deduction may then be taken to the extent of any excess

[35] See the discussion of the timing of tax payment and carry-over below.

[36] Depreciation taken before taxable years beginning in 1962 is exempted to avoid retroactive application of this provision. (See Internal Revenue Code, Section 1245.) Moreover, Section 1238 denies capital-asset and Section 1231 treatment on gains that can be attributed to amortization in excess of ordinary depreciation. Group accounts do not recognize either gain or loss on the disposition of assets and are not affected.

FIGURE 2-3 Derivation of the Gain or Loss Included in Adjusted Gross Income

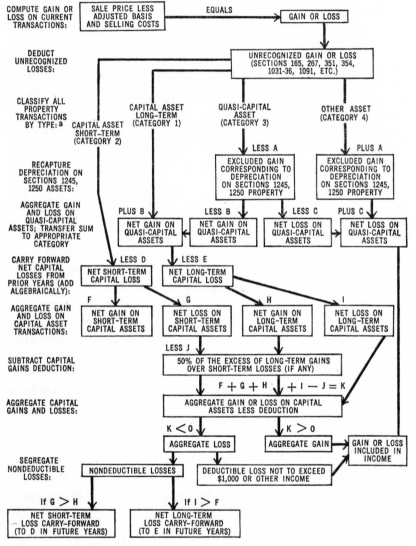

Categories are defined in the text, pp. 29-30.

of net long-term gain over net short-term loss. The remaining amount of gain (if any) is included in income.

If all capital asset transactions result in a net loss, the amount that may be deducted from other income is limited. For an individual, no more than $1,000 of the amount of capital losses may be offset against other income. No capital loss deductions can be taken if other income sources show a net loss. This limitation on capital loss deductions means that a dollar of loss on a capital asset may not always cancel a dollar of income from other sources. Nevertheless, a dollar of long-term capital gain cancels a dollar of short-term loss, and conversely. Any nondeductible losses are legally defined as net capital losses. Corporations may not deduct any capital loss from ordinary income. Net capital losses thus occur whenever the aggregation of all capital gains and losses is negative.

The net effect of the rules that define the eligible asset, the holding period, and the amount of gain or loss is summarized in Table 2-1.

Timing of the Tax Payment and Carry-over

The fourth element in the capital gains tax provisions—timing of the tax payment—is the most significant one. Generally, capital gains are taxed upon realization of the value inherent in the property through sale or exchange. The many situations in which property is disposed of by other means or in which gain and loss are not recognized at the time the property is transferred are enumerated above.

For individuals, the rules on basis and recognition permit the exemption of gain passing into the taxpayer's estate and the postponement of recognition of gain on donations. Accrued capital gains on the property of a taxpayer at the time of his death are not recognized as income on the final return of the decedent. At the same time, the property passes to the heirs with a stepped-up basis so that the appreciation that took place during the decedent's lifetime is never subject to income tax. If property is transferred by gift, a gain is not recognized to the donor. However, in this case the donee acquires the basis of the donor and must pay tax in the future if the property has accrued a gain. If the property would produce a loss, his basis is the market value on the day of transfer plus the gift tax paid by

TABLE 2-1. Treatment of Gains and Losses by Type of Asset and Holding Period

Type of asset	Holding period	Treatment of gain	Treatment of loss
Capital, long-term (category 1)*	6 months or more	Partially included in income as the result of the capital gains deduction for individuals; 100 percent included for corporations	Limited deductibility from income other than capital gains for individuals[d] Only deductible from capital gains for corporations
Capital, short-term (category 2)*	Less than 6 months	100 percent included in income	Limited deductibility from income other than capital gains for individuals[e] Only deductible from capital gains for corporations[f]
Quasi-capital (category 3)*	6 months or more[a]	If all transactions lead to a net gain, treated as category 1[b]	If all transactions lead to a net loss, treated as category 4
Other business or investment-related (category 4)*		100 percent included in income	100 percent deductible
Non-business, non-investment-related property (whether or not a capital asset)			
(a) casualty losses			100 percent deductible in excess of $100 per casualty
(b) residence		Recognition deferred if another residence is purchased or constructed[c]	No deduction
(c) other		100 percent included	No deduction

* Categories are defined in the text on pp. 29-30.
[a] Twelve months for livestock.
[b] Subject to Section 1245 and Section 1250 adjustments.
[c] Subject to exclusion available for aged taxpayers and purchase or construction of a new residence within the specified periods.
[d] Including individual net long-term loss carry-over.
[e] Including individual net short-term loss carry-over.
[f] Including all corporate loss carry-over from the previous 5 years.

the donor. Nonrecognition of losses in transfers by gift is a logical extension of nonrecognition of losses on sales or exchanges between related parties.[37]

For corporations, the opportunities for postponing realization of gains are also legion. Yet little is known about the permissible use of roll-over or its economic significance.

Limitations on the deduction of capital losses from ordinary income create a situation in which the tax is not reduced concurrently with the realization of a loss. To avoid permanent nonrecognition of net capital losses, the law provides that any capital losses that are not deductible in a particular taxable year may be carried forward indefinitely to offset the capital gains in succeeding years. For individuals, the carry-forward must offset gains of like kind. That is, an excess of short-term capital losses can be used only to offset short-term gains in the year to which they are carried; an excess of long-term capital losses can be used only to offset long-term gains in future years.

Carry-forward of net capital losses is limited to the five succeeding years for corporate taxpayers.[38] However, net capital losses are always considered short-term capital losses in the year to which they are carried.

Rates Applicable to Gains and Losses

The tax treatment of capital gains or capital losses depends on how those gains and losses are divided between short-term and long-term capital asset categories.

Individual Net Gains

If the aggregate of gains and losses on short-term and long-term capital asset transactions results in a net gain, three tax treatments are possible:

1. If both long-term and short-term transactions result in a net gain, half of the net long-term gain and all of the net short-term gain are included to determine taxable income. Alternatively, the net long-term gain may be excluded from taxable income, the tax liabili-

[37] See pp. 17-18, above, and Figure 2-1.
[38] When losses are the result of foreign expropriation, they may be carried forward ten years (Internal Revenue Code, Section 1212).

ty computed on the remaining income, and 25 percent of the net long-term gain added to determine total tax liability. The options available imply that incremental net long-term gains actually increase tax liability at one-half the legal rates up to the point at which the effective marginal rate on ordinary income is 50 percent; the alternative tax option then imposes a ceiling on rate progression.

2. If the short-term transactions result in a net loss, half of the excess of net long-term capital gains over net short-term capital losses is included in taxable income; alternatively, the tax liability is computed at 25 percent of the sum of such net gains and losses, plus the tax liability on other income. In effect, short-term losses are deducted only partially from income, just as gains are added only partially to income.

3. If the long-term transactions result in a loss, they are deducted from short-term gains, and all of the net capital gains are taxed at the rates on ordinary income. Note that a net long-term capital gain fractionally increases adjusted gross income; a net long-term capital loss is fully deductible from short-term capital gains.

Individual Net Losses

If the aggregate of gains and losses on long-term and short-term capital asset transactions is negative, that sum is deducted in full from other taxable income, leading to a reduction in tax at the marginal rates applicable to ordinary income. The extent of such tax reductions is limited by the deductibility of losses from ordinary income.

The above rules are represented mathematically in Appendix A, pages 233-39.

Corporate Net Gains

The corporation may avail itself of an alternative tax computation similar to that available to individuals. Corporations do not receive any deduction from income for long-term capital gains. If there are both short-term and long-term gains, the short-term gains are fully included in income, and the long-term gains may be taxed under the alternative rate. Any net long-term capital gains are taxed at marginal corporate rates, or 25 percent (whichever is less). (Thus corporations with less than $25,000 of income obtain no tax advantages on capital gains.) If long-term gains or short-term losses occur, the alternative tax is 25 percent of the excess of long-term gains over short-term losses. If short-term gains exceed long-term losses, both are treated as ordinary gains and losses and are fully taxed.

Corporate Net Losses

Net capital losses are not deductible and do not affect the corporate tax computation in the year in which they are realized.

Legislative Intent of the Present Law

These various provisions combined constitute preferential capital gains taxation. They are a patchwork aimed at carving out a meaningful area for preferential tax treatment. Unfortunately the line of demarcation between capital gains and ordinary gains is not based on simple logic. Moreover, the intent underlying preferential rate treatment is not clear.

There are several reasons for preferential capital gains taxation.[39] It has been favored as a means of: (1) securing more equitable tax treatment for investment gains which have accrued over long periods of time and which would be assessed in a single year under progressive income tax rates; (2) reducing the inequitable taxation of increments to capital that arise from illusory revaluations, such as inflation; and (3) minimizing interference with the operation of assets markets, which, in many cases, are characterized by a limited number of buyers and sellers. Congress has sought to limit the special treatment to only bona fide investments and to restrict the postponement and avoidance of taxes through the manipulation of sales of capital assets. The latter set of considerations has produced the complex and frequently amended provisions concerning the deductibility of losses and the taxability of sales of depreciable property.

Another motive, and perhaps a more recent one, underlying capital gains legislation has been to reduce the progression on earned in-

---

[39] Given the conflicting motives of legislators and the numerous forces that are resolved in any given piece of legislation, it is not possible to define legislative intent more clearly than by a few rather sweeping generalizations. However, several good histories of the law and legislative discussions provide insight into the validity of these generalizations. See Wells, *op. cit.*, pp. 12-32; Lawrence H. Seltzer, *The Nature and Tax Treatment of Capital Gains and Losses* (National Bureau of Economic Research, 1951), pp. 30-46; and U.S. Treasury Department, Tax Advisory Staff, *Federal Income Tax Treatment of Capital Gains and Losses* (1951), pp. 20-41.

come arising in certain unusual situations. The total income may have accrued over more than one year, may represent a unique situation in the lifetime of the investor, or may be closely related to other transactions eligible for capital gains.[40] Finally, preferential capital gains taxation is considered necessary to provide a needed stimulus to investment and to spur growth of the economy.

However, the mixture of tax treatments that has resulted from these various motives is contradictory for similar situations. Moreover, it is uncertain how well preferential taxation accomplishes any of the avowed goals.

Inequities in Present Capital Gains Taxation

A number of writers have carefully surveyed the anomalies of capital gains taxation to search for inequities and applications of the law that appear inconsistent with the objective of minimizing opportunities for tax avoidance.[41] Without going into detail, a few examples of the way in which the law presently discriminates in favor of certain situations are given here.

Tax Premium for Appreciation

Assume that an individual A purchases $1,000 worth of securities yielding 5 percent in dividends. His marginal tax rate is 40 percent. At the end of the year he pays $20 tax on his dividend income. B purchases $1,000 of growth securities at the same time, sells at the end of the year, and is entitled to capital gains treatment on the 5 percent appreciation that has accrued. His marginal tax rate is also 40 percent, but he pays only $10 tax. Clearly the law encourages the holding of appreciating securities and the retention of earnings by corporate managers to minimize the individual tax burden.

Tax Premium for Deferral

The second major inequity of the law permits the deferral of taxes so as to reduce the progressivity of statutory tax rates. Consider an

[40] It can be argued that the special provisions for gains on the sale of coal and iron ore through royalty contracts, patents, and lump-sum distributions from pension funds reflect these motives.

[41] Slitor, *op. cit.*; Leonard L. Silverstein, "The Capital Asset Definition," in House Committee on Ways and Means, *Tax Revision Compendium* (1959), Vol. 2, pp. 1285-99; Surrey, *op. cit.*, pp. 1203-32.

extension of the situation just described. *A* retains $1,000 of securities yielding 5 percent in dividends annually for ten years; *B* retains equally profitable appreciating securities for the same length of time. Both *A* and *B* pay tax at a marginal rate of 40 percent during the entire period. Both *A* and *B* pay a total tax of $200. However, *B* does not sell any of the appreciated assets until he reaches the end of the period, and he has been able to invest $20 more than *A* each year. The amount of earnings on that investment will provide an incentive to defer the tax, quite apart from any special tax rates that may apply to capital gains as opposed to ordinary income.

Trading vs. Investing

The dealer in real estate who holds appreciated and unimproved land as part of what he regards as his personal portfolio must pay tax at the full rate when he sells those properties. His properties are not capital assets because they are held for sale in the ordinary course of trade or business. However, a wealthy corporate executive who holds the same properties for a period of five years or more and subdivides them in the same manner as the real estate dealer (without making any improvements) pays a capital gains tax on the appreciation of the properties. A third person, who finds it necessary to improve the properties in order to market them, may find that he is denied the capital gains tax advantage.

The treatment of receipts in these and similar situations depends on whether the assets in question were held for sale in the business, or whether they were held as an investment and were not for sale to customers. Dealers in securities may designate their investments to obtain capital gains advantages; real estate dealers may not. Although the question of whether capital gains treatment is appropriate hinges broadly on the nature of the activity and its volume in relation to the primary business activity of the individual, imprecision in the capital asset definition leads to anomalous situations. The individual may realize more income from "occasional investment activities" than from his primary business.

Compensation vs. Investment Profits

There are various routes whereby an investor can convert a portion of his wages into income subject to capital gains treatment. He may defer a portion of the income in pension rights that are payable in a lump sum at death and will be subject only to capital gains rates,[42] or he may develop and promote a fledgling corporate enterprise in which he owns a substantial interest and receive capital gains treatment on the resulting appreciation. A large portion of that appreciation reflects a return on the organizing efforts and labor of the promoter. In contrast, the wage or salary earner without direct control over a property interest pays taxes on the entire amount of wage income he receives.

The multiplicity of routes by which the return for personal services can be converted into capital gains has led to many adjuncts to the tax law restricting collapsible corporations, corporate distributions, and the accumulation of income within corporations. At least one scholar concludes that such changes have only extended and complicated the practice of tax avoidance through capital gains without eliminating the basic problem.[43] Another fails to find a coherent rationale underlying the present provisions for taxing capital gains related to personal services.[44]

Conversion of Recurrent Income into Capital Gains

The legal distinction between an individual and a business enterprise that he operates through a closely held corporation facilitates large-scale conversion of profits into capital gains. Rather than pay dividends the owner may accumulate retained earnings without any increase in his tax. It is difficult to prove that earnings retained in the corporation are excessive (and are therefore subject to penalty taxes). The accumulation of such retained earnings is ultimately reflected in appreciation of the corporation's securities. That appreciation can easily be liquidated by selling the original securities or selling new securities distributed through spin-offs, split-ups, and split-offs. When earnings are retained in the corporation, recurrent payouts, which are similar to dividends, can be realized, but they are taxed only at capital gains rates.

Present provisions for tax-free reorganizations seem reasonable in view of the need for flexibility in corporate organization. However, it does not appear equitable for these provisions to create an avenue for

[42] Internal Revenue Code, Section 403(a) (2).

[43] Surrey, *op. cit.,* p. 1228.

[44] Peter Miller, "Capital Gains Taxation of the Fruits of Personal Effort: Before and Under the 1954 Code," *Yale Law Journal,* Vol. 64 (November 1954), pp. 1-83.

tax avoidance that is available to a select group of corporations. How to distinguish those reorganizations in which tax avoidance is incidental from those in which the primary objective is tax avoidance remains an unsolved, and perhaps insoluble, problem.

Excessive Deductions and Capital Gains

If an individual understates his income from a particular asset over a period of years and then sells the asset, some income that should have been taxed at ordinary rates will be taxed as capital gains. For example, deductions for depreciation on real property reduce the amount of taxable income in the year in which they are taken. If those deductions overstate the actual loss in market value of the property, final sale of the property will result in a capital gain. Given the many unpredictable factors that affect the economic life of a building, it is quite likely that such gains will occur, even after the recapture adjustments under Section 1250 of the Internal Revenue Code have been made. The net result is that taxes due on ordinary income in prior years have been converted to capital gains taxes. Payment has been deferred, and the rate of tax has been reduced.

The conversion of income from one form into another would be of less significance if the rate of tax payment on all forms of income were equal. It is the preferential capital gains treatment that confers such importance on the legal form in which the income is received.

Sales of Rights to Future Income

One additional case should be noted. The *xyz* corporation finds a new process the use of which is expected to increase its earnings by 10 percent in future years. Stock of the *xyz* corporation appreciates to reflect the increased present value of the earnings of the corporation. The investor who sells his holdings today receives capital gains treatment on that appreciation; but the investor who retains his interest must pay regular income tax rates on the higher dividends in the future. This is basic to the tax discrimination between capital gains and ordinary income. However, it is possible to terminate ownership through contracts that represent intermediate positions between sale and continued ownership. The property may be sold in installments or for royalties. It may be sold in parts with idiosyncratic division of contractual rights, equity, and control. Each case leads to the question of where the dividing line should be drawn between an income stream and an exchange of capital assets. The actual line drawn by the law and the courts discriminates in favor of coal, timber, and patents that are sold with a retained economic interest, and royalty payments. Oil and gas contracts of the same nature require ordinary income treatment.[45]

To summarize, under the present law, persons similarly situated with regard to the type of work they do and the type of investments they hold often pay different taxes. If the legal screen is appropriate, earnings can be taxed at the capital gains rate instead of at graduated income tax rates, recurring income such as rent or dividends can be converted into capital gains, and the investor can defer taxes from high-tax years to years in which his marginal tax rates are low. If no legal screen is present, these items are taxed currently according to statutory rates.

[45] The problems in defining a class of dispositions that constitute a final sale or exchange have been analyzed exhaustively in *Discussion Draft of a Study of Definitional Problems in Capital Gains Taxation* (American Law Institute, Oct. 20, 1960).

CHAPTER III

Taxable Capacity

TAXES CAN BE LEVIED on many bases—on stocks, such as real property, or on flows, such as the ordinary flow of income received by the individual through his annual productive efforts and contractual rights. They may be levied personally and tailored to the individual characteristics of the taxpayer, or they may be levied as *ad rem* taxes without regard to these characteristics.

In theory, taxes should be levied according to the benefits received by individuals from public services, or to their ability to pay for these services. In practice, these criteria offer no general solution to the problem of an appropriate rate structure or an appropriate tax base.[1] If either of these criteria is significant, however, it is clear that the tax structure should rely primarily on personal taxation. Otherwise the tax burden cannot be adequately tailored to the tremendous variation among individuals in ability to pay or in consumption of public services.

In the discussion that follows, some general considerations that are relevant to the balance of different taxes in the overall tax structure will be outlined. The question of exactly what might be an optimum tax structure cannot be settled here, but this chapter will discuss the reform of the capital gains tax in an appropriately broad context

[1] See Richard A. Musgrave, *The Theory of Public Finance* (McGraw-Hill, 1959), pp. 61-115, for a discussion of these theories.

rather than focusing entirely on the relationship of the capital gains tax to an ideally defined income tax.

Criteria Governing the Choice of Tax Formulas

The choice of an appropriate measure of taxable capacity depends on the nature of the financing problem and the level of government concerned. There are several areas in which the concept of taxable capacity used later in this study may be neither appropriate nor desirable. The revenue needs of governments at all levels must be considered.

1. Government enterprises require financing to cover the cost of services rendered. Since the consumer of public enterprise services reveals his preferences through the ordinary operation of the market, some type of benefit taxation is both desirable and feasible as the taxable capacity criterion.

2. Governments operating in an open economy, such as the state and local governments in the United States federal system, must measure taxable capacity in such a way that taxes can be collected with a minimum of compliance costs. Moreover, since such governments have little power to compensate for fluctuations in economic activity, they have to use a concept of taxable capacity that implies a relatively stable tax yield in spite of fluctuations in economic activity within the state. That is, the state might appropriately use wealth as a measure of taxable capacity, since wealth does not fluctuate as markedly as does income. Such stability would be necessary if the deficits associated with declines in revenue were to exceed the borrowing capacity of the state, or if they entailed an incremental financing cost greater than the social cost of stable tax yields.

3. Central government financing must not curtail private expenditures to a level that would lead to unemployment or idle industrial capacity. Yet taxes must be high enough to curtail private expenditures to a level consistent with only modest increases (if any) in the price level.

4. Finally, to achieve intergenerational equity, there may be a need for taxes on stocks, capital levies, and similar devices. This question will not be explored further here.

These special requirements for a tax system determine only a limited part of the tax structure and provide a unique basis for the collection of only a small portion of the government sector's revenue. The major sources of revenue must be based on additional principles. The preceding considerations do not uniquely determine the tax structure because there is no objective way of assessing the entire cost of public services—according to either ability to pay or benefit received. In fact, there is no objective criterion for determining the level of government expenditures because the satisfaction of public wants and income redistribution are interdependent. Therefore, an ethical choice is made when a tax formula is selected and the specific form of redistribution of income and a specific set of resulting public social products are determined.[2] For that reason the principle of benefit taxation cannot be extended to the provision of all public wants, even if these wants could be adequately revealed through the voting process.

The nature of social benefits provided by the government sector does not offer a clue as to the appropriate base for taxation. However, it is clear that revenues should be raised through a personal form of taxation to assure that the distributive objectives established are carried out efficiently and with a minimum of interference with the pricing of private goods. Furthermore, as the revenues are to be used to produce a flow of public services, it seems most appropriate to collect taxes on the basis of a flow of economic activity rather than of the stocks that produce the flow.[3]

Capital Gains and Expenditure Taxation

Kaldor has presented a persuasive argument for using personal expenditures as the tax base.[4] This criterion would exempt current savings of individuals from taxation. Each taxpayer would be assessed, at progressive rates, on the amount of his total expenditures. Expenditures could probably be measured most easily as total in-

[2] See Paul A. Samuelson, "The Pure Theory of Public Expenditure," *Review of Economics and Statistics*, Vol. 36 (November 1954), pp. 387-89.
[3] Further justification for taxing flows arises from the intrinsic difficulties of valuing stocks of human wealth directly. Since human wealth is a major component of total national wealth, a tax that does not assess human wealth would be highly discriminatory.
[4] See Nicholas Kaldor, *An Expenditure Tax* (London: George Allen and Unwin, 1955). Kaldor's discussion of income concepts (see pp. 54-78) is particularly relevant to this section.

come less change in net worth. If this were the measure of expenditure, capital gains would be measured as they accrued, and they would be taxed insofar as they were realized and spent on consumption goods. Personal expenditures are a theoretically plausible tax base, although the administrative problems that would be involved in levying the tax were close to insuperable until electronic computers made possible extensive audits of tax returns.

Expenditure taxation would obviate the need for taxing capital gains as they accrue and are reinvested, since with rare exceptions such gains constitute a saving that does not increase a taxpayer's expenditures.[5] While a pure system of expenditure taxation would preclude corporation and personal income taxes, any mixture of tax bases would leave some part of the dilemma that is involved in taxing capital gains under an income tax. For example, a combination of personal expenditure taxation and corporate income taxation would entail the administrative burden of defining two tax bases. The avoidance of corporate income taxes by large payouts of profits in interest and the avoidance of personal expenditure taxes by using the corporation as a screen for personal consumption expenditures would constitute problems as difficult as that of the lock-in effect under the present federal income tax.[6]

Preferential taxation of capital gains under an income tax bears little relationship to a pure expenditure tax. Although appreciation of assets is partially exempted from the income tax, other forms of saving are not. Moreover, under the income tax, a person's tax remains unchanged if appreciation of assets (saving) is offset by equal increases in debt (dissaving), so that consumption rises by the full amount of appreciation without any realization of capital gains. Thus preferential capital gains taxation under an income tax is not necessarily analogous to a selective expenditure tax. The analogy is appropriate only to the extent that appreciation of assets is matched by increased saving, and this saving is exempted from tax, or taxed at a preferential rate.

---

[5] Appreciation of residential property would be an exception. An increase in the value of the property increases the value of housing services consumed.

[6] The problem of consumption expenditures disguised as business expenditures would be more serious than the present one of tax avoidance through excessive travel and entertainment expenses. Under the present tax system marginal rates of tax are less than 70 percent. Under an expenditure tax system with equal yield the rates on expenditures could easily rise to 100 percent or more.

Although an expenditure tax would obviate the need for taxing capital gains, the effect on the tax structure would be far greater than if capital gains were exempted from taxation under the present income tax. The radical character of the change in the tax structure that would be required by an expenditure tax leads us to focus on income as the criterion of personal taxable capacity. Historically the income tax has been most widely accepted as the prime source of government financing. Measures of income have been well developed and tested in many different tax jurisdictions. Income taxes have been collected by withholding and by individual declaration. This is not true of a broad-based expenditure tax.

Concepts of Income

What then is an appropriate measure of income for tax purposes? The individual's share of net national product at factor cost might be taken as a logical measure. The income of each individual would simply be the return he received for real services rendered to the economy. Rent would be included for the services of land and property; wages, for labor services; profits, for entrepreneurial services; and so on.

There are two major difficulties with the factor income approach. First, substantial differences may arise between payments received for services rendered and income actually available for consumption and saving. Transfers of income in the form of pensions, alimony, voluntary support, social insurance, and welfare mean that some individuals have far larger disposable incomes than would be indicated by payments received for services rendered. If the ability to pay of such individuals is to be taxed, income received through transfers must also be taxed. Second, increments to individuals' incomes arise indirectly from corporate saving. Business profits reinvested in the enterprise generate an expectation of increased future profits, which are then reflected in the valuation of shares in the business. Furthermore, revaluations may occur because of changes in the price level, or in the expected rate of return associated with the current capital stock, or because of fluctuations in the rate of interest. Clearly, revaluation of real and financial assets by the market creates even larger discrepancies between factor incomes and funds available for current consumption and savings. Such revaluations do not affect the factor cost of the real net national product and factor incomes. For the economy as a whole, the transfer of assets between persons does not increase the total amount of real capital or the total amount of goods and services produced; hence such transactions are not reflected in factor incomes.[7]

When the taxable capacity of individuals is considered, revaluations cannot be ignored if the tax base is to measure ability to pay. An increase in the value of property in central cities, for example, benefits persons who hold that type of property. Their economic power increases at the expense of those who do not hold such property. Similarly, a general rise in the prices of equity assets increases the potential for consumption and savings of the group that owns those assets. Holders of debt and other fixed-value financial assets suffer.

Actually, the inclusion of revaluations of assets in the tax base does not necessarily mean that all revaluations would have to be included. An equitable tax base requires recognition of only those revaluations that result in changes in the distribution of economic power or disposable income. Uniform percentage increases in the level of incomes that arise from revaluations of assets can be ignored.[8] Several who have argued that capital gains are illusory because they reflect only a general revaluation of property prices have advocated some form of partial inclusion of gains in the tax base. While such a modification of the taxable income concept is theoretically feasible, there would be serious difficulties in measuring income for tax purposes on the basis of real rather than money income. If only real gains are to be included in income, then presumably only real deductions for operating costs should be permitted.[9] Moreover, real losses experienced by bondholders and others holding contracts fixed in nominal terms should be deductible from taxable income.

Even if the problems involved in choosing a measure of prices and the computation of revenue and deductions on a real basis could be surmounted, the amount of real gain on the sale of assets could be

[7] This statement is not completely accurate, as the transfer of property increases the value of services rendered by brokers and agents, thereby increasing the gross national product.

[8] If average incomes rise in equal proportions, the distributional shares are unaffected, and progression will rise on all income unless tax rates are changed.

[9] Price adjustment of depreciation has often been suggested as a *real* deduction for tax purposes, but few propose a parallel adjustment of other income items, such as interest, wages, and so on.

measured by several formulas. In Equation 3.1, below, the real value is measured as the difference between the actual increase in the asset price and an increment corresponding to the average increase in asset prices. In Equation 3.2, the real gain is measured by the difference in real value of the property at the end and at the beginning of the holding period.[10]

$$(3.1) \qquad \Delta R_j = (V_{2j} - V_{1j}) - (P_2 - P_1)V_{1j}$$

$$(3.2) \qquad \Delta R_j = \frac{V_{2j}}{P_2} - \frac{V_{1j}}{P_1}.$$

In both equations, V_{1j} and V_{2j} represent the value of the property in the initial and terminal periods; P_1 and P_2, the price of real assets in those periods; and ΔR_j, the measure of the real gain or loss on the revaluation of the property. In general, these equations will give different results, and a choice between them is not dictated by obvious a priori principles. This problem alone makes it impossible to adopt a compelling definition of real income for tax purposes. In addition, however, real income as a tax criterion may not provide the stabilizing effect of a monetary tax criterion when the economy is experiencing inflation or deflation.[11] For all these reasons, it seems desirable to restrict the following discussion to a money concept of income.

The definition of income used here includes factor income, transfer payments, and revaluations. Conceptually this is the same as the well-known Haig-Simons definition—consumption enjoyed during a particular period, plus any accretion (or less any diminution) to net worth.[12]

Opponents of the accretion definition of income have used numerous arguments to exclude capital gains from the concept of taxable

---

[10] These formulas are discussed in George F. Break, "On the Deductibility of Capital Losses Under the Income Tax," *Journal of Finance*, Vol. 7 (May 1952), pp. 214-29.

[11] See E. Cary Brown, "Analysis of Consumption Taxes in Terms of the Theory of Income Determination," *American Economic Review*, Vol. 40 (March 1950), pp. 74-89. See also Amotz Morag, *On Taxes and Inflation* (Random House, 1965).

[12] See William S. Vickrey, *Agenda for Progressive Taxation* (Ronald Press, 1947), pp. 5-7; and Henry C. Simons, *Personal Income Taxation* (University of Chicago Press, 1938), p. 50. Net worth implicit in human training and its resultant earning capacity is disregarded.

income.[13] Two that have been the focus of recent controversy should be mentioned:

1. The inclusion of all capital gains in the concept of taxable income causes it to differ from the concept of net national product at factor cost—a point that was discussed above.

2. The appropriate income concept should be determined by the behavior of individuals with regard to components of income. That is, since increments to income (as used in aggregate economic studies) tend to produce proportional increments to consumption, receipts that do not do so should not be included in taxable income.

The first argument can be dismissed by observing that there is no necessary connection between the *personal* taxable income concept and a particular definition of a national aggregate. Indeed, many transactions that have no net effect on the national aggregate must be counted in taxable income to preserve equity.

The second argument in fact says that consumption ought to be used as an index of taxable capacity. That is, no income that does not lead to increases in consumption ought to be considered as taxable capacity. While this view is valid, it seems peculiar to designate the resulting measure of taxpaying ability as *taxable income.*[14] In any case, no definition of income has been offered that systematically excludes capital gains and remains consistent with some fairly appealing notions, such as Hicks' *ex ante* definition of income:

> Income No. 1 is thus the maximum amount which can be spent during a period if there is to be an expectation of maintaining intact the capital value of prospective receipts (in money terms).[15]

---

[13] See the conference summary in Chap. X for the discussants' views on this problem.

[14] Moreover the defense of this view is weak, since it hinges on an empirical estimate of the propensity to consume out of capital gains. If income from other sources accruing to persons whose incomes are far above the mean could be as readily identified as capital gains, it seems likely that a low marginal propensity to consume could be obtained for those items of income as well. The distinction proposed has the interesting effect of subjugating Friedman's transitory income to the same non-income role of capital gains, given that the marginal propensity to consume out of transitory income is zero, as Friedman hypothesizes. (Milton Friedman, *A Theory of the Consumption Function* [National Bureau of Economic Research—Princeton University Press, 1957].)

[15] J. R. Hicks, *Value and Capital* (Oxford: Clarendon Press, 1939), p. 173.

The corresponding *ex post* definition is the accretion definition cited above—in which capital gains constitute income as they accrue.[16]

To summarize, the source of a large part of the financing of government expenditures is not clearly determined by the character of government services or by the fiscal limitations of the government sector. This financing must be met by some general form of taxation.

Differences in ability to pay taxes and society's desire to reduce inequities in the market process through differential taxation require that taxation be assessed on a personal basis.

Personal taxation can be levied on stocks or on flows. The difficulties in assessing personal and human wealth, the problems of administering and creating an expenditure tax system, and the historical precedent created by half a century of income taxation have led to the assumption that the burdens of personal taxation are met primarily through income taxes.

Equity demands that the income concept on which such taxation is based accurately reflect differences in the ability to pay of different taxpayers. Examining various alternatives leads to an accretion definition of income defined in money terms.

Receipts for services rendered, transfer income, and the gain or loss from revaluations of property are all appropriately included in a concept of taxable income.

Period of Income Measurement

Although the scope of the income measure is set by the accretion concept, determining the period over which income will be measured for tax purposes entails three further questions:

1. The most fundamental concerns the frequency of assessment of income for tax purposes. Months, quarters, or years could be chosen as the basic income accounting period. The use of twelve months as the basis for measuring tax income is an arbitrary compromise between shorter periods, for which it might be difficult to value certain necessary expenses incurred in earning income, and longer periods,

---

[16] The reader who would like to explore these arguments further is referred to Henry C. Wallich, "Taxation of Capital Gains in the Light of Recent Economic Developments" and the comments by Walter J. Blum, "Taxation of Capital Gains in the Light of Recent Economic Developments—Some Observations," *National Tax Journal,* Vol. 18 (June and December 1965), pp. 133-50 and 430-36.

during which substantial variation in the actual rate of income flow might occur. That variation is not measured in a long-period total amount.

2. Once twelve months is accepted as the basic tax accounting period, a second question arises. Should the accrual of income or the realization of income in cash be used in the tax base? The problem can be resolved easily, at least in theory.[17] As the accrual of receipts gives rise to accounts receivable, contracts, and other evidences of obligation, the economic power of the recipient also increases. In many cases, the value of accruing receipts can be used as collateral for loans, so that the actual receipt of cash can be anticipated, and the accrued funds can be used immediately.

The ability to manipulate rights to accrued receipts implies that an appropriate concept of taxable capacity must be based on accruals. Otherwise taxable capacity and tax liability will not be synchronized, or tax liability will be based on an understatement of taxable capacity.[18]

3. The third problem in the timing and measurement of income for tax purposes revolves about the question: Should income information from tax periods other than the current year be used in computing the tax liability? Such information might be relevant, depending on social welfare judgments as to the appropriate basis for progression in the tax system.

Progression in the tax system reflects a political judgment that market forces do not distribute incomes in socially desirable ways. To reduce the inequality in the distribution of incomes that naturally results from monopoly elements in the market and the premiums paid for scarce services, relatively larger amounts of tax are collected from high-income than from low-income individuals. But how should "high-income" and "low-income" be defined? Income received during the current tax period, income received over some pe-

---

[17] In practice, evaluating accrued liabilities and accrued costs creates enormous accounting problems. These issues will be discussed in Chaps. VII and X.

[18] In fact, the distinction between accrual and cash receipts as a basis for taxation is associated largely with the two most highly debated aspects of income taxation—deductions for capital costs and the taxing of gains from asset revaluations. The latter subject is somewhat more extensive than the question of capital gains taxation, since it includes the monetary valuation problem and questions related to the taxability of accounting adjustments associated with reorganizations, mergers, and liquidations.

riod in the past, or the expected lifetime patterns of income of different individuals are possible measures of relative income position. The choice of one of these as the basis for progression requires a collective welfare judgment by the community. If the community chooses either historical income or lifetime income as the measure of relative income position, data relating to income in years other than the current one must be used to compute the tax liability for the current year. An averaging scheme of some kind would be an appropriate mechanism for taking into account information on income history. Differential rates for persons with different educational attainments or different occupations might be appropriate for progression on the basis of lifetime income.[19]

The need for averaging arises from an ethical or a political judgment that determines the criterion for progression in the tax structure. If information on taxable income in other years is relevant, it will be relevant for computing the tax liability on *all* components of current income. Thus, it does not seem to be consistent that averaging be incorporated into the tax scheme for some components of income and not for others.

If capital gains are taxed when they are realized, rather than when they accrue, this statement must be modified. In that case, gains that accrue over several years may be taxed in a single year. The degree of progression in the year of realization might be chosen on the basis of an average of marginal tax rates applicable to annual accruals. If gains were taxed as they accrued, however, it would be quite consistent to rule that only this year's marginal tax rate is appropriate for computing liability on the gain. If another principle were chosen for determining the rate of progression, it clearly should apply to all forms of income-producing elements in the tax base.

Equity, Taxable Capacity, and Capital Gains

Once a measure of taxpaying ability has been established, equity can be defined with some precision. Horizontal equity implies that taxpayers of like ability to pay taxes must bear equal tax burdens. Vertical equity requires that those with greater than average taxpay-

---

[19] See Harold Watts, "An Objective Permanent Income Concept for the Household," Cowles Foundation, Discussion Paper No. 99, unpublished, Nov. 23, 1960.

ing ability pay taxes at a higher average rate, in accord with a social consensus on the appropriate degree of progression.

On the assumption that capital gains are income, preferential capital gains taxation robs the tax structure of both kinds of equity. Persons with equal ability to pay, in terms of the income concept developed above, may pay quite different taxes. Those with wages or interest income pay at the full rates. But income in the form of capital gains is more accessible to high-income taxpayers, and thus, as income rises, effective tax rates depart increasingly from the legally established rates.[20] Rate progression thus depends on the extent to which an individual realizes capital gains. Certain taxpayers may pay much less (or possibly more) than the amount that would be demanded by an agreed-upon desirable rate progression.

The system not only reduces the progression implicit in the structure of legal bracket rates, it also creates a situation in which the tax increase experienced by persons with more rapidly growing incomes (at income levels above $100,000) is less than the increase for those whose incomes are growing more slowly.[21] This can be attributed to the ability of high-income persons to use their wealth for tax avoidance through the capital gains provisions at the same time that they are able to take advantage of their skills and knowledge of the asset market to maximize return.[22]

---

[20] See Chap. IV, Table 4-18.

[21] Douglas Dosser discusses the incidence of taxes on increased income, which he calls "dynamic incidence," in "Tax Incidence and Growth," *Economic Journal,* Vol. 71 (September 1961), pp. 572-91. Dynamic regression occurs if:

$$\left(\frac{dR_{1s}/dt}{dR_{2s}/dt} \right) \div \left(\frac{dR_{1f}/dt}{dR_{2f}/dt} \right) < 1,$$

where R is realized income; s and f denote income classes whose income is growing relatively more "slowly" or "fast" in terms of R. Subscripts 1 and 2 denote before-tax and after-tax magnitudes.

[22] Dynamic regression apparently occurred during the 1958-59 bull market and may be influenced by the general conditions in the market. (Harley H. Hinrichs, "Dynamic-Regressive Effects of the Treatment of Capital Gains on the American Tax System During 1957-1959," *Public Finance,* Vol. 19, No. 1 [1964], pp. 73-83.) Hinrichs used data on aggregate income classes in making the comparison. Persons may have moved between income classes in the years that he studied. Thus it is possible, but unlikely, that the increase in tax for individuals is different from that calculated for an income group.

The Double Taxation Argument

One additional problem in income analysis should be examined. Does the taxation of changes in capital value subject changes in earning power to double taxation, once at the time when a change in income is anticipated by the market and once when income is actually realized? The point of view taken here can be expressed in the following rate-of-return formulations.

If R reflects the market rate of return and a stream of real income G_k is anticipated from a given investment for a period of N years, then:

$$(3.3) \qquad V = \sum_{k=1}^{N} \frac{G_k P_k}{(1 + R)^k},$$

where V expresses the present money value of that investment and P_k reflects a suitable price index for expressing G_k in money terms. Taxation of income clearly reduces the present value of an asset by a factor of $(1 - t)$ if the tax rate is fixed and uniform over time:[23]

$$(3.4) \qquad V_t = V(1 - t) = \sum_{k=1}^{N} \frac{G_k P_k (1 - t)}{(1 + R)^k}.$$

If valuations change because of changes in the expected yield of the investments, these rate-of-return formulas suggest that the change in capital value ought not to be taxed. If capital value is also taxed at a rate g, then the holder of a capital asset can realize a larger present value by retaining the asset until maturity than by selling it on the open market; sales are inhibited by the transaction cost implied in the tax rate g; buyers are forced to accept somewhat less than the prior rate of return on their assets; and the allocation of resources is distorted in directions that require labor or nontransferable capital.

This argument convinces many that capital gains ought to be exempted from the personal income tax base. Paradoxically that ex-

[23] Actually this equation reflects the effect of the average tax rate on the average taxpayer-investor. Someone whose marginal tax rate is extremely high would normally expect a lesser return on his investment than the market rate since all income-earning possibilities are more heavily taxed to him than to the average investor.

emption shatters the firm connection between a personal basis for taxation and actual assessments. As soon as a form of exemption enters the tax computation that is not related to personal characteristics but rests on the nature of income sources, or on the conditions of income receipt, individuals may avoid taxation by taking their income in the favored type of income or the favored form of receipt.

Fortunately, the paradox is apparent rather than real. A change in the present value of an investment ought to be subject to tax under the above circumstances, since the change in value generally corresponds to investment that was in some way added to the original asset value by the present owner or his agents. The reinvestment of savings by a corporation produces gains that are naturally associated with returns from additional physical capital. This process is identical to that by which the investor diverts a part of his receipts to new savings—a process in which a tax is levied on the receipts.

A change in the present value of an investment may also be derived from changes in P_k or R. It was indicated above that revaluations associated with price level changes are not easily excluded from a definition of taxable income. Gains associated with changes in R are even less easily segregated from a flow of other types of income. Changes in R are associated with physical changes in the productivity and longevity of the nation's capital stock or with explicit fiscal and monetary measures designed to influence the allocation of the nation's product between consumption and investment. In the former case, revaluation is again associated with the corporate reinvestment process discussed in the paragraph above. In the latter case, revaluation derives from overt policy, and it would appear that no purpose is served by insulating individuals from the intended allocation effects of government fiscal policy by some contrived definition of taxable income. No argument presented thus far makes a good case for considering gain and loss as anything but income.

One instance appears to create some difficulties. Suppose the investor in question had done nothing to produce the additional increment in value corresponding to the increased general income anticipated for this investment. Then the income and the increase in value would be a true windfall. If windfall gains and windfall losses cancel out in the aggregate, the assessment of capital gains taxes does not discriminate against capital investments. Assessment causes some income redistribution and distortion in tax burden to the extent that windfalls form a part of the distribution of income. While there may be discrimination against some taxpayers due to the asymmetric tax rates associated with windfall gains and losses of equal size, the adverse taxation of gains is a secondary effect. The argument that taxation of gains discriminates against capital loses much of its force.

If windfall gains and losses do not cancel out in the aggregate, it is clearly possible for the tax to discriminate in favor of, or against, capital investments. However, it is not clear that such discrimination is undesirable. Inflation-induced gains would be automatically taxed at discriminatory rates, favoring the substitution of labor-intensive rather than capital-intensive techniques in production and restricting the extent to which paper gains can be converted into cash items disposable for the limited supply of real commodities available in the economy. The effect would be a desirable fluctuation in tax yields over the business cycle.

If net windfall gains are induced by declines in the market rate of interest, the resulting capital gains taxes will not have desirable counter-cyclical effects. However, the equity of this one case in which the taxation of gains is both discriminatory and undesirable must be assessed by considering the other fiscal and monetary policies that precipitated or endorsed such a change.

The case for taxing capital gains as income is even stronger than the above argument would suggest. Even the taxation of a windfall gain is not "double taxation." Given a sudden increase in the valuation of a particular productive opportunity—such as a uranium mine—the investor may realize his income over the life of the investment. In that case he is permitted to amortize his investment in computing taxable income. If the asset is sold and capital gains are realized, the buyer obtains both the real yields of the investment *and* an *increased basis* from which amortization may be computed. Thus the buyer pays less taxes in an amount algebraically equivalent to that on which the seller has paid capital gains taxes.[24]

---

[24] If the investment has an indefinite lifetime, the result is equivalent. Capital gains taxes would be paid either by the seller at the time of accrual or by his estate at death if the gains were constructively realized. The buyer or heir would acquire an asset which has the same basis as the sum of the original owner's cost and capital gain. Assuming a constant market rate of return, the buyer would sell the asset at cost, realize no gain or loss, and pay tax on only the current yield of the investment. If capital gains were not taxed in this instance, the original owner would be able to sell an asset, after which there would be an increase in basis implying *less* taxation in the aggregate when the owner of a windfall sells in preference to holding the asset.

The extent of double taxation thus appears to depend on the effectiveness of tax rules for recovering basis on assets with a limited life. Premiums paid for bonds, for example, can be amortized over the life of the bonds, and so on.

These arguments may be summarized as follows, with a classification based on the source of change in the present value V of an investment:

1. Change in real income prospects G_k:
    a. Association with investment of business saving: gains taxable as income, since this event is identical to explicit receipt of income followed by investment.
    b. Windfall, not associated with business saving: gains necessarily taxable as income; taxation of gains implies no "double taxation"; if asset is sold, capital gains taxes are levied; but new owner acquires increased basis (against which to charge depreciation if asset has a finite life).
2. Change in expected prices P_k: gains properly included in income so long as taxation is accounted in *nominal,* not real, terms.
3. Change in market rate of return R: gains taxable as income; revaluation associated with level of business investment as well as government's fiscal policy.

Thus it is concluded that:

1. Under an income tax system individuals who have the same potential for consumption and saving should be taxed equally to meet a large part of the public sector's financing requirements. Equity requires that taxable income should include receipts for services rendered to the economy, transfer payments, and the gain or loss from revaluations of property on a money basis.
2. The choice of a basic period over which income is measured is arbitrary and conventional.
3. Since accruing rights to income give rise to potential consumption or savings, these accrued rights should in principle be taxed in the period when they accrue, not in the period when they appear as cash receipts. Difficulties of valuation and compliance may warrant taxing rights when they are realized, but this should be recognized as a compromise of the underlying income concept.

4. The decision that establishes the progression of rates on taxable income embodies a social welfare judgment by the entire community. The rate structure need not be based on the measure of taxable income in any one year, but may depend on broader criteria, such as the income history of the individual or his expected lifetime income. If the progression of tax rates is based on long-term considerations, those considerations determine a formula under which capital gains are taxed. Conversely, if it is the social welfare judgment of the community that progression should be determined by the measure of taxable income in a single year, it is not generally appropriate for multi-period considerations to enter the *tax rate* formula for capital gains.

5. In most instances taxation of capital gains is appropriate as a technique for levying personal taxes against values created and retained within the corporate business.

CHAPTER IV

Statistical Background

THE INFORMATION NEEDED TO evaluate properly the alternative approaches to capital gains taxation is hard to obtain. Some of the central questions concern the reactions of investors to alternative tax structures—a subject about which little is known. Moreover, much of the appreciation that might be taxed under alternative schemes lies hidden in private portfolios. Their value is rarely measured, and therefore it is not known precisely how much they have appreciated. Realized capital gains, which have been reported on individual and corporate income tax returns, constitute only a small fraction of the appreciation that has accrued to households and corporations since preferential capital gains taxation was introduced in 1922.

A variety of statistics can be used to show that the major portion of appreciation in the economy has escaped taxation as capital gains. Although a part of the appreciation extant at present may be taxed in future years, if past upward trends in asset values continue, the major portion of appreciation will continue to escape taxation.[1] Computations by Martin Bailey suggest that 80 to 90 percent of the approximately $700 billion of appreciation on corporate shares between 1926 and 1961 has never been taxed. McClung's estimate suggests

[1] This is strictly analogous to Eisner's well-known argument concerning the deferral of taxation under programs of accelerated depreciation. See Robert Eisner, "Accelerated Amortization, Growth, and Net Profits," *Quarterly Journal of Economics,* Vol. 66 (November 1952), pp. 533-44.

that 60 percent of some $400 billion accruing on shares between 1922 and 1963 has never been realized.[2] (The difference between the two figures lies both in the period of time over which appreciation was estimated and in the method by which realizations of capital gains were estimated. The estimates are critically analyzed on pages 93-99.)

Both of the foregoing estimates are concerned with appreciation accruing on particular sources of wealth and the corresponding realizations. A broader picture of the problem, as well as an insight into the significance of recent developments, can be obtained by studying increments to national wealth in the period 1951-58. To what extent increments in the wealth of different individuals and corporations should be consolidated for this computation is not entirely clear. Because of intercorporate shareholdings, a given increase in the valuation of real operating assets may be reflected several times in the value of different corporate equities and may mean more than one corresponding increase in potential capital gains liability. In addition, both the increment in value of real assets and the increment in value of shares may create capital gains and potential tax liabilities. Thus it may be appropriate to measure realized capital gains against the aggregate appreciation of real and financial assets, although this would clearly involve some double counting of the nation's wealth.

To add to the difficulties, nonprofit corporations and beneficial trusts may not be liable to capital gains taxation. Thus increments to their wealth are irrelevant unless changes in their tax-exempt status are contemplated. Less than $100 billion of capital gains were realized during a seven-year period when the relevant appreciation in assets of the economy was somewhere between $250 billion and $1,000 billion, according to Table 4-1.

Most of the data that follow pertain to gains that have been realized and taxed in the postwar period.[3] While the figures cover only

[2] Martin J. Bailey, "Capital Gains and Income Taxation," in Arnold C. Harberger and Martin J. Bailey (eds.), *Taxation of Income from Capital* (Brookings Institution, 1968), and Nelson McClung, "The Distribution of Capital Gain on Corporate Shares by Holding Time," *Review of Economics and Statistics*, Vol. 48 (February 1966), pp. 40-50. See Table 4-23, below.

[3] Further historical data can be obtained covering experience under the capital gains law from 1917 through 1946 in Lawrence H. Seltzer's classic study, *The Nature and Tax Treatment of Capital Gains and Losses* (National Bureau of Economic Research, 1951). Data included in this chapter pertain almost exclusively to the period since 1948.

TABLE 4-1. Appreciation in National Wealth, 1951–58
(In billions of 1958 dollars)

Item	Net stock of tangible assets only (1)	Noncorporate tangible assets plus increase in the value of shares held by households (2)	Aggregate of assets held by major sectors of the economy (3)
Change in asset value, 1951–58	459	—	1,200
Less net investment in tangible assets during the period	204	—	204
Appreciation subject to capital gains taxation	255[ab]	324[ac]	996[d]

Source: The estimates in Cols. (1) and (2) were made by Samuel B. Chase, Jr., of the Brookings Institution. The underlying statistics come from Raymond W. Goldsmith and Robert E. Lipsey, *Studies in the National Balance Sheet of the United States* (Princeton University Press for National Bureau of Economic Research, 1963), Vol. 1, p. 46 and elsewhere.

[a] Possibly an understatement due to multiple increments in equity values associated with a given increase in real tangible asset values.

[b] Based on the replacement cost of tangible assets.

[c] Exceeds Col. (1), since the value of corporate equities has historically been less than Goldsmith's values for the replacement cost of corporate assets, although the former has grown more rapidly.

[d] May overstate taxable appreciation, since assets of tax-exempt trusts and nonprofit corporations are included

a small fraction of the potential gains on property, they provide significant insight into the distributional consequences of changes in capital gains taxation.

Outlined below are the recent trends in capital gains reported on federal income tax returns and the characteristics of those who have taken advantage of the preferential rates. The rest of the chapter is devoted to data on the impact of major reforms in the capital gains tax on individuals.

Recent Trends in Reported Capital Gains

From 1948 to 1963 the yield of capital gains taxes rose markedly; it more than trebled on both corporate and noncorporate tax returns. Roughly one-fourth of all taxes paid on capital gains were paid by corporate taxpayers. The greater portion of the yield came from individual returns, although enough appeared on fiduciary returns that they cannot be disregarded altogether.

Reported realizations of capital gains have not conformed closely to the major business cycle movements during the postwar period.

FIGURE 4-1. Growth of Estimated Capital Gains Tax and Income Tax Yields, 1948–63

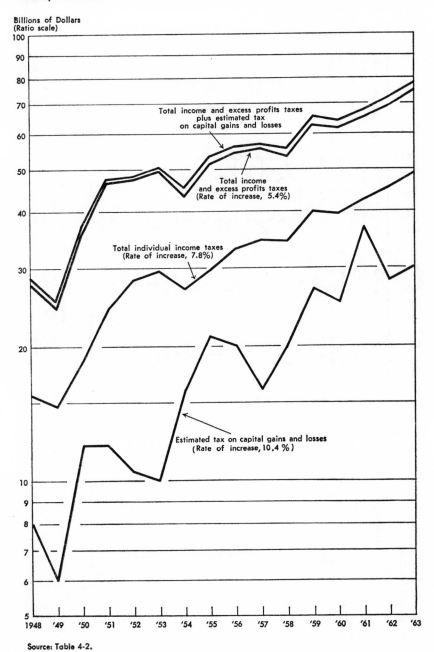

Source: Table 4-2.

TABLE 4-2. Estimated Revenue Yield from Capital Gains and Income Taxation, 1948–65ᵃ
(Dollar amounts in billions)

Calendar year of liability	Individuals and fiduciaries			Corporations			Individuals, fiduciaries, and corporations		
	Total income taxes	Estimated tax on capital gains and losses		Total income and excess profits taxes	Estimated tax on capital gains and losses		Total income and excess profits taxes	Estimated tax on capital gains and losses	
		Amount	As a percentage of total tax		Amount	As a percentage of total tax		Amount	As a percentage of total tax
1948	$15.6	$0.6	3.8	$11.9	$0.2	1.7	$27.5	$0.8	2.9
1949	14.7	0.4	2.7	9.8	0.2	2.0	24.5	0.6	2.4
1950	18.5	0.9	4.9	17.3	0.3	1.7	35.9	1.2	3.3
1951	24.4	0.9	3.7	22.1	0.3	1.4	46.5	1.2	2.6
1952	28.0	0.8	2.9	19.1	0.3	1.6	47.2	1.1	2.3
1953	29.7	0.7	2.4	19.9	0.3	1.5	49.6	1.0	2.0
1954	26.9	1.1	4.1	16.9	0.5	3.0	43.8	1.6	3.7
1955	29.9	1.6	5.4	21.7	0.5	2.3	51.6	2.1	4.1
1956	33.1	1.5	4.5	21.4	0.5	2.3	54.5	2.0	3.7
1957	34.8	1.2	3.4	20.6	0.4	1.9	55.4	1.6	2.9
1958	34.7	1.4	4.0	18.8	0.6	3.2	53.5	2.0	3.7
1959	40.0	2.3	5.8	22.5	0.4	1.8	62.5	2.7	4.3
1960	39.8	1.9	4.8	21.9	0.6	2.7	61.7	2.5	4.1
1961	42.6	2.9	6.8	22.2	0.8	3.6	64.8	3.7	5.7
1962	45.3	2.1	4.6	23.9	0.7	2.9	69.2	2.8	4.0
1963	48.7	2.3	4.7	26.3	0.7	2.7	75.0	3.0	4.0
1964	47.6	2.7	5.7	n.a.	n.a.	n.a.	n.a.	n.a.	n.a.
1965	50.0	3.4	6.8	n.a.	n.a.	n.a.	n.a.	n.a.	n.a.

Source: Office of the Secretary of the Treasury, Office of Tax Analysis. The actual revenue figures are as reported in U.S Treasury Department, Internal Revenue Service, *Statistics of Income*, annual issues. Percentages are derived from rounded data.

n.a. Not available.

ᵃ The estimated tax on capital gains and losses for each of the specified years is the difference between (1) the total individual and corporation income taxes reported in *Statistics of Income*, and (2) the total of such taxes that would have been realized if capital gains and losses had been excluded entirely from the tax computation.

Estimates of capital gains tax revenue are subject to a rather significant margin of error for individuals. These estimates are approximations of the effect on tax liabilities of a recomputation of tax excluding the amount reported as capital gains and losses. These gains and losses are treated as final sources of income or deduction, and therefore the revenue effect is based on marginal rates. In addition, the estimates are based upon summary data. The possible error is reduced somewhat where cross classifications by size of adjusted gross income and size of capital gains income or loss are available.

FIGURE 4-2. Capital Gains Tax Yield As a Percentage of Total Income and Excess Profits Taxes, 1948–63

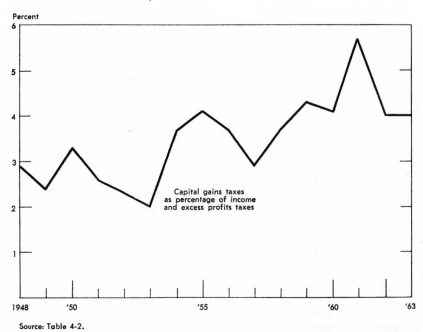

Source: Table 4-2.

They increased, for example, during the 1953-54, 1957-58, and 1960-61 recessions. In contrast, realizations declined during the 1948-49 recession.[4] Thus the yield of the capital gains tax has been destabilizing during most of the post-World War II period. (See Figure 4-1.) At present it is not known whether this pattern can be modified by structural changes in the taxation of capital gains. (This problem is discussed in Chapters V-VIII in connection with specific proposals for reform.) It is also not clear how capital asset sales are timed within the year, so it is difficult to be certain how to interpret the annual data.

The yield of the capital gains tax has risen even more rapidly than that of income taxes generally. (See Table 4-2 and Figure 4-2.) Since the income tax yield has been rising more rapidly than personal income and gross national product, it follows that the capital gains tax is becoming a more important part of the United States tax system.

[4] See Wilfred Lewis, Jr., *Federal Fiscal Policy in the Postwar Recessions* (Brookings Institution, 1962), pp. 49-50.

TABLE 4-3. Individual Income Tax Returns Reporting Net Gain or Loss on Sales of Capital Assets, 1945–64

(Number of returns in thousands)

Year	Number of Returns			Percent of returns reporting either net gain or loss
	Reporting net gain[a]	Reporting net loss[b]	Reporting either net gain or loss	
	(1)	(2)	(3)	(4)
1945	1,671	392	2,063	4.13
1946	2,245	502	2,747	5.20
1947	1,867	610	2,477	4.49
1948	1,694	586	2,280	4.38
1949	1,439	697	2,136	4.12
1950	1,896	668	2,564	4.83
1951	2,132	582	2,714	4.89
1952	2,034	666	2,700	4.78
1953	1,988	789	2,777	4.80
1954	2,411	664	3,075	5.42
1955	2,900	654	3,554	6.10
1956	3,148	784	3,932	6.64
1957	2,937	1,038	3,975	6.64
1958	3,469	921	4,390	7.43
1959	4,007	900	4,907	8.14
1960	3,842	1,154	4,996	8.19
1961	4,698	1,097	5,796	9.42
1962	4,323	1,599	5,922	9.44
1963	4,947	1,595	6,542	10.23
1964	5,321	1,502	6,822	10.44

Source: U.S. Treasury Department, Internal Revenue Service, *Statistics of Income, Individual Income Tax Returns* various issues. Details may not add to totals due to rounding.
[a] Net positive balance from sale of capital assets and loss carry-over.
[b] Net negative balance from sale of capital assets and loss carry-over.

From 1948 to 1963, yields from the capital gains tax rose approximately 10 percent a year, while the combined yield of income and excess profits taxes rose only 5 percent annually.

Capital Gains of Individual Taxpayers

The increase in capital gains taxes can be attributed to a variety of factors. The proportion of individuals reporting capital gains or losses on their income tax returns more than doubled during the period from 1945 to 1964. (See Table 4-3.) In part, that increase can be attributed to growth in the net worth of individuals over this period. From 1950 to 1962 the proportion of spending units with less than $1,000 of net worth fell from 35 to 30 percent. Between 1953 and 1962 the median net worth rose from $4,100 to $4,700, and the pro-

TABLE 4-4. Composition of Net Worth by Age Cohort, 1953 and 1962
(Assets and debt as percentages of net worth)

| Composition of net worth | Net worth of cohort identified by age of spending unit head in 1962 | | | | | |
| | 35–44 years | | 45–54 years | | 55–64 years | |
	1953	1962	1953	1962	1953	1962
Variable value assets						
Consumer capital goods	71	74	56	49	41	48
Business and investment assets	47	61	50	60	53	49
Fixed value assets	16	11	16	14	15	18
Gross worth	134	146	122	123	109	115
Less debt	34	46	22	23	9	15
Net worth	100	100	100	100	100	100

Source: George Katona, Charles A. Lininger, and Richard F. Kosobud, *1962 Survey of Consumer Finances* (University of Michigan, Institute for Social Research, Survey Research Center, 1963), Table 6–15, p. 142.

portion of spending units with more than $10,000 of net worth increased from 29 to 34 percent.[5]

Between 1953 and 1962, young and middle-aged spending units increased their holdings of equity assets substantially. That element in the increase in net worth is probably responsible for some of the increase in the proportion of taxpayers realizing capital gains. Debt also increased for all age groups under 65 and financed an expansion of portfolios greater than the increases in net worth. (See Table 4-4.)

The substantial increase in stock ownership among families in the United States is indicative of the growth in equity investments. The proportion of families owning stock has increased from 10 percent in 1955 to 14 percent in 1960 to 21 percent in 1964.[6]

Further increases in the number of taxpayers reporting capital gains are undoubtedly associated with the broadened eligibility for capital gains treatment. Preferential capital gains treatment was granted in 1950 to stock purchased under restricted employee stock options; in 1951, to proceeds of the sale of livestock; and in 1954,

[5] George Katona, Charles A. Lininger, and Richard F. Kosobud, *1962 Survey of Consumer Finances* (University of Michigan, Institute for Social Research, Survey Research Center, 1963), p. 128.

[6] *Survey of Consumer Finances,* 1960 and 1964 volumes (University of Michigan, Institute for Social Research, Survey Research Center, 1961, 1965), pp. 95 and 96, respectively.

TABLE 4-5. Capital Gain and Loss Reported on Individual Income Tax Returns, 1952–64

Year	Net gain (including loss carry-over)[a] (millions) (1)	Net loss (including loss carry-over)[b] (millions) (2)	Total net gain less net loss (millions)[c] (3)	Average net gain less net loss on returns with sales of capital assets (4)
1952	$5,635	$1,354	$4,764	$1,764
1953	5,092	1,806	3,943	1,420
1954	7,388	1,446	6,656	2,164
1955	10,135	1,456	9,328	2,625
1956	9,995	1,599	8,970	2,281
1957	8,474	2,401	6,931	1,744
1958	9,777	2,335	8,583	1,955
1959	13,553	2,282	12,333	2,513
1960	12,140	2,834	10,377	2,077
1961	16,546	2,851	14,752	2,545
1962	14,034	4,354	11,014	1,860
1963	15,168	4,579	12,852	1,964
1964	18,127	4,733	15,709	2,303

Source: U.S. Treasury Department, Internal Revenue Service, *Statistics of Income, Individual Income Tax Returns,* various years.

[a] Sum of (1) net short-term gain and (2) net long-term gain on returns with net gain and (3) net short-term gain and (4) net long-term gain on returns with net capital loss. Loss not deductible in prior years is treated as a short-term capital loss to arrive at the net balance on short-term transactions. This amount is less than the gross gain on sales with net gain, since transactions are aggregated within short-term and long-term categories.

[b] Similar to Col. (1), except all net losses reported are summed.

[c] All capital loss carry-overs are added to the sum of Cols. (1) and (2). If the sum of Cols. (1) and (2) equals $A + C$, where A is the net proceeds of capital asset sales this year and $C < 0$ is the loss carry-over from prior years, A can be derived by subtracting C from the sum of Cols. (1) and (2).

to royalties on patents. Furthermore, during the last few years the number of returns reporting net gains appears to have risen in relation to the number reporting net losses.

While the amounts of capital gains and losses realized have increased substantially in the aggregate, the average net increase in returns reporting gains or losses on the sale of capital assets has not occurred systematically. (See Table 4-5.) Average net gain fluctuates erratically, showing no obvious correlation with Arthur M. Okun's estimates of the relative GNP gap or with changes in the Consumer Price Index.[7] (See Appendix B for statistical qualifications.)

[7] Okun's series, which were used by the President's Council of Economic Advisers, are quoted in Table A-2, p. 124, of Michael E. Levy, *Fiscal Policy, Cycles and Growth,* Studies in Business Economics, No. 81 (National Industrial Conference Board, 1963).

TABLE 4-6. Estimate of Underreporting by Individuals of Capital Gains Realized on Corporate Stock Traded in 1959 and 1961

(In billions of dollars)

Item	1959	1961
1. Volume of shares traded	$80.0	$103.5
2. Shares traded by individuals	42.8	53.2
3. Long-term capital gains		
a. Estimated	27.6	33.0
b. Reported (*Statistics of Income*)	17.5	21.3
4. Net long-term gains realized by individuals		
a. Estimated	8.1	9.7
b. Reported (*Statistics of Income*)	5.1	6.2
5. Unreported net long-term gains	3.0	3.5
6. Underreporting as a percentage of all gains	37%	36%
7. Revenue loss from underreporting (millions of dollars)	645	750

Source: Harley H. Hinrichs, "Unreporting of Capital Gains on Tax Returns or How To Succeed in Gainsmanship Without Actually Paying Taxes," *National Tax Journal*, Vol. 17 (June 1964), p. 159.

For criticism and rejoinder on these statistics see: Stan West and James W. Riley, "How to Succeed in Figuremanship Without Having All the Figures," and Harley H. Hinrichs, "Altruism on Wall Street or Who's Afraid of the IRS? A Reply to West and Riley," *National Tax Journal*, Vol. 18 (March 1965), pp. 78–90 and 91–96, respectively.

Actually, the percentage of individuals receiving capital gains and the amounts received are probably grossly understated. Hinrichs estimates that at least one-third of individuals' capital gains on traded corporate securities are never reported. (See Table 4-6.) While underreporting is probably not related to current business conditions, it is likely to be inversely related to the frequency of asset transactions and the taxpayer's adjusted gross income. Tax returns by individuals in high income brackets are more widely and systematically audited than are tax returns of low income recipients. The scope of underreporting unfortunately implies that there may be a substantial bias in the tax return data.[8]

Capital Gains of Corporate Taxpayers

Net long-term capital gains have become increasingly important in the corporate tax base. (See Table 4-7.) The aggregate of net long-term capital gains (less short-term losses) more than trebled in the period from 1952 to 1964.[9] A modest increase in the amount of gain

[8] The gap has closed considerably as the increased use of information on returns and electronic processing of tax returns after 1962 have made taxpayers aware that relatively small or infrequent receipts can be detected by the Internal Revenue Service.

[9] A part of that gain probably reflects an increased turnover of capital assets.

TABLE 4-7. Net Long-Term Gain on Sales of Capital Assets Reported on Active Corporation Income Tax Returns, 1952-64

Year	Excess of net short-term capital gain over net long-term capital loss (millions) (1)	Net long-term capital gain reduced by net short-term capital loss (millions) (2)	Total gain on capital assets[a] (1)+(2) (millions) (3)	Average net long-term capital gain less short-term capital loss[b] (4)	Net long-term capital gain less short-term capital loss as a percentage of net income[c] (5)	Ratio of total gain on capital assets to net income[d] (6)
1952	$ 25	$ 1,354	$ 1,379	$2,014	3.5	3.6
1953	30	1,235	1,265	1,770	3.1	3.2
1954	71	1,930	2,001	2,670	5.3	5.5
1955	46	2,205	2,251	2,731	4.6	4.7
1956	45	2,332	2,377	2,633	5.0	5.1
1957	50	2,100	2,150	2,234	4.7	4.8
1958	76	3,027	3,104	3,057	7.9	8.1
1959	72	2,971	3,043	2,766	6.4	6.5
1960	84	3,058	3,142	2,681	7.0	7.2
1961	90	4,458	4,547	3,745	9.7	9.9
1962	85	3,767	3,852	2,970	7.6	7.8
1963	89	3,943	4,033	2,980	7.3	7.4
1964[e]	86	4,360	4,446	3,174	7.1	7.2
All years	$850	$36,739	$37,589	$2,807	6.2	6.3

Source: U.S. Treasury Department, Internal Revenue Service, *Statistics of Income, Corporation Income Tax Returns*, various years. Calculations and totals are based on unrounded data.
[a] This item includes only capital asset transactions resulting in net long-term capital gains over net short-term capital losses and net long-term capital gains over net short-term capital losses. It excludes net gains arising from sales of capital assets, which amounts to $13,739 million from 1952 to 1962. It is possible that realized gains may have been somewhat understated.
[b] Col. (2) divided by number of active corporation returns.
[c] Col. (2) divided by total net income (less deficit).
[d] Col. (3) divided by total net income (less deficit).
[e] Preliminary.

TABLE 4-8. Net Gain Less Net Loss from Sales of Capital Assets Reported on All Fiduciary Returns, 1947–62[a]

Year	Number of returns	Total income[b] (thousands)	Net gain less net loss from sales of capital assets[c] (thousands)	Average net gain less net loss from sales of capital assets per return
1947	109,997	$ 973,583	$ 142,903	$1,299
1948	101,283	986,806	140,925	1,391
1949	99,577	926,806	105,511	1,060
1950	115,252	1,233,957	210,804	1,829
1951	116,210	1,202,376	210,015	1,807
1952	422,663	2,788,160	268,564	635
1954	424,915	3,861,924	826,241	1,944
1956	490,696	4,884,419	1,172,568	2,390
1958	558,357	5,055,057	1,060,193	1,899
1960	579,660	5,267,022	1,237,221	2,134
1962	598,160	5,937,095	1,589,087	2,657

Source: U.S. Treasury Department, Internal Revenue Service, *Statistics of Income, Fiduciary, Gift, and Estate Tax Returns*, various years.

[a] For 1951 and earlier years, data include only taxable returns. Data for nontaxable returns are not available.

[b] Total income includes 100 percent of capital gains; it excludes net capital losses in excess of $1,000.

[c] Any loss carry-over from prior years is treated as a short-term capital loss. Hence these figures understate the true amounts of gains on the returns.

per active corporation indicates that the growth is not due solely to the increase in the number of corporations. Corporate enterprise has clearly moved toward greater use of the preferential capital gains tax provisions. Although these data provide no clues to the underlying causes of this trend, it is likely that accelerated depreciation, in conjunction with Section 1231, accounts for a part of the increase in gains. The remainder is probably associated with the same recapitalization of shares, increased valuation of good will, and inflationary pressures that account for a large part of the increase in capital gains of individuals.

Capital Gains of Fiduciary Taxpayers

The increase in capital gains reported on fiduciary returns has been phenomenal. Both the numbers of fiduciary returns and the amount of total income reported on those returns have grown more than five-fold from 1947 to 1962. (See Table 4-8.) That rate of increase accounts for the major part of the more than ten-fold increase in capital gains reported on fiduciary returns. The remaining increase

TABLE 4-9. Net Gain Less Net Loss from Sales of Capital Assets Reported on Fiduciary Returns with Capital Gain and Loss, 1947–62

Year	Total number of returns	Number of taxable returns	Amount of net gain reported on returns with net gain (thousands)[a]	Amount of net loss reported on returns with net loss (thousands)	Net gain less net loss as a percentage of total income[b]	Average net gain less net loss per return	Average net gain less net loss per taxable return
1947	n.a.	56,830	$ 146,535	$ 3,632	14.7	n.a.	$ 2,515
1948	n.a.	48,843	144,583	3,658	14.3	n.a.	2,885
1949	n.a.	47,621	108,968	3,457	11.4	n.a.	2,216
1950	n.a.	62,038	213,237	2,433	17.1	n.a.	3,398
1951	n.a.	64,112	212,407	2,392	17.5	n.a.	3,276
1952	196,367	73,354	292,837	24,273	9.6	$1,368	3,661
1954	172,896	73,790	835,779	9,538	21.4	4,779	11,197
1956	213,214	98,722	1,188,508	15,940	24.0	5,499	11,877
1958	245,244	105,852	1,073,400	13,207	21.0	4,323	10,016
1960	244,561	125,722	1,259,297	22,076	23.5	5,059	9,841
1962	276,025	153,166	1,617,386	28,299	26.8	5,757	10,375

Source: U.S. Treasury Department, Internal Revenue Service, Statistics of Income, Fiduciary, Gift, and Estate Tax Returns, various issues.
n.a. Not available.
[a] Any loss carry-over from prior years is treated as a short-term capital loss. Hence these figures understate the true amounts of gains on the returns.
[b] Total income includes 100 percent of capital gains; it excludes net capital losses in excess of $1,000.

in capital gains is accounted for by the increased share of total income that is derived from sales of capital assets. Between 1947 and 1962 capital gains grew from roughly one-sixth to over one-fourth of total income.[10] This increase amounts to a quadrupling of the average net gain (less net loss) reported on taxable returns of fiduciary taxpayers who sold capital assets. (See Table 4-9.)

Characteristics of Transactions Producing Capital Gains

Internal Revenue Service data give some clues as to the nature of transactions that produce capital gains. A detailed tabulation of transactions reported on individual tax returns for 1962 indicates the relationship between gains, gross proceeds, and the type of transaction, as well as the relationship between the gains realized in particular types of transactions and the income level of the taxpayer. These data are summarized in Tables 4-10 to 4-12.[11] The degree of appreciation of assets sold, the period held, and the distribution of types of assets sold are probably all sensitive to economic conditions generally. Therefore, the statistics shown must be interpreted as general magnitudes that may vary substantially over a business cycle.

Table 4-10 shows the distribution of capital asset sales by type of asset. Capital assets most frequently reported are corporate stock, capital gain dividends, livestock, assets used in trade or business, and proceeds of installment sales of prior years. Proceeds from the sale of corporation stocks and nonbusiness real estate constitute three-fifths of the value of gross proceeds of capital asset sales.[12] These asset types also produced more than one-third of total gains less losses.

Appreciation realized on the sale of capital assets represents almost a third of the gross proceeds of sales of stock and of business

[10] On fiduciary returns total income includes 100 percent of all capital gains; on individual income tax returns, only 50 percent of net long-term gains less short-term losses is included in adjusted gross income. Hence the ratio of net long-term gains less losses to income on fiduciary returns and the corresponding ratio on individual returns are not comparable. The amount of net gain less net loss in Tables 4-5 and 4-8 is comparable.

[11] Seltzer has tabulated similar data for samples of high-income taxpayers and traders in stock in selected years, 1917-37. See Seltzer, *op. cit.*, Tables 42-65, pp. 449-89; and Tables 82-86, pp. 518-21.

[12] No amount corresponding to gross proceeds could be assigned to certain types of transactions, such as distributions of capital gains dividends from corporations.

TABLE 4-10. Distribution of Long-Term Capital Asset Sales Reported on Individual Income Tax Returns, by Type of Asset, 1962[a]

Type of asset	Each asset type as a percentage of		Percentage of gross proceeds		Each asset type as a percentage of total long-term gain less loss
	Total returns with long-term asset sales (A)	Total gross proceeds of sales (B)	Long-term capital gain (C)	Long-term capital loss (D)	(E)
Corporate stock	35.1	54.6	31.5	15.0	30.1
U. S. government obligations	0.7	1.6	2.7	1.1	0.1
State and local securities	0.9	2.2	6.8	2.6	0.3
Other bonds, notes, and debentures	0.7	0.9	9.8	17.6	−0.2
Insurance and annuities	0.1	0.1	51.0	4.7	0.1
Options to buy or sell	0.1	0.1	51.0	9.7	0.1
Commodities including future contracts	0.2	0.3	13.3	7.6	0.1
Capital gain dividends	28.9	c	c	c	4.4
Share of capital gain (loss) from partnerships and fiduciaries	6.7	c	c	c	8.0
Capital gain distributions from small business corporations	0.5	c	c	c	0.5
Liquidation distributions	0.8	c	c	c	4.4
Retirement plan distributions	1.1	c	c	c	2.6
Livestock	12.3	2.5	74.8	3.0	6.1
Timber and coal	1.1	0.4	81.6	2.8	0.9
Oil and mineral interests	0.4	0.3	67.8	12.7	0.6
Partnership interests	1.5	1.9	47.4	3.6	2.8
Assets used in trade or business	7.7	8.7	30.4	4.3	7.6
Property held for personal use	0.8	0.4	27.8	5.9	0.3
Residences	3.1	6.8	21.2	—	4.8
Nonbusiness real estate	6.0	9.0	28.1	3.7	7.3
Real estate subdivided	2.6	4.7	37.1	1.7	5.5
Farmland with unharvested crops	0.1	0.3	49.9	2.2	0.4
Other farmland	1.3	3.2	35.2	2.7	3.5
Proceeds from prior year installment sales	7.5	c	c	c	12.8
Other types of assets	8.0	2.1	77.2	117.3	−2.9
All assets					
Percent	b	100.0[d]			100.0[d]
Number of returns	5,552,815				
Amount (billions)		$39.2	$16.7	$4.9	$11.8

Source: U.S. Treasury Department, Internal Revenue Service, *Statistics of Income—1962, Supplemental Report, Sales of Capital Assets Reported on Individual Income Tax Returns* (1966).

(A) =Table C, p. 4, Cols. (6)+(8)/Total; (B) =Table 5, p. 47, Cols. (15)+(20)/Total; (C) =Table 6, p. 61, Col. (31)+Table 9, p. 87, Col. (31)/Table 5, p. 47, Cols. (15)+(20); (D) =Table 6, p. 61, Col. (33)+Table 9, p. 87, Col. (33)/Table 5, p. 47, Cols. (15)+(20); (E) =[Table 6, Col. (31)+Table 9, Col. (31)]−[Table 6, Col. (33)+Table 9, Col. (33)]/Total.

[a] Includes capital assets exchanged in a transaction where gains or losses on capital assets are recognized
[b] Total does not equal 100, since there are individual returns with more than one type of capital asset sale.
[c] Not applicable. Taxpayer reports only gain or loss.   [d] Details do not add to totals due to rounding.

assets. As might be expected from their nominal basis, sales of livestock produce taxable gains corresponding to about three-fourths of gross proceeds.

The percentage of capital gains arising from sales of corporate shares increases as adjusted gross income rises. On the other hand, the percentage of net gain or loss reported on sales of real estate decreases with increasing income. (See Table 4-11.)

Table 4-12 shows net appreciation in 1959 and 1962 as a percentage of gross proceeds for selected asset types by adjusted gross income groups. For corporation stocks, business assets, and nonbusiness real estate and farmland, appreciation constituted an increasing fraction of gross proceeds as income rose. There seems to have been no similar relationship for U.S. obligations and other bonds and certificates of indebtedness. The increase in net appreciation as a percentage of net proceeds is partly a question of definition. Realization of a large gain will also increase adjusted gross income. Despite that definitional linkage, Table 4-12 indicates clearly that taxpayers are willing to realize appreciation even though it is taxed at the highest rates applicable to capital gains. Lock-in may occur for some gains, but it does not entirely inhibit realization.

Great care is needed in interpreting statistics on how long assets have been held. Table 4-13 shows the distribution of holding periods on corporate stock traded during 1962. If there is any lock-in effect from the capital gains tax, the assets traded after short holding periods should produce little appreciation or loss, while those held for more than six months should produce relatively larger realized gains. Assets that have appreciated substantially will be traded only rarely if lock-in is important. Statistics derived from sales thus are for a specialized subgroup of capital assets. McClung estimates that nearly half (by value) of the 1963 holdings of corporate stocks had been held for nine or more years, while tax returns filed for 1962 indicated that more than four-fifths of the assets sold had been held for less than five years.

If the foregoing qualifications can be discounted, a study of the two series would suggest that the holding-period requirement of the law has a subtle effect on the timing of asset sales. McClung's constant turnover model generates approximately equal proportions of assets that have been held for one, two, and three years. It suggests a pattern that might occur if the holding period and lock-in did not

TABLE 4-11. Distribution of Gain Less Loss on Long-Term Capital Asset Sales Reported on Individual Income Tax Returns, by Type of Asset and by Adjusted Gross Income Class, 1959 and 1962[a]

(In percent)

Type of asset	Adjusted gross income class			
	Under $10,000[b]	$10,000 under $50,000	$50,000 under $100,000	$100,000 or more
1959				
Corporation stocks, including rights	18.1	41.7	53.4	63.3
U. S. obligations	−0.1	−0.2	−0.3	−0.1
Other bonds and certificates of indebtedness[c]	1.5	1.6	2.1	2.0
Distributions from regulated investment corporations	3.8	4.0	2.2	0.6
Share of gain or loss from partnerships and fiduciaries	7.2	8.8	9.9	7.4
Livestock	16.3	2.2	1.0	0.4
Natural resources[d]	3.5	1.2	0.9	2.0
Business assets including real estate used in trade or business	5.9	5.9	2.2	1.3
Real estate not used in trade or business and farmland[e]	29.4	18.2	11.3	7.3
Other types of assets	13.9	16.6	17.3	15.8
Total[f]	100.0	100.0	100.0	100.0
Amount of gain less loss (billions)	$3.55	$4.35	$1.45	$2.97
1962				
Corporate stock[g]	−0.3	22.5	44.8	60.1
U. S. government obligations	0.1	h	0.1	0.1
State and local securities	0.3	0.3	0.3	0.3
Other bonds, notes, and debentures	−1.1	−0.1	0.1	0.2
Insurance and annuities	i	0.2[i]	i	h
Options to buy or sell	h	0.1	0.1	0.1
Commodities including future contracts	0.2	h	0.1	h
Capital gain dividends	7.2	5.6	2.8	1.0
Share of capital gain (loss) from partnerships and fiduciaries	7.4	9.4	10.0	5.9
Capital gain distributions from small business corporations	0.3	0.6	0.4	0.4
Liquidation distributions	1.7	2.0	4.8	9.6
Retirement plan distributions	2.5	4.3	2.1	0.8
Livestock	19.9	2.4	0.7	0.4
Timber and coal	i	0.9[i]	i	0.4
Oil and mineral interests	0.4	0.6	0.5	1.0
Partnership interests	2.6	4.1	2.3	1.5
Assets used in trade or business	12.5	9.1	4.0	2.8
Property held for personal use	0.5	0.3	0.2	0.2
Residences	11.0	5.3	1.1	0.2
Nonbusiness real estate	9.4	10.5	5.6	2.5
Real estate subdivided	9.9	6.9	2.8	1.0
Farmland with unharvested crops	0.4	0.7	0.4	0.1
Other farmland	6.6	4.0	2.2	0.8
Proceeds from prior year installment sales	15.1	14.9	12.8	8.1
Other types of assets	−8.5	−4.5	1.0	2.5
Total[f]	100.0	100.0	100.0	100.0
Amount of gain less loss (billions)	$3.00	$3.99	$1.42	$3.35

Note: See footnotes on following page.

affect investor behavior. Actual reported sales indicate that a greater proportion are sold within six months of purchase than are sold after the six-month holding period, which currently distinguishes long-term from short-term capital asset sales. Although this is undoubtedly determined largely by early realization of losses, it is somewhat surprising because of the higher rates applicable to short-term gains.[13]

A different perspective on the holding period for capital assets can be obtained from 1961-64 data by relating the presence of short-term and long-term capital asset transactions to the number of taxpayers with capital asset transactions. (See Table 4-14.) One-fifth of the returns with capital asset transactions reported short-term gains or losses; more than 90 percent reported long-term gains or losses. Somewhat more than half of all returns with short-term capital asset transactions must, therefore, have both types of transactions.

Short-term transactions are substantially more frequent for tax-

[13] See Nelson McClung, "The Distribution of Capital Gain on Corporate Shares by Holding Time," *Review of Economics and Statistics,* Vol. 48 (February 1966), pp. 40-50. The comparison is suggestive, although one would expect substantial differences because of the difference in the weighting of the two distributions. Reported capital asset sales are weighted according to the number of distinct holding periods reported by different taxpayers, regardless of the value of assets sold. That is, each transaction is classified by holding period, and the percentages shown reflect the distribution of holding periods over all transactions, not a distribution of holding periods in which each asset is weighted by its value. McClung's distribution is weighted according to the 1963 value of corporate shares. It is likely that assets in which the ownership interest is not easily divisible may account for relatively more of the total value of appreciation than the relative frequency of sales would suggest. If such assets are also held for longer periods of time, then some difference between the distribution of holding periods by number of transactions and the distribution by value would be expected.

Notes to Table 4-11
Sources: U.S. Treasury Department, Internal Revenue Service, *Statistics of Income—1959, Supplemental Report Sales of Capital Assets Reported on Individual Income Tax Returns for 1959,* Table 3, p. 11, Col. (5) for each asset/ Col. (5), corresponding total for all asset types in that income class; *Statistics of Income—1962, Supplemental Report, Sales of Capital Assets Reported on Individual Income Tax Returns,* Table 6, p. 61, Col. (31)+Table 9, p. 87, Col. (31)=Table 6, p. 61, Col. (33)—Table 9, p. 87, Col. (33) for each asset/Corresponding total for all asset types in that income class.
 [a] Includes capital assets exchanged in a transaction where gains or losses on capital assets are recognized.
 [b] Includes class designated "no adjusted gross income" in 1959, and "nontaxable returns" in 1962.
 [c] Includes state and local bonds; other bonds, notes, and debentures; and mortgages.
 [d] Includes timber, coal, and oil and mineral interests.
 [e] Includes residences, nonbusiness real estate, real estate subdivided, farmland with unharvested crops, and other farmland.
 [f] Percentages do not always add to 100 because of sampling variability, combined income classes (for insurance and annuities, and timber and coal), discrepancies in the underlying data, and rounding.
 [g] Net gains on corporate stock were relatively depressed in 1962 because of the decline in the stock market.
 [h] Less than 0.05 percent.
 [i] Figure in $10,000 under $50,000 gross income class applies to adjusted gross income under $100,000; the breakdown is not available.

TABLE 4-12. Gain Less Loss on Long-Term Capital Asset Sales Reported on Individual Income Tax Returns as a Percentage of Gross Proceeds, by Type of Asset and by Adjusted Gross Income Class, 1959 and 1962

Adjusted gross income class	Corporate stock	U. S. government obligations	Other bonds and certificates of indebtedness[a]	Assets used in trade or business	Real estate not used in trade or business and farmland[b]
		1959			
Under $10,000[c]	17.2	−5.8	15.6	15.1	16.6
$10,000 under $50,000	22.5	−6.7	6.7	30.1	27.1
$50,000 under $100,000	35.4	−1.9	5.8	36.8	35.7
$100,000 under $200,000	39.5	−2.9	7.7	49.9	66.4
$200,000 under $500,000	57.3	−1.0	4.5	48.9	53.2
$500,000 under $1,000,000	71.4	−5.0	14.5	66.9	64.2
$1,000,000 or more	76.9	−6.2	13.2	60.2	67.5
All classes	29.3	−3.7	7.9	22.3	22.2
		1962			
Under $10,000[c]	−0.2	4.6	−13.2	19.7	20.9
$10,000 under $50,000	9.5	0.6	1.8	29.9	32.5
$50,000 under $100,000	21.2	1.1	2.4	40.9	46.4
$100,000 or more	51.4	2.5	5.2	60.5	50.6
All classes	16.5	1.6	0.7	26.1	27.0

Sources: U.S. Treasury Department, Internal Revenue Service, *Statistics of Income—1959, Supplemental Report, Sales of Capital Assets Reported on Individual Income Tax Returns*, Table 3, p. 11, Col. (5)/Col. (2), by income class; *Statistics of Income—1962, Supplemental Report, Sales of Capital Assets Reported on Individual Income Tax Returns*, Table 6, p. 61, Col. (31)+Table 9, p. 87, Col. (31)−Table 6, p. 61, Col. (33)−Table 9, p. 87, Col. (33)/Table 6, p. 61, Col. (27)+Table 9, p. 87, Col. (27), by income class.
 [a] Includes state and local securities and other bonds, notes, and debentures.
 [b] Includes residences, nonbusiness real estate, real estate subdivided, farmland with unharvested crops, and other farmland.
 [c] Includes class designated "no adjusted gross income" in 1959, and "nontaxable returns" in 1962.

payers with high levels of adjusted gross income than for those with low adjusted gross income.

On balance, short-term transactions give rise to small gains or losses, while long-term transactions produce substantial gains. (See Table 4-15.) But taxpayers with incomes over $10,000 regularly report smaller losses or larger gains on short-term transactions relative to their gains on long-term transactions than do taxpayers with lower incomes.[14] The result again casts doubt on the tax sensitivity of capi-

---

[14] In part this may be attributed to the fact that classification by income sorts those with losses into lower income groups and those with gains into higher income groups. The amount of such sorting is limited, however, by the fact that only $1,000 of net losses from capital transactions may be used to offset adjusted gross income.

TABLE 4-13. Distribution of Sales of Corporate Stock Reported on 1962 Individual Income Tax Returns, by Holding Period, and Estimated Holding Period of Entire Stock of Corporate Equities, 1963

Length of period held	Weighted percentage of transactions, 1962[a]	McClung's estimated holding period for corporate stock, 1963 (as a percentage of value of stock)
1 year	49.1	7.7
Under 1 month	4.9	
1 month under 2 months	4.7	
2 months under 3 months	4.4	
3 months under 4 months	4.0	
4 months under 5 months	3.9	
5 months under 6 months	4.3	
Over 6 months under 7 months	4.8	
7 months under 8 months	3.8	
8 months under 9 months	3.9	
9 months under 10 months	3.4	
10 months under 11 months	3.6	
11 months under 12 months	3.4	
1 year under 2 years	15.3	7.2
2 years under 3 years	9.2	6.0
3 years under 5 years	11.0	11.5
5 years under 10 years	9.2	22.3
10 years under 15 years	3.2	15.4
15 years under 20 years	1.4	10.9
20 years or more	1.6	19.0
Total (percent)	100.0	100.0
Values of shares (billions)	$28.6	$592.3

Sources: U. S. Treasury Department, Internal Revenue Service, *Statistics of Income—1962, Supplemental Report, Sales of Capital Assets Reported on Individual Income Tax Returns*, Table 12, p. 112; Nelson McClung's data were derived from "The Distribution of Capital Gain on Corporate Shares by Holding Time," *Review of Economics and Statistics*, Vol. 48 (February 1966), pp. 40–50.

[a] Each holding period reported on a given return was given a weight of one regardless of the number or value of transactions having that holding period. The percentage obtained therefore emphasizes those returns with multiple capital asset sales, each of which falls into a different holding period. Returns with no holding period reported are not shown.

tal gains recipients. The observed differences between the rate of gain on short-term and that on long-term transactions may be the result of differences in portfolio size; some may result from differences in the business acumen and investment talents of taxpayers at different levels of income.

TABLE 4-14. Sales of Short-Term and Long-Term Capital Assets on Individual Income Tax Returns Reporting Sales of Capital Assets, by Adjusted Gross Income Class, 1961–64

Year and adjusted gross income class	Percentage of returns reporting net short-term gain or loss on sales of capital assets[a] (A)	Percentage of returns reporting net long-term gain or loss on sales of capital assets (B)	Number of returns reporting short-term or long-term gain or loss from sales of capital assets (thousands) (C)
1961			
Total[b]	23.3	93.4	5,796
Under $5,000	14.0	94.2	2,049
$5,000 under $10,000	22.2	92.3	1,798
$10,000 or more	34.2	93.6	1,949
1962			
Total[b]	20.4	93.4	5,922
Under $5,000	13.6	94.5	2,022
$5,000 under $10,000	18.7	92.0	1,823
$10,000 or more	28.7	93.6	2,077
1963			
Total[b]	20.6	93.2	6,543
Under $5,000	13.3	94.5	2,133
$5,000 under $10,000	18.7	91.7	2,017
$10,000 or more	28.7	93.3	2,392
1964			
Total[b]	20.8	93.3	6,822
Under $5,000	13.8	94.2	2,080
$5,000 under $10,000	17.4	92.7	2,088
$10,000 or more	28.8	92.9	2,654

Sources: U.S. Treasury Department, Internal Revenue Service, *Statistics of Income, Individual Income Tax Returns*— 1961, Table 16, p. 85; 1962, Table 10, p. 70; 1963, Table 15, p. 57; 1964, Table 10, p. 31. (A)=[Cols. (5)+(7) +(17)+(19)]/Col. (1); (B)=[Cols. (9)+(11)+(21)+(23)]/Col. (1); (C)=Col (1).
[a] Including returns with carryover of losses from prior years.
[b] Cols. (A) and (B) add to more than 100 percent, since there are individual returns with more than one type of capital asset sale. Details may not add to totals in Col. (C) due to rounding.

For each of the recessions since 1952 more short-term losses were realized in the year of the preceding peak than in the year of the succeeding trough.[15] It is difficult to draw any inferences from this rela-

[15] See Figure 4-3.

tionship, since the accrual of gains and losses within any year is not known. Losses accrued in peak years may or may not be realized after the peak of stock prices; the same may be said of gains in trough years. (Data on individuals' capital asset transactions, the timing of such transactions, and incomes are the only sure test of any hypotheses concerning investor behavior.)

The ratio of short-term to long-term gains follows the same anticyclical pattern as does the absolute amount of short-term gains, despite substantial variation in the amount of long-term gains realized during the period 1952-64. (See Figure 4-3.) Investors seem to prefer to offset long-term gains and other income in peak years by realizing short-term losses. However, it is quite possible that the losses and gains are incurred by different taxpayers so that the losses offset ordinary income (at a dollar-for-dollar rate) rather than capital gains, which are preferentially taxed in any case.

Characteristics of Taxpayers Reporting Capital Gains

Some of the characteristics of capital gains recipients—individual, fiduciary, and corporate—may be gleaned from available statistics.

Individual Taxpayers

Data for 1962 show that individual taxpayers receiving capital gains were wealthier and had a higher current income than did the average taxpayer. (See Table 4-16.) The majority of capital gains recipients had an interest in a business or received property income, and the amounts that they realized from these sources exceeded the average for all taxpayers.

Taxpayers reporting capital gains received nearly one-fifth of adjusted gross income. They received two-fifths of rental income, half of all interest income, and half of net partnership income. Taxpayers reporting capital gains accounted for three-fourths of the total amount of dividends reported. If this proportion has persisted from year to year, at least half of dividend income is received by taxpayers who realize capital gains annually. By the same logic, an appreciable proportion of partnership income must also be received by annual recipients of capital gains, since more than 50 percent of part-

TABLE 4-15. Net Gain or Loss on Sale of Short-Term and Long-Term Capital Assets on Individual Income Tax Returns Reporting Sales of Capital Assets, by Adjusted Gross Income Class, 1952–64

Year and adjusted gross income class	Net short-term capital gain or loss[a] (millions of dollars)	Net long-term capital gain or loss (millions of dollars)	Short-term as a percentage of long-term capital gain or loss
1952			
Total	− 9	4,773	−0.2
Under $5,000	− 17	910	−1.9
$5,000 or more	8	3,863	0.2
1953			
Total	−138	4,081	−3.4
Under $5,000	− 30	706	−4.2
$5,000 or more	−109	3,375	−3.2
1954			
Total	157	6,499	2.4
Under $5,000	− 8	1,099	−0.7
$5,000 or more	165	5,400	3.1
1955			
Total	146	9,182	1.6
Under $5,000	− 13	1,231	−1.1
$5,000 or more	159	7,951	2.0
1956			
Total	− 68	9,038	−0.8
Under $5,000	− 23	1,304	−1.8
$5,000 or more	− 45	7,734	−0.6
1957			
Total	−320	7,250	−4.4
Under $5,000	− 75	1,161	−6.5
$5,000 or more	−244	6,089	−4.0
1958			
Total	89	8,494	1.0
Under $5,000	− 27	1,479	−1.8
$5,000 under $10,000	1	1,196	0.1
$10,000 or more	114	5,819	2.0
1959			
Total	95	12,238	0.8
Under $5,000	− 11	1,765	−0.6
$5,000 under $10,000	14	1,606	0.9
$10,000 or more	92	8,866	1.0
1960			
Total	−256	10,633	−2.4
Under $5,000	− 45	1,617	−2.8
$5,000 under $10,000	− 66	1,363	−4.8
$10,000 or more	−145	7,653	−1.9
1961			
Total	− 6	14,758	0.0
Under $5,000	−108	1,617	−6.7
$5,000 under $10,000	0	1,781	0.0
$10,000 or more	101	11,360	0.9

TABLE 4-15. Continued

Year and adjusted gross income class	Net short-term capital gain or loss[a] (millions of dollars)	Net long-term capital gain or loss (millions of dollars)	Short-term as a percentage of long-term capital gain or loss
1962			
Total	−744	11,759	−6.3
Under $5,000	−124	1,596	−7.8
$5,000 under $10,000	−169	1,311	−12.9
$10,000 or more	−451	8,851	−5.1
1963			
Total	− 68	12,920	−0.5
Under $5,000	− 23	1,546	−1.5
$5,000 under $10,000	− 75	1,584	−4.7
$10,000 or more	30	9,790	0.3
1964			
Total	−279	15,988	−1.7
Under $5,000	− 79	1,557	−5.1
$5,000 under $10,000	−125	1,768	−7.1
$10,000 or more	− 75	12,662	−0.6

Source: U.S. Treasury Department, Internal Revenue Service, *Statistics of Income, Individual Income Tax Returns*, various years. Details may not add to totals due to rounding.
[a] Not including losses carried forward from earlier years.

nership income is reported on returns with capital gains or losses.[16]

Net gains from the sale of capital assets included in income rise sharply as a proportion of adjusted gross income as the individual's adjusted gross income increases. Table 4-17 probably understates the proportion of total income that represents capital gains. The numerator of the proportion shown includes only the net gain included in adjusted gross income (approximately half of the total net gain), less a limited portion of net capital losses[17]; adjusted gross in-

---

[16] If taxpayers receiving half of the dividends paid report capital gains in two successive years and if recipients of exactly half of the remaining dividend income report capital gains in alternate years, the recipients of capital gains will represent three-fourths of dividend income annually. Such a large fraction of dividend income would not consistently be reported by capital gains recipients if recurrent annual capital gains were realized by individuals representing a smaller fraction of dividend income.

Steger also found that capital gains were a recurrent source of income for most taxpayers. See Wilbur A. Steger, "Averaging of Income for Income Tax Purposes" (Doctoral thesis, Harvard University, 1956).

[17] If the proportion of total gain N included in adjusted gross income is αN, then the proportion shown is $y(\alpha) = \{\alpha N \div (Y - [1 - \alpha]N^{-1})\}$, where Y is total income. Adding the excluded fraction would increase the proportion, since $y(\alpha) < y(1)$.

FIGURE 4-3. Net Short-Term Gain as a Percentage of Net Long-Term Gain on Individual Income Tax Returns Reporting Sales of Capital Assets, 1952–64[a]

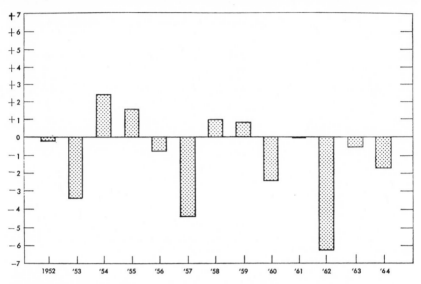

[a] Amounts are for calendar years.

come in the denominator also includes those portions of gains and losses. Despite the understatement, capital gains constitute as much as *one-half* of the income of high-income taxpayers.

Since, as income rises, capital gains constitute an increasing portion of the total, the marginal and average tax rates on income are limited by the extent to which it is realized in the form of capital gains.

This is reflected in the average rate of tax on all income (shown for all taxpayers in Table 4-18). Effective average tax rates reach a peak of just over 31 percent for individuals whose total gross income lies between $150,000 and $200,000. Effective average tax rates are somewhat lower for persons in higher income brackets.

It is less obvious that high-income taxpayers also have enough deductions from income that their marginal rates are considerably lower than would be suggested by the legally established marginal tax rates. A simulated recomputation of taxes for individuals to include one dollar of additional wages and salaries produces the effective marginal rates shown in the last column in Table 4-18. The aver-

TABLE 4-16. Sources of Income and Loss Reported on Individual Income Tax Returns, 1962

Source of income and loss	Returns with capital gain or loss			All returns			Capital gains recipients' share of this source	Returns reporting capital gain or loss as percentage of all returns in each income category
	Amount	Number of recipients	Average income from this source for recipients	Amount	Number of recipients	Average income from this source for recipients		
1. Adjusted gross income, total	$65.3ᵃ	5,922ᵇ	$11,019	$348.7ᵃ	62,712ᵇ	$5,560	18.7%	9.4%
2. Wages and salaries	49.6%	63.2%	8,645	81.3%	87.8%	5,143	11.4	6.8
3. Net profit or loss on business, farm, or profession	12.6	35.2	3,942	6.9	13.8	2,773	34.4	24.2
4. Net gain or loss on sales of capital assets	8.8	100.0	974	1.7	9.4	974	100.0	100.0
5. Dividends (after exclusions)	12.2	48.3	2,774	3.1	9.3	1,825	74.6	49.1
6. Interest	5.2	65.8	865	2.1	23.5	486	47.1	26.4
7. Rents, net income or loss	1.7	26.3	699	0.8	9.5	481	37.9	26.1
8. Partnership, net profit or loss	7.3	13.0	6,133	2.7	3.1	4,778	50.7	39.5
Total of items 2–8	97.4	ᶜ		98.6	ᶜ			

Source: U.S. Treasury Department, Internal Revenue Service, *Statistics of Income—1962, Individual Income Tax Returns,* Tables 4 and 11, pp. 38, 73.
ᵃ Billions of dollars.
ᵇ Thousands of recipients.
ᶜ Adds to more than 100 percent, since capital gains recipients have several income sources.

TABLE 4-17. Adjusted Net Gain Less Net Loss on Sales of Capital Assets Reported on Individual Income Tax Returns, by Adjusted Gross Income Class, 1964

Adjusted gross income class	Adjusted gross income (millions)	Net gain minus net loss on sales of capital assets	
		Amount[a] (millions)	As a percentage of adjusted gross income
	(1)	(2)	(3)
Under $5,000	$ 76,643[b]	$ 766	1.00
$5,000 under $10,000	164,488	835	0.51
$10,000 under $15,000	78,094	695	0.89
$15,000 under $20,000	24,772	501	2.02
$20,000 under $50,000	34,408	1,653	4.81
$50,000 under $100,000	10,429	1,037	9.94
$100,000 under $500,000	5,649	1,460	25.85
$500,000 under $1,000,000	700	360	51.34
$1,000,000 or more	952	521	54.70
All income classes	$396,660[b][c]	$7,939[c]	2.00

Source: U.S. Treasury Department, Internal Revenue Service, *Statistics of Income — 1964, Individual Income Tax Returns*, Table 4, p. 13; Col. (3)=Col. (2)/Col. (1), before rounding.

[a] Not comparable with net gain shown in Table 4-5. Only the gains includable in income and allowable losses are shown. In addition, loss carry-forward is included in the net.

[b] Adjusted gross income less deficit.

[c] Detail does not add to total because total includes nontaxable returns in adjusted gross income classes above $10,000, for which income class breakdown is not available.

age marginal rate simulated for 1965 reaches a maximum of just under 60 percent for taxpayers in the $200,000 to $500,000 adjusted gross income class. This finding suggests that the effect of marginal tax rates on investor choices will never reach the level suggested by the statutory 70 percent ceiling rate set for 1965. (See also Figure 4-4.) Of course, the result does not imply that the 70 percent rate is not a key consideration in motivating tax avoidance.

Fiduciary Taxpayers

Little is known generally about the conditions that give rise to fiduciary income, although tax avoidance is certainly an important motivation. Fiduciaries are handled primarily by professional investors who have good access to investment markets and legal services. Therefore, one would expect fiduciaries to be particularly sensitive to the tax avoidance opportunities offered by the capital gains tax.

FIGURE 4-4. Erosion of Statutory Bracket Tax Rates Through Various Provisions of the Individual Income Tax, 1964 Act[a]

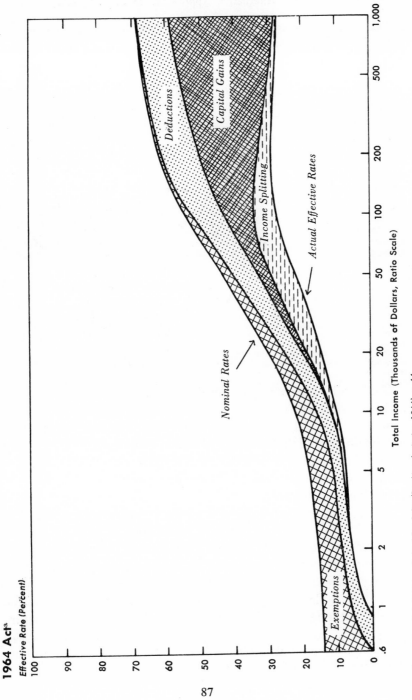

Effective Rate (Percent)

Total Income (Thousands of Dollars, Ratio Scale)

Source: Joseph A. Pechman, *Federal Tax Policy* (Brookings Institution, 1966), p. 66.
[a] Based on 1962 incomes, with rates applicable beginning Jan. 1, 1965.

87

TABLE 4-18. Estimated Average and Marginal Individual Income Tax Rates, by Income Class, 1965

(In percent)

Total income class	Average tax rate on total income[a]	Adjusted gross income class	Average tax rate on adjusted gross income[b]	Estimated marginal tax rate on wages and salaries[c]
0 under $5,000	5.61	0 under $5,000	5.64	9.83
$5,000 under $10,000	9.16	$5,000 under $10,000	9.28	17.66
$10,000 under $15,000	11.92	$10,000 under $15,000	12.10	21.18
$15,000 under $20,000	14.08	$15,000 under $20,000	14.55	25.00
$20,000 under $25,000	15.83	$20,000 under $25,000	16.56	28.84
$25,000 under $50,000	19.92	$25,000 under $50,000	21.06	37.46
$50,000 under $100,000	27.51	$50,000 under $100,000	30.37	51.78
$100,000 under $150,000	30.89	$100,000 under $150,000	36.61	57.41
$150,000 under $200,000	31.21	$150,000 under $200,000	39.34	59.11
$200,000 under $500,000	30.49	$200,000 under $500,000	41.00	59.39
$500,000 under $1,000,000	28.41	$500,000 under $1,000,000	42.42	55.66
$1,000,000 or more	27.07	$1,000,000 or more	41.66	51.35
All classes	11.28		11.47	14.70

Source: Joseph A. Pechman, Brookings Institution, unpublished tabulations.

[a] Income for 1965 was estimated by applying uniform ratios to individual income reported on 1962 tax returns. Tax liability for 1965 was estimated by simulation of the Internal Revenue Code applicable to 1965. Total income includes all capital gains plus dividends and sick pay exclusions from adjusted gross income.

[b] The same as note a, except that the rate is computed on adjusted gross income, which is total income minus the excluded portion of capital gains and losses, minus sick pay and excluded dividend income.

[c] Computed by simulating taxes on actual income and deductions plus an additional one dollar of wage and salary income, and taking the average difference between the recomputed liability and actual liability within income groups.

Table 4-19 indicates that fiduciaries avail themselves of preferential capital gains taxes to a far greater extent than do individuals generally. In 1964, only among individuals with more than half a million dollars did the incidence of capital gains exceed the incidence on fiduciary returns in general. (See Table 4-17.) The frequency of capital gains income shown for fiduciaries with more than $10,000 of income is remarkable.[18]

Corporation Taxpayers

In the decade 1952-61, capital gains income constituted a larger fraction of net corporate income for corporations with small asset holdings than for corporations with average or substantial asset holdings. (See Table 4-20.) Since assets and income are correlated, the ratio of net long-term gains less short-term losses (if any) to net in-

---

[18] Strictly speaking the comparison is biased by the exclusion of long-term capital gains in computing the ratios shown in Table 4-17. (See note 17, above.) However, it is unlikely that the conclusion is affected. The data shown in Table 4-17 for individuals are for 1964, but the comparable figures for 1962 do not differ appreciably.

TABLE 4-19. Net Gain and Net Loss from Sales of Capital Assets Reported on Fiduciary Returns, by Income Class, 1962

Total income class	Number of estates and trusts	Total income[a] (thousands)	Average income per estate or trust	Net gain from sales of capital assets[b]		Net loss from sales of capital assets[b]	
				Number of estates and trusts as a percentage of total	Amount as a percentage of total income	Number of estates and trusts as a percentage of total	Amount as a percentage of total income
	(A)	(B)	(C)	(D)	(E)	(F)	(G)
Under $5,000	384,036	$731,235	$1,904	33.2	10.5	6.4	−2.6
$5,000 under $10,000	97,054	686,625	7,075	46.0	13.9	6.5	−0.6
$10,000 or more	117,071	4,519,234	38,603	57.0	32.0	5.3	−0.1
All income classes	598,160	5,937,095	9,926	40.0	27.2	6.2	−0.5

Source: U.S. Treasury Department, Internal Revenue Service, *Statistics of Income—1962, Fiduciary, Gift, and Estate Tax Returns* (1965), Table 2, p. 16; (A)=Col. (1); (B)=Col. (2); (C)=Col. (2)/Col. (1); (D)=Col. (17)/Col. (1) (E) =Col. (18)/Col. (2); (F) =Col. (19)/Col. (1); (G) =Col. (20)/Col. (2). Details may not add to totals due to rounding.
  [a] "Total" income estimates from fiduciary returns should not be compared with adjusted gross income estimates from individual income tax returns, because total income includes gross rents and royalties, gross profits, and net gain from sales of assets.
  [b] See notes to Table 4-8.

come also declines as net corporate income rises. (See Table 4-21.) This is the reverse of the situation for individual taxpayers, where an *increase* in gains is associated with increased income.

The inverse relationship can be explained by the different character of the business activities of small and large corporations. Capital gains constitute a substantial proportion of net income for corporations that are engaged primarily in agriculture, mining, and construction. These industries are characterized by a large number of corporations with relatively small assets and net incomes. They are the ones that are favored by the inclusion of livestock and timber in Section 1231 assets.

Manufacturing and utilities report only nominal amounts of capital gains in relation to their total income, but real corporate assets are

TABLE 4-20. Amount of Net Long-Term Gain Less Short-Term Loss on Sales of Capital Assets Reported on Active Corporation Income Tax Returns, by Asset Size Class, 1952–61[a]

Year	Total assets $50,000 under $100,000			Total assets $100,000 under $250,000		
	Net long-term capital gain reduced by net short-term capital loss (millions)	Average net long-term capital gain less short-term capital loss	Net long-term capital gain less short-term capital loss as a percentage of net income	Net long-term capital gain reduced by net short-term capital loss (millions)	Average net long-term capital gain less short-term capital loss	Net long-term capital gain less short-term capital loss as a percentage of net income
1952	$29	$267	7.5	$81	$664	7.4
1953	31	269	10.4	59	463	6.7
1954	30	255	11.5	75	562	9.1
1955	37	282	10.5	94	623	8.0
1956	41	274	9.9	104	608	8.1
1957	43	269	12.7	89	495	8.3
1958	49	294	14.5	118	603	10.5
1959	60	338	12.2	136	642	9.4
1960	53	279	14.0	137	599	11.3
1961	70	338	17.6	172	719	12.6

Year	Total assets $50,000,000 under $100,000,000			Total assets $100,000,000 or more		
	Net long-term capital gain reduced by net short-term capital loss (millions)	Average net long-term capital gain less short-term capital loss	Net long-term capital gain less short-term capital loss as a percentage of net income	Net long-term capital gain reduced by net short-term capital loss (millions)	Average net long-term capital gain less short-term capital loss	Net long-term capital gain less short-term capital loss as a percentage of net income
1952	$100	$142,000	3.7	$265	$310,000	1.4
1953	92	124,000	3.4	319	348,000	1.5
1954	205	258,000	7.8	637	684,000	3.2
1955	153	184,000	5.0	632	615,000	2.4
1956	222	248,000	6.6	732	678,000	2.9
1957	155	162,000	5.0	764	676,000	3.0
1958	222	222,000	8.1	1,336	1,111,000	6.3
1959	218	209,000	6.5	1,119	877,000	4.4
1960	237	207,000	7.7	1,232	925,000	4.8
1961	334	278,000	10.8	1,944	1,361,000	7.2

[a] See notes to Table 4-7.

Source: U.S. Treasury Department, Internal Revenue Service, Statistics of Income—1961–62, Corporation Income Tax Returns, pp. 282–84.

TABLE 4-21. Net Long-Term Capital Gain Reduced by Net Short-Term Capital Loss as a Percentage of Net Corporate Income, by Net Income Class, 1961[a]

Type of return and size of income taxed at normal tax and surtax rates	Net long-term gains reduced by net short-term losses[b] (millions)	Net long-term gains reduced by net short-term losses as a percentage of net income
Size of income taxed at normal tax and surtax rates, total	$2,340	4.83
Under $5,000	141	25.09
$5,000 under $50,000	435	9.11
$50,000 under $100,000	107	6.02
$100,000 under $500,000	362	7.64
$500,000 under $1,000,000	136	6.10
$1,000,000 under $5,000,000	346	5.83
$5,000,000 under $10,000,000	127	3.79
$10,000,000 under $25,000,000	235	4.90
$25,000,000 under $50,000,000	135	2.86
$50,000,000 under $100,000,000	122	2.60
$100,000,000 or more	196	1.82
Returns with no income taxed at normal tax and surtax rates, total	1,599	
Taxable	518	
Nontaxable	1,080	
Returns without net income, total	369	
Taxable	2	
Nontaxable	367	
Total[c]	$4,308	

Source: U.S. Treasury Department, Internal Revenue Service, *Statistics of Income—1961–62, Corporation Income Tax Returns* (1964), Table 9, p. 192.
[a] Excludes corporations filing small business returns (Form 1120-S).
[b] See notes to Table 4-7.
[c] Total differs from total for all active corporations shown in Table 4-7 because of exclusion of corporations filing small business returns.

concentrated in a few firms in these two industries. These firms constitute more than half of all firms that report more than $1 million of net income annually. Thus a considerably higher ratio of capital gains to income might have been anticipated.

Corporate Section 1231 Transactions

Gains on sales of property eligible for capital gains treatment under Section 1231 of the Internal Revenue Code constituted more than one-third of net long-term capital gains of corporations in 1962.

TABLE 4-22. Corporation Net Long-Term Capital Gains on Sales of Capital Assets and on Section 1231 Property, by Industrial Divisions, 1962

Industrial division	Total capital asset gain, including Section 1231 gain		Gain on sales of Section 1231 property		
	Net long-term capital gain less net short-term capital loss (thousands) (A)	Average gain as a percentage of corporate net income (B)	Net long-term capital gain less net short-term capital loss (thousands) (C)	Average gain as a percentage of corporate net income reported by corporations with Section 1231 gain (D)	Number of returns reporting Section 1231 gain as a percentage of total number of active corporation returns (E)
Agriculture, forestry, and fisheries	$ 75,757	47.1	$ 26,366	38.9	8.4
Mining	113,913	14.4	72,308	11.3	10.4
Construction	101,707	16.5	50,746	32.3	5.9
Manufacturing	1,096,838	4.3	632,759	4.8	8.4
Transportation, communication, electric, gas, and sanitary services	275,423	3.4	172,698	6.7	7.1
Wholesale and retail trade	228,410	4.4	107,087	9.7	4.5
Finance, insurance, and real estate	1,666,748	19.2	290,102	18.9	2.4
Services	205,913	24.7	90,084	39.1	3.9
All industrial groups	$3,766,543a	7.6	$1,442,620a	7.4	4.7

Source: U.S. Treasury Department, Internal Revenue Service, *Statistics of Income—1962, Corporation Income Tax Returns* (1966), Table 2, p. 58. (A) = line 12; (B) = line 12 /line 35; Table 27, p. 282, (C) = Col. (14)/Col. (16); (E) = Col. (13), Table 27/Col. (1), Table 2.
a "All industrial groups" does not equal the sum of the components because industries with nature of business not allocable are included in the total.

These gains were concentrated among 5 percent of all active corporations and accounted for 7 percent of their income. (See Table 4-22.) Section 1231 gains were most prevalent in agriculture, construction, and services. The amount of Section 1231 gains claimed in the future will be somewhat limited by the recapture provisions of Sections 1245 and 1250 of the Internal Revenue Code. However, the special rules for livestock and timber, iron, and coal mining royalties will continue unless the relevant code provisions are eliminated.

Unrealized Capital Gains and Related Issues

Unrealized capital gains can be estimated by subtracting the gains and losses reported on tax returns from the appreciation that has accrued on assets held by individuals, fiduciaries, and corporations.[19] But application of this simple concept to the experience in the United States is difficult for several reasons. Except for publicly traded corporate equities and marketed debentures, little is known about the price variation of capital assets. The amount of realized gains is not fully reported because taxpayers understate gains realized during their lifetime (that is, they neglect to report some capital asset transactions on income tax returns). In addition, some gains cease to be taxable when assets are transferred at death. To add to the difficulties, gains and losses of tax-exempt corporations do not appear in any of the available data sources.

Unrealized capital gains include: gains on which capital gains taxes are potentially due and gains on which accrued tax liability has been forgiven. Forgiveness arises from step-up in the basis of the asset on the death of an individual or from tax exemption of a corporate owner. Of particular interest are estimates of realized capital gains, gains on which tax has been forgiven, and potentially taxable gains associated with individual taxpayers or households, since lock-in is more likely to affect individual portfolios subject to the provisions on the step-up in basis. The estimates concerning individuals are unfortunately unreliable. Little is known about the wealth of the household sector and the characteristics of that wealth, particularly in the years prior to World War II.

[19] Tax-exempt corporations are not required to report capital gains and losses, and are an important exception to the general rubric described.

TABLE 4-23. Estimated Realized and Accrued Capital Gains on Corporate Shares, Turnover Method, 1922–63, and Stock Price Method, 1926–61

(Dollar amounts in billions)

Item	Turnover method (McClung)[a] 1922–63	Stock price method (Bailey)[b] 1926–61
1. Current value	$592.3	$810.5
2. Value at time of issue	192.1	
3. Accrued gains (A)	400.2	695.0
4. Unrealized gains (U)	233.0	558.4
5. Step-up in basis at death (S)	—	
6. (U+S)/A	—	80.4%
7. U/A	58.2%	—
8. Ratio of unrealized gains plus step-up in basis to current share values	—	68.8%
9. Ratio of unrealized gains to current share values	43.1%[c]	—

[a] Assumes that turnover is independent of holding period. See Nelson McClung, "The Distribution of Capital Gain on Corporate Shares by Holding Time," *Review of Economics and Statistics*, Vol. 48 (February 1966), Table 6, p. 49.
[b] Assumes that annual accrued gains can be approximated by the product of the ratio of the stock price index at the beginning of period $t+1$ to its value in t times the beginning of the period value of corporate shares. Martin J. Bailey, "Capital Gains and Income Taxation," in Arnold C. Harberger and Martin J. Bailey (eds.), *Taxation of Income from Capital* (Brookings Institution, 1968).
[c] U divided by current value less share disappearances of $52 billion (McClung, op. cit.).

The unrealized appreciation of corporate shares has been estimated in two ways. McClung drew up a distribution of holding periods for all corporate shares from a simple probability (Markov) process. He then inferred the tax basis of shares from their estimated date of acquisition. The current value of shares less their estimated basis then yielded an estimate of unrealized gains.[20] Bailey estimated annual appreciation in shares held by households at the beginning of the year by using Standard and Poor's stock price indices. He then estimated unrealized gains by subtracting realized gains reported on individual and fiduciary tax returns from the estimated aggregate appreciation of households.[21]

McClung's estimates depend critically on the assumption that the period for which shares have already been held does not affect the

[20] McClung, *op. cit.*, pp. 40-50.
[21] Bailey, *op. cit.*

likelihood that they are traded in the present. While this assumption is questionable, it provides us with a minimal estimate of unrealized capital gains, since the shareholder is likely to be inhibited from trading shares that have been held for some period due to the tax on the positive appreciation in value. Bailey's estimates depend critically on the estimated capital gains realized, which were obtained from *Statistics of Income* for individual and fiduciary taxpayers. Bailey makes no effort to account for realizations of capital gains on corporate shares held by corporations; moreover, the estimate implicit in Table 4-23 includes all realized capital gains of individuals and fiduciaries; downward adjustment, prorating the total realizations in the proportion that gain on corporate shares bore to all gains in 1959, results in an estimate of unrealized gains in excess of 90 percent.

Differences in the measure of share value used by McClung and Bailey account for the difference between the two numbers in Line 1 of the table. Consequently the most meaningful comparison of the two methods lies in the ratio of unrealized gains, or unrealized gains plus step-up in basis, to the total accrual. Unfortunately, the methods cannot be compared directly.

Unlike the stock price estimates, the turnover-based estimates implicitly include transfers at death as realizations. The distribution of holding periods that is obtained is derived from the rate of turnover of *all* shares (volume of sales per year divided by the outstanding stock issues). The rate includes transfers of shares by executors who are liquidating estates; thus the turnover of assets associated with portfolio adjustment for inherited wealth is part of McClung's basic turnover figure. For this reason alone, McClung's estimates of unrealized gains should fall short of the stock price method, in which only *taxed* realizations are subtracted from accruals to arrive at unrealized gains plus step-up.

To eliminate the inconsistencies between Bailey's accrual estimate and the tax data used for realizations and to provide an independent estimate of step-up, the estimates shown in Table 4-24 were prepared. The stock price method was applied to household shareholdings of securities listed on major exchanges. Limiting the base for the accrual estimate to that definition means that: (1) only individual and fiduciary realizations of capital gains need be considered in estimating R (corporate gains on intercorporate sharehold-

TABLE 4-24. Comparison of Turnover and Stock Price Methods for Estimating Realized and Accrued Capital Gains on Corporate Shares, 1922–63

(In billions of dollars)

		Stock price method	
	Turnover method	All corporate equities less tax-exempt and intercorporate shareholdings	
Item	All corporate equities[a]		
		Estimated realized gains[b]	Estimated realized gains adjusted for unreporting[c]
	(1)	(2)	(3)
1. Realized gains (R)	219.2	43.7	56.8
2. Step-up in basis at death (S)		48.3	43.3
3. Total (R+S)	219.2	92.0	100.1
4. Accrued gains (A)	400.2[d]	272.9	272.9
5. Unrealized gains (A−R−S)	233.0	180.9	172.8
6. Unrealized gains plus step-up (A−R)	—	229.2	216.1
7. (A−R−S)/A	58.2%	66.3%	63.3%
8. A−R/A	—	84.0%	79.2%

[a] From Table 4-23.

[b] It is assumed that 0.485 of individual and fiduciary net capital gain less capital loss represents gain on corporate equities. The ratio is the same as the proportion of sales involving corporate equities to sales of all capital assets, 1959, as reported in U.S. Treasury Department, Internal Revenue Service, *Statistics of Income—1959, Supplemental Report on Sales of Capital Assets Reported on Individual Income Tax Returns* (1962). The gain on corporate equity is then allocated to listed securities in proportion to their share of total equity value.

[c] Realized gains are inflated by 30 percent to allow for underreporting.

[d] Less than the sum of realized and unrealized gains, since some gains have been realized on shares that are retired or have been sold abroad.

ings need not be considered; individual gains on noncapital assets are unlikely to include any listed securities); and (2) 1959 data on the ratio of gains on shareholdings to all gains may be used to derive an estimate of gains realized on shareholdings for other years. (While the same method could be applied to a universe consisting of all shares held by households, it proved easier to estimate listed shareholdings of households.)

The value of listed shares held by households may be derived as a residual by subtracting the value of listed shares held by corporations, beneficial trusts, and nonprofit institutions from the total value of listed shares. Constructing such a residual isolates the portion of listed shareholdings from which individuals and fiduciaries benefit directly. The gain on shares owned by beneficial trusts and nonprofit institutions will not directly benefit households. Moreover, because of intercorporate shareholdings, some of the increase in value of publicly traded shares may be counted twice in the value of shares and stock price indices, while the household ultimately benefits only once from the increase in value of the shares which it holds in the parent company. Column (2), line 4, in Table 4-24 indicates the estimated accrued gains to households when the tax-exempt sector and intercorporate shareholdings are removed from the base to which stock price indices are applied. (The accrued gain is likely to be understated under the stock price method because of the exclusion of gains on stocks in the year of issue.)

There appears to be no radical difference in the proportion of accrued gains that has not been reported as realized when attention is focused on individuals and on listed securities. (See Table 4-23, line 6, and Table 4-24, Column 2, line 8.) However, the ratio obtained for the household sector is likely to be more accurate for the reasons given above. Column (3) in Table 4-24 gives a crude estimate of the ratio of realizations to accrued appreciation, taking into account unreported realizations of capital gains, following Hinrichs' estimates in Table 4-6.

Since tax return data do not include gains on which taxation is forgiven due to the step-up in basis at death, further computations are necessary to provide a direct comparison of McClung's figures with those presented in Columns (2)-(3), line 8. The step-up in basis at death was estimated by applying a constant mortality rate to stockholders' potentially taxable gains in each year. The procedure logically allocates gains originating in a given period of time to step-up in basis in subsequent years unless the gain is realized in a lifetime transaction.

The mortality rate used was 26.4 per 1,000, which is a mean estimated as an average of age-specific rates reported in the *Statistical Abstract of the United States: 1965*.[22] The average was weighted according to the age distribution of the stockholding population. The estimate is critically dependent upon the mortality rate used. Since the age distribution of the stockholding population is not known for the years before World War II, the mortality rate of 26.4 is uniformly applied for the entire period 1922-63. (Increased stockholding by younger persons during the post-World War II period, compounded by the secular decline in mortality rates in those years, made it

[22] U.S. Bureau of the Census, Table 63, p. 56, and Table 651, p. 475.

TABLE 4-25. Ratio of Estimated Step-up in Basis at Death[a] to Unrealized Gains Before Step-up, 1922–63[b]

(In percent)

Initial year in calcula- tion	Terminal year in calculation								
	1922	1930	1935	1940	1945	1950	1955	1960	1963
1922		23.15	204.26	31.78	19.92	24.92	14.27	20.12	20.50
1931			53.62	−15.68	16.00	26.36	12.86	19.79	20.30
1936				10.62	10.42	17.45	11.92	18.51	19.34
1941					10.27	20.97	12.07	19.11	19.81
1946						47.08	12.39	20.16	20.58
1951							9.58	18.79	19.68
1956								34.38	27.03
1961									21.49

Source: See Appendix C for a description of the method of estimation.

[a] Step-up in basis at death using data adjusted for intercorporate shareholdings and nontaxable sectors and unreporting of gains.

[b] Listed corporate shares only. This calculation corresponds to Col. (3) of Table 4-24 and represents a smaller estimate of step-up in basis than would be obtained from reported realizations in Col. (2) of that table.

impossible to estimate a trend in mortality of shareholders.) For each year the rate was applied to the cumulative amount of accrued gains less gains realized or forgiven in prior years. The step-up in basis so estimated amounts to approximately 21.5 percent of unrealized gains before step-up.

Use of the actual annual mortality rate for all ages from 1922 to 1963 and treatment of all capital gains as realizations on corporate equities sets an extreme lower bound on our estimate of step-up. Both the mortality rate, which averages 1.05 per 1,000, and the gains used to offset annual accrued value would lead to an understatement of step-up. The resulting estimate of step-up was half as large as the estimate based on the more likely mortality rate above.[23]

The ratio of estimated step-up in basis to unrealized gains before step-up is sensitive to the period covered and has been rising since 1955. It was substantially higher in the early postwar period than it is now. (See Table 4-25.)

Naturally it is somewhat difficult to draw definite conclusions from the broad range of estimates of unrealized gains shown in Tables 4-23 and 4-24. However, it does appear that a 20 percent loss in potentially taxable gains due to step-up in basis is a conservative esti-

[23] The formulas used to obtain the estimates are reported in Appendix C.

mate of the loss. No effort has been made in these computations to account for the lock-in effect on persons approaching death. That is, large unrealized gains may be correlated with a high rate of expected mortality. Independence has been assumed here. The Bailey estimate that 0.67-0.85 of gains escape taxation through step-up lies at the other extreme.

Table 4-24 suggests that the stock price method may not estimate high enough accrued gains or high enough realized gains (because of underreporting of realizations). If the understatement of realizations exceeds the understatement of accrual, one would expect a less extreme effect of step-up than Bailey hypothesized. It has been shown here that, with reasonable assumptions, realizations before step-up may amount to 15-20 percent of gains. The conservative estimate of step-up made above implies that the ratio of unrealized gains to accrued gains does not exceed McClung's estimate by a large margin (Table 4-24, line 6). If the estimates by both methods are accurate, the implied lock-in effect must be small, since McClung's estimates are based on random turnover with no lock-in.

McClung's method sets a lower bound of 58 percent on unrealized gains in the portfolio of a decedent, since he assumes that trading occurs independently of the period for which assets have been held. On the average, decedents should have the same proportion of unrealized gains as the aggregate. The stock price estimates suggest that unrealized gains passing into estate must be approximately 84 percent, again assuming that turnover is not affected by the anticipation of death. Thus a combined "minimum reasonable" estimate of unrealized gains passing into estate is about 75 percent of the total gain accrued in the holding period. Given the issue values estimated by McClung, this would suggest that more than half of the current portfolios of decedents probably consist of unrealized gains. Any lock-in would increase that ratio.

The foregoing argument suggests that half of the shareholdings of decedents could be taxed if gains were presumed to be realized at death. Quite independently, Harley Hinrichs has constructed estimates of step-up in basis at death from estimates of the national balance sheet and the wealth of the estate tax population. (See Table 4-26.)[24] Hinrichs assumes that the ratios of appreciation to current

---

[24] I am indebted to Harley Hinrichs for these hitherto unpublished estimates.

TABLE 4-26. Basic Data Summary for Presumptive Realization of Capital Gains at Death, 1953, 1958, and 1963

(In billions of dollars)

Appreciable assets	Individual wealth			Decedents' wealth			Decedents' unrealized capital gain		
	Total	Top wealth-holders[a]	Other wealth-holders	Total	Top wealth-holders[a]	Other wealth-holders	Total	Top wealth-holders[a]	Other wealth-holders
1953									
Real estate	442.6	70.1	372.5	9.757	1.552	8.205	4.545	0.853	3.692
Stock[b]	127.2	105.7	21.5	3.487	2.983	0.504	1.463	1.312	0.151
Noncorporate equity	187.4	20.0	167.4	4.498	0.480	4.018	1.397	0.192	1.205
Total	757.2	195.8	561.4	17.742	5.015	12.727	7.405	2.357	5.048
1958									
Real estate	633.3	114.0	519.3	13.934	2.509	11.425	6.521	1.380	5.141
Stock[b]	252.0	216.7	35.3	5.797	4.985	0.812	2.437	2.193	0.244
Noncorporate equity	243.8	31.7	212.1	5.850	0.760	5.090	2.059	0.304	1.755
Total	1,129.1	362.4	766.7	25.581	8.254	17.327	11.017	3.877	7.140
1963 (low)[c]									
Real estate	800	160	640	17.600	3.520	14.080	7.390	1.760	5.630
Stock[b]	400	350	50	9.200	8.050	1.150	3.890	3.540	0.350
Noncorporate equity	300	45	255	7.200	1.080	6.120	2.270	0.430	1.840
Total	1,500	555	945	34.000	12.650	21.350	13.550	5.730	7.820
1963 (probable)[c]	1,500	555	945	34.000	12.650	21.350	17.000	9.490	7.510

Sources: From data in Robert J. Lampman, The Share of Top Wealth-holders in National Wealth, 1922–1956 (Princeton Univ. Press for National Bureau of Economic Research, 1962); Lampman updated figures to 1961 in Business Week, January 27, 1962, pp. 30–31; Raymond W. Goldsmith, The National Wealth of the United States in the Postwar Period (Princeton Univ. Press for National Bureau of Economic Research, 1962); Raymond W. Goldsmith, A Study of Saving in the United States (Princeton Univ. Press, 1955); Wilbur A. Steger, "The Taxation of Unrealized Capital Gains and Losses: A Statistical Study," National Tax Journal, Vol. 10 (September 1957), pp. 266–81; Securities and Exchange Commission, Statistical Bulletin, April 1962; and others. Data for 1963 estimated by "devolution" method consistent with techniques of Lampman, Steger, and Horst Mendershausen, using death rates of 2.2, 2.3, and 2.4 percent for real estate, stock, and noncorporate equity, respectively. Unrealized gain share of wealth at death is estimated as 50, 44, and 40 percent, respectively, for top wealth groups, and 40, 30, and 30 percent, respectively, for other wealth groups in the low estimate. The probable estimate assumes 50 percent unrealized gain share for the top wealthholders.

a Gross estate tax filers with assets over $60,000.
b Stock held by individuals, but excluding stock held by personal trust funds
c See Sources, above, for explanation of low and probable estimates.

value of household shareholdings is 30 percent for decedents as a whole and 44 percent for wealthy shareholders. A revision of his original estimates based on 50 percent and 75 percent for the two groups is given in Table 4-26. The conclusion obtained in McClung's calculation that about 40 percent of the value of shares held by households reflects potentially taxable gains provides a reasonable corroboration of the *ad hoc* statistics presented in Table 4-26.

If unrealized gains that accrued in past years were subject to taxation at death, the annual increment to the tax base would substantially exceed the current reported net gains. For the 1960-64 period, reported net gains less net losses on individual income tax returns averaged $13 billion a year. Decedents' wealth was estimated at some $34 billion for 1963 by Hinrichs; of that amount, $13.4 billion is estimated as unrealized capital gains.[25] Exemptions and underreporting would reduce the amount actually taxed. Unless the percentage of appreciation in decedents' wealth is substantially smaller (which is unlikely) or individuals respond to taxation of unrealized gains with sizable lifetime realizations, the yields from the taxation of unrealized gains would equal or exceed the yields from taxing lifetime realizations. Since deaths are not cyclical, the overall yield of the capital gains tax would become relatively more stable. The reader may make his own judgment about the magnitude of capital gains constructively taxed at death by modifying appropriately the fractions of wealth included as unrealized gains in the last three columns of Table 4-26.

Changes in investor behavior in response to a system of presumptive realization would mean a reduction in the current level of unrealized gains. Investors would be more likely to trade assets prior to death. While this would mean a decline in revenue from the taxation of decedents' wealth, it would not cause a reduction in the aggregate yield from the capital gains tax. Increased lifetime sales of assets would mean correspondingly greater realized capital gains.

In the hearings on the President's 1963 Tax Message[26] the Treasury estimated the prospective revenue gain from the proposed taxation of unrealized gains at $0.3 billion after the provision was fully in

[25] Our estimate of accrued gain on listed shares held by households shows about $21 billion of unrealized capital gains in 1963. (See Appendix Table C-1, Cols. 6 and 7.)

[26] *President's 1963 Tax Message,* Hearings before the House Committee on Ways and Means, 88 Cong. 1 sess. (1963), Part I, revised, p. 709.

TABLE 4-27. Increase in Effective Average Rates of Tax on Total Income Under Alternative Definitions of Taxable Income, 1965
(In percent)

Total income class[a]	Average tax rate on total income before credits and not allowing income splitting[b] (1)	Alternative capital gains tax (2)	50 percent long-term capital gains exclusion (3)	Limited inclusion of capital losses (4)
0 under $5,000	5.48	0.00	0.06	−0.03
$5,000 under $10,000	9.52	0.00	0.12	−0.03
$10,000 under $15,000	13.56	0.00	0.28	−0.06
$15,000 under $20,000	16.90	0.00	0.87	−0.14
$20,000 under $25,000	20.20	0.00	1.46	−0.26
$25,000 under $50,000	26.00	0.01	2.48	−0.34
$50,000 under $100,000	33.33	0.28	5.27	−0.32
$100,000 under $150,000	34.43	1.18	10.59	−0.22
$150,000 under $200,000	33.26	1.97	14.49	−0.21
$200,000 under $500,000	30.96	3.59	18.68	−0.09
$500,000 under $1,000,000	28.15	5.51	23.31	−0.05
$1,000,000 or more	26.27	6.86	26.46	−0.12
All income classes	11.96	0.09	0.88	−0.09

The header for columns 2-4: *Increase in tax rate associated with sequential elimination of[c]*

Source: Joseph A. Pechman, Brookings Institution, unpublished tabulations.
[a] Total income includes all capital gains plus dividend and sick pay exclusions from adjusted gross income.
[b] Based on 1962 tax returns. For methods of estimating 1965 income and tax, see Table 4-18, note a.
[c] Col. (2) refers to the increase in taxes over Col. (1) associated with the elimination of the alternative tax. Col. (3) refers to the increase in taxes over the level that obtains when *both* the reforms applicable to Col. (1) and Col. (2) are already in effect. Col. (4) refers to the increase over the tax in effect when all of the conditions of Cols. (1), (2), and (3) are already in effect. Thus the impact of eliminating all preferential provisions of the capital gains tax can be measured by the sum of Cols. (2), (3), and (4).

effect. This was based on (1) a 30 percent rate of inclusion of unrealized gains in income; (2) the restriction of presumptive realization to the estate tax population; (3) liberal exemptions for household effects, the personal residence, and the initial $15,000 of appreciation; and (4) offsetting reductions in estate tax receipts. The tax yield would be substantially larger if the tax were levied on a greater proportion of the appreciation shown in Table 4-26.

If unrealized capital gains were presumed to be realized at death, a large part of the increment to the tax base would be taxed at the alternative rate of 25 percent if present capital gains rates remained unchanged. However, if the taxation of capital gains generally is revised to eliminate a ceiling rate, the inclusion of unrealized capital

TABLE 4-28. Tax Liability as Percentage of Taxable Income Plus the Excluded Portion of Long-Term Capital Gains Under Alternative Tax Computation Procedures, Returns with Long-Term Capital Gains, 1965[a]
(*In percent*)

		Tax computation procedure		
			Proration of long-term capital gains[c]	
Adjusted gross income class	Present law[b]	Over 3 years	Over 5 years	Over 10 years
	(1)	(2)	(3)	(4)
0 under $5,000	8.8	9.3	8.5	8.0
$5,000 under $10,000	15.1	15.8	15.5	15.3
$10,000 under $15,000	16.9	17.7	17.5	17.3
$15,000 under $20,000	18.4	19.5	19.4	19.2
$20,000 under $25,000	20.2	21.2	20.9	20.7
$25,000 under $50,000	24.2	25.6	25.2	24.9
$50,000 under $100,000	31.8	35.4	34.4	33.6
$100,000 under $150,000	35.0	44.0	42.2	40.4
$150,000 under $200,000	35.7	49.2	47.0	44.6
$200,000 under $500,000	34.7	55.0	52.0	48.2
$500,000 under $1,000,000	31.4	61.7	58.7	53.5
$1,000,000 under $10,000,000	32.1	65.4	63.6	59.6
All adjusted gross income classes	21.8	25.2	24.6	23.9

Source: Joseph A. Pechman, Brookings Institution, unpublished tabulations.
[a] The effective tax rate shown here slightly understates the true rate on total income less deductions, since only the allowable portion of net capital losses is included in the denominator. The rate shown is total tax liability as a percentage of total taxable income plus long-term capital gains excluded from income. The figure is the average effective rate, not the rate that would be obtained by calculating accumulated tax liability as a percentage of total income within each class.
[b] Provisions of the individual income tax law applicable in 1965 were applied to actual income data from the 1962 taxpayer population. For method of calculation, see Table 4-18, note c.
[c] Proration is accomplished by computing the tax on taxable income including all short-term losses less long-term capital gains or losses (T_1). The tax is recomputed on this amount of income plus the amount of long-term capital gains (or losses) divided by the proration period (T_2). The tax attributed to long-term capital gains is $N(T_2 - T_1)$, where N is the proration period. The total tax is $T_1 + N(T_2 - T_1)$.
All short-term losses are assumed to be 100 percent deductible in computing net capital gains.

gains could substantially increase the effective marginal tax rates applicable to upper-income taxpayers. Some insight into this problem can be obtained by applying the proposed revised tax to tax returns actually filed in 1962.

Impact of Alternative Reforms on Marginal and Average Tax Rates

Simulation studies of tax liabilities under alternative definitions of the taxable income concept produced the results shown in Table

4-27.[27] Eliminating the current preferential capital gains tax provisions would increase the average tax rate on all taxpayers by nearly 1 percentage point to 13 percent, provided that no change in the dollar volume of capital gains realized would be induced by the shift in the tax law.[28] For individuals with incomes over $100,000, elimination of the preferential provisions would increase the average rate of tax on *total* income by 12 to 33 percentage points, depending on the income class. Most of the benefits of preferential capital gains taxation are conferred by the percentage inclusion feature of the law. Repeal of the alternative tax would cause many taxpayers to change the method by which they compute tax liability, but the increase in tax yield would be small compared with that which would result from reducing further the capital gains deduction. Disallowing losses would have the greatest impact on average tax rates on deficit returns, because net losses are concentrated on such returns.

Table 4-28 shows the increase in average tax rates that would result if a proration procedure were adopted to determine marginal tax rates on long-term capital gains. Under this proposal there would be no limitation on the net capital loss allowed on income. Average effective tax rates on taxable income plus the excluded portion of long-term capital gains would rise by 2 to 3.5 percentage points from the current level of 22 percent. Proration of gains over five years would increase average tax rates by 7 to 31 percentage points for individuals in adjusted gross income brackets over $100,000.

Some indication of the incentive effects of such a provision is given in Table 4-29. The average tax rate applied to long-term capital gains is computed by calculating the ratio of incremental taxes associated with capital gains to the amount of those gains. In the top brackets, the average marginal rates on capital gains would more than double, even with a ten-year proration period.[29]

[27] I am indebted to Joseph A. Pechman of the Brookings Institution, who designed these studies, for access to the findings.

[28] Due to the sequence of the calculations, the method also assumes that the rate advantages of income-splitting on joint returns are removed.

[29] Incremental tax rates on long-term gains do not rise to the statutory bracket rates. However, the *true* marginal rate on the last dollar of capital gains income is higher than the *average* marginal rate shown. That rate is computed from the statutory bracket rates that are successively applied to the prorated amount of capital gains. The *true* marginal rates would exceed those shown in Table 4-29, since the amount of prorated long-term capital gains could be a sizable increment to other income.

TABLE 4-29. Tax on Long-Term Capital Gains as Percentage of Amount of Such Gains Under Alternative Tax Computation Procedures, Returns with Long-Term Capital Gains, 1965[a]

Adjusted gross income class	Present law (1)	Proration of long-term capital gains		
		Over 3 years (2)	Over 5 years (3)	Over 10 years (4)
0 under $5,000	2.8	3.7	2.3	1.3
$5,000 under $10,000	7.3	12.7	10.8	9.4
$10,000 under $15,000	9.6	17.3	15.8	14.4
$15,000 under $20,000	11.2	19.8	18.6	17.4
$20,000 under $25,000	12.1	21.0	19.1	17.6
$25,000 under $50,000	15.5	26.8	24.4	22.5
$50,000 under $100,000	21.5	38.9	35.0	31.8
$100,000 under $150,000	23.1	46.5	42.3	38.0
$150,000 under $200,000	23.8	51.7	47.3	42.6
$200,000 under $500,000	24.0	56.7	52.0	46.0
$500,000 under $1,000,000	24.4	62.4	58.6	52.2
$1,000,000 under $10,000,000	24.6	65.3	63.2	58.2
All adjusted gross income classes	15.2	31.0	28.3	25.6

Source: Joseph A. Pechman, Brookings Institution, unpublished tabulations.
[a] See notes to Tables 4-18 and 4-28.

TABLE 4-30. Revenue Attributable to Taxation of Long-Term Capital Gains Under Alternative Schemes, 1965[a]

(In millions of dollars)

Tax attributable to long-term capital gains	Present law (1)	Proration of long-term capital gains		
		Over 3 years (2)	Over 5 years (3)	Over 10 years (4)
1. Proration applied to all returns with long-term capital asset transactions	1,752	3,574	3,269	2,948
2. Proration applied to returns with net long-term capital gains	1,900	3,952	3,663	3,354
3. Provisions of 1965 tax law applied to returns with net long-term capital losses[b]	−148	−148	−148	−148
4. Line 2+Line 3	1,752	3,804	3,515	3,206

Source: Joseph A. Pechman, Brookings Institution, unpublished tabulations.
[a] See notes to Tables 4-18 and 4-28.
[b] That is, losses may be used to offset short-term gains or a limited amount of current income from other sources.

While Tables 4-27 to 4-29 demonstrate the impact of proposed major changes in capital gains taxation, they do not show potential reactions to higher tax rates. Moreover, the tables do not account for the distributional impact of a change in tax rates that would be required to maintain constant aggregate tax yields. Thus the change in rate structure must be regarded as a crude approximation that undoubtedly exaggerates the increase in tax rate progression.

Proration over a period of five years results in average tax rates on capital gains that exceed 50 percent only for taxpayers with more than $200,000 of adjusted gross income.

The increase in incremental tax rates associated with decreases in the proration period provides an insight into the effect of increases in the capital gains tax base that might be associated with presumptive realization. For example, assume that presumptive realization of gains would double the amount of capital gains subject to tax. Assume also that unrealized gains are distributed within each income group shown in Table 4-29 in the same way as are realized gains. Then the incremental tax rate associated with constructive realization would be the same as the incremental rate associated with the current realized capital gains and a proration period half as long. For example, if the proration period were ten years under the assumed conditions, the rates shown for a proration period of five years would actually apply to the total of realized and constructively realized gains. Those rates are shown in Table 4-29, Column (3).

The revenue effects of the proration proposals can be seen in Table 4-30. These estimates take no account of induced changes in taxpayer behavior.

Conclusions

The growth in the frequency and the amount of capital gains realized over the past decade clearly indicates that capital asset transactions are playing an increasingly important role in producing income for individuals, corporations, and fiduciaries. The present rate of growth of income and net worth suggests that capital gains will continue to rise in the future, causing the tax treatment of capital gains income to dominate the incentive and equity characteristics of the tax structure.

The available data on the amount of capital gains realized by corporate and fiduciary entities indicate that these entities cannot be ignored in a discussion of alternative approaches to capital gains taxation. Fiduciaries appear to be highly conscious of the tax advantages available under the present tax and able to take advantage of its preferential features. Moreover, fiduciaries have been growing rapidly as a legal means through which individuals have accommodated their increasing income to a progressive tax structure. The tax treatment of fiduciaries, therefore, is increasingly important in the overall personal income tax structure.

Corporate realizations of capital gains appear to be highly concentrated among smaller enterprises in particular industry sectors. In part this arises from the special treatment accorded to certain elements of recurrent income in Section 1231. The recent growth in the proportion of corporate net income realized in the form of capital gains, as well as the increase in the corporate population, makes the tax treatment of corporate capital gains a significant problem both in aggregative and in equity terms.

A study of individual tax liabilities under alternative definitions of the contribution of capital gains to taxable income indicates clearly that both the alternative tax rate and the percentage inclusion features of the present law must be amended if the marginal tax rates of high-income individuals are to approach the levels set by statute. It is also clear from available data on the recipients of capital gains that capital gains income is a recurrent source of income for individuals reporting the largest dollar volume of gains. These individuals own most of the country's corporate equities; and the bulk of corporate equities traded on the market have been held less than five years. These facts would indicate that the largest volume of trading does not require special tax treatment to avoid inappropriate tax progression. However, an unknown number of individuals who hold assets on which gains have *not* been realized would be inequitably treated by a law that did not provide some averaging feature for capital gains income.

The need for an averaging feature (or other device to mitigate the impact of capital gains on the income tax liability of a particular year) becomes apparent when the amount of appreciation in decedents' wealth is estimated. If appreciation were taxed constructively in the year of a taxpayer's death, the resulting gains could easily double the amount of capital gains included in the tax base. Conservative assumptions about holding patterns and lock-in suggest that at least half of current shareholding wealth held by households is unrealized capital gain. Again, conservative assumptions indicate that one-fifth, and possibly a much greater fraction, of the potential gains escape taxation due to step-up in basis at death.

The foregoing data do not reveal the observed behavior that produced capital gains income in the past. The extent to which realizations of gains were associated with conscious recognition of the opportunities for tax avoidance, rather than being responses to other economic and noneconomic events, remains undetermined. Some guess concerning motivation is of critical importance in assessing the effects of major changes in the tax treatment of capital gains. In the chapters that follow some aspects of these effects will be discussed, and a possible alternative approach to capital gains taxation will be proposed.

CHAPTER V

Proposals for Reform

THE PRESENT CAPITAL GAINS TAX structure invites a variety of proposals for change. Some of them would base the tax treatment of capital gains on an accretion concept of income. Others reflect concern over the impact of the capital gains tax on financial markets and on saving and investment. Some proposals reflect the personal interest of those who seek a further reduction in their tax liability.

Dimensions of Reform

Proposals for change in the capital gains tax provisions can be classified as were the provisions of the present law in Chapter II. Thus, reform proposals may affect: (1) the class of eligible transactions, (2) holding period criteria, (3) the definition of the value of gains and losses, (4) the timing of tax payment, (5) the rate to be paid on net gains, and (6) the rate to be paid on net losses. The proposals discussed in Chapter VI are developed within the framework of these present dimensions of capital gains taxation, the suggested changes being concerned specifically with the first three dimensions listed above. In Chapter VII the tax treatment of assets transferred by gift or bequest is discussed. Chapter VIII considers a variety of proposals that would do away with preferential rate treatment for capital gains, that is, proposals for a more complete overhaul of the concepts underlying the present capital gains tax. In

109

FIGURE 5-1. Dimensions and Interdependence of Capital Gains Reform Proposals[a]

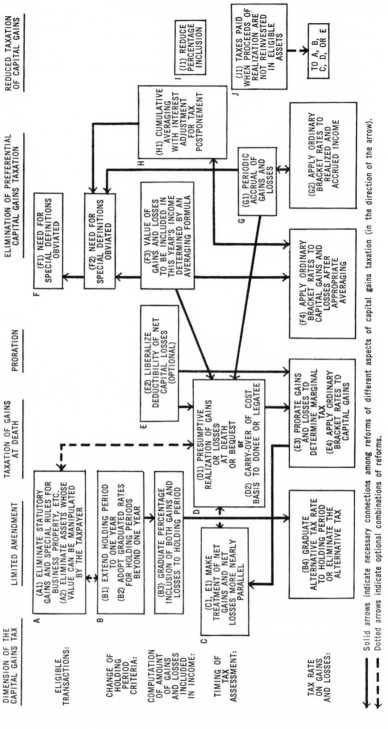

Solid arrows indicate necessary connections among reforms of different aspects of capital gains taxation (in the direction of the arrow).

---- Dotted arrows indicate optional combinations of reforms.

[a] See Chap. II.

Chapter IX roll-over and other proposals for reducing taxes on capital gains and losses are taken up.

The limited number of proposals discussed in these four chapters were selected to represent the principal types of reform suggested, although many variants would accomplish similar results.

Figure 5-1 shows how the present dimensions of capital gains tax treatment would be altered by each of the proposals considered in the following chapters. In the analysis below an attempt is made to develop some perspective on (1) the extent of the change in present tax treatment that is implied by a particular proposal, (2) the necessary corollaries of a given reform proposal, (3) the consistency of the proposal with the accretion concept of taxable capacity defined in Chapter III, and (4) the administrative impact of the proposed changes. Equity, as well as the incentive effects, will be analyzed, together with the legal basis for the changes, probable compliance problems, and the problems that would be associated with the transition from the present to the proposed system.

The various proposals that were selected for discussion represent increasing departures from the precedent established by the present capital gains tax. The less extreme changes in the present tax contained in proposals A-D do not represent points on a continuum of treatment that logically culminates in the treatment suggested under proposals E-H. Nevertheless, they suggest useful changes that would increase equity and eliminate some of the major inequities under present law.

Narrowing the scope of transactions eligible for preferential capital gains taxation (proposal A), would be a major step in eliminating possibilities for converting ordinary income into capital gains. A change in the taxation of assets transferred by gift or bequest (proposal D) would eliminate another, perhaps the largest, tax benefit conferred by the present system,[1] Changes in the holding period requirements (proposal B) and loss offset provisions (proposal C) would create minor, but desirable, changes in the existing disincentives to sell appreciated assets. The proration of gains (proposal E) would make the full inclusion of gains in income reasonably equitable under a progressive tax system.

---

[1] Martin J. Bailey, "Capital Gains and Income Taxation," in Arnold C. Harberger and Martin J. Bailey (eds.), *Taxation of Income from Capital* (Brookings Institution, 1968).

Figure 5-1 shows clearly that reforms that are comprehensive enough to eliminate problems associated with the definition of eligible transactions (proposals F, G, and H) would also require simultaneous alterations in several, if not all, dimensions of the capital gains tax. The less comprehensive proposals might be combined to provide varying degrees of change, but would not produce a tax system in which eligible transactions do not need to be defined. Proposals G and H would both eliminate the definitional problems in the present law; moreover, they would reduce present incentives to deferment (lock-in) to minimal levels.

Clearly, proposals I and J stand apart as changes that would greatly reduce asset taxation and increase deferral of taxes on capital gains. They deserve a place in the discussion since they offer a solution to the problem of lock-in created by the capital gains tax.

Revenue Effects[2]

Eliminating the alternative tax, constructive realization of gains when assets are transferred by gift or bequest, or eliminating Subchapter P differentials for the taxation of gains on capital assets would substantially increase the revenue yield of the income tax at present statutory rates. Data from the 1962 *Statistics of Income*[3] suggest that the increase in revenues might be about $1 billion if the alternative tax were eliminated, $2 billion to $4 billion if constructive realization were imposed (depending on the exclusions and estimated appreciation in the portfolios of decedents), and $2 billion if capital gains deductions were eliminated and some system for averaging gains introduced (see pages 99-106).

While these magnitudes are not large when compared with the revenue yield of the entire federal tax structure, they are substantial in comparison with the revenue cost of other major structural changes in the federal personal income tax and transfer taxes. For example, a reduction of tax rates to a maximum of 39 percent would have cost $4.8 billion in 1963. That amount is probably less than would be yielded by a combination of constructive realization, together with proration and full taxation of capital gains. (See Tables

[2] For the views of the conference participants on this subject, see Chap. X.
[3] U.S. Treasury Department, Internal Revenue Service, *Statistics of Income, Individual Income Tax Returns—1962* (1965).

4-26 and 4-30.) An increase in exemptions of $100 would reduce tax yields by $3 billion, while a reduction in marginal tax rates of 1 percent would cost about $2.5 billion.[4] By comparison, the *entire* yield of the federal estate tax was $2.4 billion in 1964. Clearly, enough revenue could be obtained from a revision of the capital gains tax to provide some appreciable changes in the current structure of personal taxation at the federal level.

The choice among alternative uses of the revenues obtained from a revision of capital gains taxes would depend on a resolution of the following policy questions:

1. Should income taxation be based on the accretion concept (discussed in Chapter III), or on some alternative base that exempts certain monetary gains or the gains from certain investment activities?

2. Should the progression of the tax structure be altered? If so, in which tax brackets should effective rates be increased or reduced?

3. Should more or less emphasis be placed on the income tax as a device to limit lifetime accumulation of wealth?

4. Given the established levels of income taxation, does the estate tax appropriately limit the transmission of wealth from one generation to the next?

The nature of these choices can best be seen by examining alternative uses for the revenue yield that would result if specific proposals for revising capital gains taxation were adopted. Constructive realization of gains when assets are transferred through gift or at death illustrates some of the competing views. It would increase the tax burden on the estate of a decedent. (It might also increase lifetime taxation as individuals respond to a reduction in the lock-in effect on their portfolios.) Constructive realization would increase the coverage of the personal income tax in relation to the base defined by the accretion definition of income, but it would not mean any particular resolution of the second and third questions. If the revision were adopted as a measure to assure the taxation of income accrued over the lifetime of the decedent, it would be reasonable to apply additional revenues to the reduction of income tax rates generally. The decision whether to apply rate reduction within the taxpayer group that bears the burden of constructive realization depends upon one's view of the progression of the present tax structure. If the tax struc-

[4] Derived from Appendix Table B-6 in Joseph A. Pechman, *Federal Tax Policy* (Brookings Institution, 1966), p. 265.

ture is judged sufficiently progressive in the upper-income groups, revenues ought to be allocated to the reduction of upper-income sur-tax rates. Alternatively, constructive realization might be viewed as a net increase in taxation applied to the estate of the decedent. In that case, revenues should be applied to the reduction of the estate tax rates to whatever extent is needed to adjust the balance of income and estate taxes to some appropriate equilibrium. Finally, constructive realization may be regarded primarily as a technique for reducing the lock-in effect of the present capital gains tax. From that point of view, it would be appropriate to allocate a part of the revenue yield to the reduction of the percentage inclusion or the alternative tax rate. (Some revenues would have to be used for other purposes, since the entire yield of the capital gains tax is roughly of the same order of magnitude as that which would result from constructive realization.)

A similar set of considerations would apply to any general averaging scheme for eliminating the distinction between capital gains and ordinary income. To the extent that such a provision would increase investor lock-in, it would be appropriate to apply revenues to the reduction of marginal tax rates in the upper-income groups. Such a revision in the taxation of capital gains would make it possible to reduce the top bracket rates to 50 percent, or possibly somewhat less. Alternatively, if the revision were regarded as a technique for enforcing the progression that is already implied by statutory bracket rates, it would be appropriate to apply revenue yields to an across-the-board reduction in taxes via increased exemptions or possibly a percentage reduction in all bracket rates. Finally, if the revision were regarded primarily as a means of simplifying the tax and reducing compliance costs, it would be most appropriate to distribute the revenue to those income brackets that are likely to experience increases in effective tax rates.

The analysis that follows is concerned largely with the consequences of proposed capital gains tax revisions in which additional revenues would be used to reduce tax rates in each income bracket in proportion to the additional taxation of capital gains imposed. Although alternative points of view could be pursued with equal validity, to assume that revenues are used to prevent increases in the effective rate of taxation within each tax bracket appears consistent with the spirit of tax rate reduction incorporated into the Revenue Act of

1964. It also would assure that the increase in tax burden on investors consequent to revision of capital gains would be minimized, together with any investment disincentive effects.

It can thus be seen that both the choice of revision in capital gains taxation and the concomitant changes in the personal tax structure are not determined entirely by economic considerations. The analysis that follows does suggest, however, that certain revisions ought to be undertaken if one is willing to accept the accretion measure of income discussed in Chapter III.

CHAPTER VI

Limiting Eligibility

TWO STEPS COULD BE TAKEN to reduce the applicability of preferential capital gains taxation to situations that permit gross and inequitable tax avoidance. First, income arising from a number of *special situations* accorded capital gains treatment could be returned to the ordinary income category, with the income-averaging provisions enacted in 1964 applying. Second, preferential capital gains tax privileges could be withdrawn from owner-management situations where it is not possible to distinguish elements of compensation from changes in investment value.[1]

Both of these categories require early and careful attention if additional erosion of the ordinary income concept is to be avoided. Under both, the fruits of personal effort can be converted into forms that are taxable at capital gains rates.[2] And under both, the manipulation of ordinary property income into capital gains is encouraged.

The conversion of ordinary income into capital gains takes several routes. For example, the compensation of a manager may understate the true value of services received. If he holds a controlling interest in

[1] Any differential in tax rates needed to sustain or to encourage initiation of small business enterprises could be granted directly. The existing indirect subsidy through the tax avoidance permitted under the preferential capital gains tax is an obscure and inequitable form of incentive to small business.

[2] A review of legislative intent and judicial interpretation of the appropriateness of such conversions was prepared by Peter Miller in "Capital Gains Taxation of the Fruits of Personal Effort: Before and Under the 1954 Code," *Yale Law Journal,* Vol. 64 (November 1954), pp. 1-83.

a corporation, he receives some compensation in the appreciation of his equity interest. That accretion in value may later be liquidated as a gain on the sale of a capital asset.[3]

Alternatively, current deductions to arrive at adjusted gross income may exceed their real cost to the taxpayer. The accelerated depreciation of real property or the expensing of development costs permitted for certain mineral-producing properties and for raising livestock do not reflect current costs that actually reduce income or income prospects. Yet taxable income is reduced in the year in which such deductions are taken. The tax basis of the asset is understated by the amount of the excess depreciation deduction and the failure to account properly for capital expenditures. The difference between market value and the understated basis of asset can be realized as a capital gain when the asset is ultimately sold. Income that would otherwise be taxed at ordinary rates is once more converted into capital gains.

Finally, the conversion of return to labor services into capital gains is directly sanctioned by special provisions in the law. Capital assets, as defined in the Internal Revenue Code (Section 1221), do not include patents or royalty contracts on timber, iron, and coal, though income from such patents and royalties may be treated as capital gains.

The opportunities for tax avoidance presented by these legal provisions are significant primarily for two groups of taxpayers—those whose business activities lend themselves to the organization of small and closely held corporations and those who are free to direct production into fields where current income is legally taxed as a capital gain. Investors with small portfolios, with limited time for direct business management, or with limited access to tax counselling are unlikely to be among either group.

Owner-Management Investments

When the ownership of a corporation is so limited that its stock is neither widely traded nor sufficiently distributed so that one can dis-

[3] Typical of such arrangements are the personal service corporation, which is organized to sell the services of an individual or accumulate his income, and the collapsible corporation, which is organized to liquidate (by the appropriate sale of a capital asset) an economic interest that would otherwise be taxable at ordinary income rates.

tinguish between the ownership and the management of the corporate operation, the distinction between the corporation and its owners forced by the corporate tax law ceases to have empirical reality.[4]
The balance between the income and property accounts of the individual managers and the corporation can be struck at whatever level
is suitable for maximum tax avoidance. The retention of profits within the corporate body leads to changes in the valuation of its stock,
which will be taxed at capital gains tax rates when it is sold. Reducing the compensation paid to the owner-managers below the market
level further increases the profit and reduces the amount of income
taxable to the owner-managers at ordinary income rates. The owner-
managers can thereby convert their own salaries into capital gains
and limit the progression of the combined corporate-personal tax
structure on their total income.

The effective combined rate of tax on a taxpayer's share of pre-tax
corporate earnings can generally be determined by the equation:[5]

$$(6.1) \qquad t^* = c + t\rho(1 - c) + g(1 - \rho)(1 - c),$$

where:

t^* = the effective combined marginal tax rate on corporate earnings,

t = the taxpayer's marginal personal income tax rate,

ρ = the expected (average) ratio of corporate dividends to corporate
earnings (for the marginal investment in corporate stocks),

c = the corporation income tax rate, and

g = the effective marginal tax rate on capital gains, discounted on
account of deferred liability and the avoidance of taxation possible through the passage of assets into gifts or estate.

The owner-manager has the choice of ignoring corporate taxation
if he qualifies for integrated tax treatment under the provisions of
Subchapter S of the Internal Revenue Code. In that case the rates
t^* and t are equal ($\rho = 1$, $c = 0$ in Equation 6.1). If t is sufficiently
high, however, incorporation will be advantageous. With the ability
to control payout and the present low rate of taxation on capital

---

[4] The distinction is sufficiently arbitrary that the Internal Revenue Code permits
closely held corporations to be taxed as partnerships (Sections 1371-77) and certain
partnerships to be taxed as corporations (Section 1361).

[5] Martin J. Bailey, "Capital Gains and Income Taxation," in Arnold C. Harberger
and Martin J. Bailey (eds.), *Taxation of Income from Capital* (Brookings Institution,
1968).

gains, it pays the owner-manager to subject his earnings to corporate taxation, since t^* can be reduced below t if the taxpayer's income is so large that $t > 0.61$. Since ownership in the enterprise is not widely marketed, the proprietor may be able to achieve substantially more tax avoidance by this route than can be purchased in the market.

When the taxpayer is an owner-manager, tax avoidance can be enlarged beyond the levels possible through a low dividend payout in a closely held corporation. A fraction e of wage income (or earnings) can be stated as profit for accounting purposes. The effective tax rate on the combined wages E and profit P of the enterprise then becomes:

$$(6.2) \quad (E + P)t^{**} = t(1 - e)E + t^*(eE + P),$$

$$(6.3) \qquad t^{**} = t(1 - e)\frac{E}{E + P} + t^*e\frac{E}{E + P} + t^*\frac{P}{E + P}.$$

Assuming P to be at a market rate of return, the tax benefit to the owner-investor in excess of that available to other investors in the market is:

$$(6.4) \qquad\qquad tE - (t[1 - e]E + t^*eE),$$

or

$$e(t - t^*) \text{ per dollar of executive salary.[6]}$$

Efforts to limit the tax avoidance that can be effected in this manner have created a welter of special regulations concerning personal holding corporations, excessive accumulation, collapsible corporations, and other symptoms of the underlying inconsistency in the law.

The change in definition of capital assets suggested by Silverstein circumvents the problem of excessive accumulation which arises be-

---

[6] If all of the compensation paid to the owner-manager can be converted into capital gains, then $e = 1$, $p = 0$; if in addition the marginal capital gains tax rate g anticipated by the owner-manager is 25 percent (the most unfavorable possibility), then equation 6.3 above leads to the following tax rate under the combined corporate personal tax burden:

$$t^{**} = c + g(1 - c) = 0.48 + 0.25(0.52) = 0.61.$$

In a reasonably favorable situation g may be as low as 0.05 (see Bailey, *op. cit.*); then $t^{**} = 0.51$.

It should be noted that excess compensation claimed by the owner-manager will reduce the combined tax liability in any instance in which $t < t^*$. The owner-manager whose income places him in such a tax bracket will find it profitable to avoid taxation by overstating his wages in order to be able to increase the deductions from corporate income. That possibility could be reflected in the formulas above by a value of $e < 0$.

cause closely held corporations are manipulable. Silverstein proposes that capital gains treatment be limited to transactions in a circumscribed group of *investment assets,* which are a limited subset of the present class of capital assets. Investment assets would include only those securities and investments in which the taxpayer does not have sufficient ownership interest to influence management policy.[7] In other words, capital gains treatment would be limited to investments that are bought and sold on a market over which the investor has little conrol.

[7] See Leonard Silverstein, "The Capital Asset Definition," in House Committee on Ways and Means, *Tax Revision Compendium* (1959), Vol. 2, pp. 1285-99, from which the following illustrative draft of a new subchapter (Subchapter T) on investment property is reproduced:

"(a) *General Rule.* For purposes of this subtitle, the term 'investment property' means property which

(1) consists of investment securities or other investment assets

(2) has been held by the taxpayer for more than 6 months (and for this purpose, section 1223 shall apply in determining the period for which the taxpayer has held the property),

(3) is not held by the taxpayer primarily for sale to customers in the ordinary course of his trade or business,

(4) is not used in, or connected with, a trade or business of the taxpayer.

(b) *Definition.*

(1) For purposes of this section, the term 'investment securities' means

(A) stock in a corporation which does not conduct a trade or business;

(B) stock in a corporation which does conduct a trade or business unless the taxpayer owns (or is considered as owning more than 5 percent in value of the outstanding stock of such corporation). For this purpose, the ownership of stock shall be determined in accordance with the rules prescribed in paragraphs (1), (2), (3), (5), and (6) of section 544(a) (relating to personal holding companies);

(C) a bond, debenture, note, certificate, or other evidence of indebtedness issued by a corporation or other debtor.

(2) The term 'investment assets' means property other than investment securities, as described in paragraph (1), which consists of

(A) real estate or tangible personal property the ownership of which does not constitute the conduct of a trade or business;

(B) an interest in a partnership, joint venture, or other entity unless such partnership, venture, or entity is engaged in the conduct of a trade or business;

(C) an interest in a partnership, joint venture, or other entity, which does conduct a trade or business, if the interest of the taxpayer in the partnership, venture, or entity is not more than 5 percent. For this purpose, the interest of a taxpayer in a partnership, venture, or other entity shall be determined in accordance with the rules prescribed in paragraphs (1), (2), (3), (5), and (6) of section 544(a) (relating to personal holding companies) and for this purpose such interest shall be considered as stock.

The investment asset basis for determining eligibility for capital gains treatment would have a number of advantages. Capital gains taxation would apply to investments that are traded widely enough to establish reasonable market prices. On the basis of existing prices and subjective anticipations, any taxpayer may make an investment that is expected to produce a return at favored capital gains rates sometime in the future. Active trading in the market implies that assets that are expected to appreciate greatly in the future also command some premium in proportion to the tax avoidance they make possible for high-income investors.[8]

Limiting capital gains tax rates to investments in which ownership is dispersed would probably mean that some investments that are closely held under present law would become publicly traded. If ownership became more dispersed, more investors would have a chance to bid for tax avoidance opportunities. Each investor would then have to weigh the value of reductions in future tax liability against the possibly lower aggregate rate of return available on securities with low rates of current return. The market would limit the extent to which taxes could be avoided by holding appreciated securities.

At present the owner-manager can get substantially more tax avoidance benefits from a given investment than can the market at large. While it may not seem completely appropriate to eliminate this windfall to owner-managers by excluding them from capital gains treatment entirely, the special tax privileges and subsidies already accorded this group could be made to offset an equitable part of their increased tax resulting from exclusion from capital gains treatment. The owner-manager already has an opportunity to escape the burden of corporate taxation entirely if the corporation elects to be taxed under Subchapter S.[9] If it is necessary for the sake of equity, the scope of Subchapter S elections could be broadened to match the class of owner-manager investments excluded from preferential capital gains treatment by the investment asset definition.

The existence of many laws and regulations affecting the taxation of small business implies that an investment asset definition of in-

[8] See Figure 7-1, below, and the accompanying text, pp. 152-53.
[9] However, the Tax Adjustment Act of 1966 (Public Law 89-368) amended taxation of electing corporations to require that capital gains be taxed in some instances (see Internal Revenue Code, Section 1378). This restriction limits the use of the election on a selective basis in years in which the corporation disposes of large amounts of its capital assets.

come eligible for preferred tax treatment would be administratively feasible. The fact that there are already tax privileges under Subchapter S that differentiate this group from the general taxpayer makes it reasonable to think that the owner-managers could not invalidate the investment asset definition in the courts. Furthermore, the frequent legislative amendment of the area eligible for capital gains treatment and the limited extent of judicial review of the boundaries of eligibility indicate that legislative power exists to narrow the capital asset definition to an investment asset definition.[10]

The more general availability of the means of tax avoidance would reduce the present horizontal inequity affecting investors at the same marginal personal tax rate (given efficient capital markets). And the tax treatment of low-income taxpayers would correspond more closely to that available to upper-income groups. Of course, the alternative tax available to persons whose marginal tax rate exceeded 50 percent would continue to mean vertical inequity; individuals at lower income levels have a smaller margin for tax avoidance. Inequities between investor and noninvestor groups in the same marginal tax bracket would remain.

Special Situations

Ordinary Income Treated as a Capital Gain

Income received from (1) the sale of crops with land, (2) the sale of patents, (3) the sale of timber, (4) coal, timber, and iron ore royalties, and (5) the lump-sum termination of pension trusts is all entitled to capital gains treatment.[11] When these privileges were enacted, it was clearly recognized that the transactions did not involve

[10] See Lawrence H. Seltzer, *The Nature and Tax Treatment of Capital Gains and Losses* (National Bureau of Economic Research, 1951), pp. 34-36. Discussion at the conference revealed little enthusiasm for this technique for narrowing the scope of capital gains taxation. See the conference summary, Chap. X, p. 226.

[11] Internal Revenue Code, Sections 1235, 1231(b), 1240, and 631. A special problem arises with regard to restricted stock options (Section 424 of the Code). Until 1964, some income corresponding to the difference between the option price and the market price of the stock on the date of the option's issue was treated as a capital gain. While such a difference no longer receives preferential capital gains treatment, the difference between market price and sale price, with certain qualifications, may be treated as capital gains. The question remains whether the restricted stock option permits conversion of ordinary compensation into capital gains by a process similar to that discussed above in connection with owner-manager income.

the sale of a capital asset representing only a casual investment. Preferential taxation was granted in many cases because of the difficulty of distinguishing these transactions from those entitled to capital gains treatment.

Actually there are two separable areas of controversy concerning capital gains treatment of income from patents: (1) Is the sale of a patent by its creator the sale of stock in trade and therefore excluded in principle from the capital assets definition? (2) Is the licensing of a patent in return for future royalties a sale or exchange within the meaning of the law? Royalties are contracted as a variable percentage of sales or profit. They thus constitute a variable return on the initial investment much like dividends or profit. The licensor continues to enjoy the benefits and risks of his investment after license. After considerable litigation in the early 1950's the courts held that exclusive licensing (or exclusive licensing within a particular medium or area) constitutes a sale despite the character of royalty payments.[12]

Under the law and its judicial interpretations prior to 1954, the sale of a patent by an amateur was accorded capital gains treatment to the extent that the invention could be considered incidental to his primary livelihood. Sale by a professional inventor was not.

Congress felt that it was desirable to stimulate creative invention and in 1954 granted capital gains treatment to the creator of the patentable invention under Section 1235 of the Internal Revenue Code, thus resolving the first of the issues cited above. It is ironic that Congress had chosen to deny capital gains treatment to copyrights on artistic creations four years earlier in the Revenue Act of 1950.

Prior to 1943, the sale of a forested piece of property or of rights to cut timber received preferential treatment, while receipts from sales of timber cut by the owner did not. Royalties received from the sale of mining rights presented a similar problem. Outright sales were preferentially taxed, while sales including a returned or contingent interest were not always so treated.

The plight of the farmer who leased acreage for timber cutting was

[12] This problem can be solved by using the approach of the American Law Institute in its *Draft on Definitional Problems in Capital Gains Taxation* (American Law Institute, Oct. 20, 1960). Most sales in which the return is contingent on future events could not qualify for capital gains treatment under their proposed revision of Section 1222 of the Internal Revenue Code. (See pp. 29-30 of the *Draft*.)

The cases involved are discussed in an article by Reuben Clark in *Patent Licensing* (Practising Law Institute, 1958), pp. 91-113.

eased by Sections 631 and 1231(b)(2) of the Internal Revenue Code of 1954. Capital gains treatment was granted to all harvesting of timber, regardless of the legal arrangement under which cutting occurred.

While the legislative intent of Sections 631, 1231(b)(2), and 1235 may have been to increase the equity of the capital assets definition and to stimulate inventions, no clear benefit, and considerable revenue losses, resulted from these provisions for "statutory gains." The President's 1963 Tax Message called for the repeal of preferential treatment in certain cases by the following amendments:

1. Lump-sum distributions from pension plans were to be treated as ordinary income. The tax would be computed from the marginal rate obtained by prorating the distribution by a factor of five. Current income received from the employer making the distribution would be disregarded in computing the appropriate rate.

2. Patents were to be excluded from the capital asset definition. Gains on sales were to be ordinary income in the hands of the creator, just as in the case of sales of copyrights.

3. Income from the sale of timber in excess of $5,000 was to be taxed as ordinary income whether it resulted from outright sale or from royalties under a lease. The $5,000 annual exemption was expected to exclude most operators of small woodlots.[13]

4. Income from coal royalties also would be treated as ordinary income; the relevant portions of Sections 631 and 1231(b) would be repealed.

The arguments presented in favor of these proposals in 1964 remain convincing. However, Congress chose to reject them and extended ordinary income treatment to iron ore royalties.[14]

---

[13] The $5,000 exclusion applied only to individuals; no exclusion was granted to corporate sales of timber. (See *President's 1963 Tax Message,* Hearings Before the House Committee on Ways and Means, 88 Cong. 1 sess., [1963], Pt. 1, p. 151.) See also the supporting exhibit on taxation of timber, *ibid.,* pp. 388-419.

[14] However, in 1964 Congress acted to restrict capital gains treatment for amounts that corporation executives could receive by realizing gains on restricted stock options issued at a discount. The issuance of an option at less than 95 percent of its fair market value on the date of issue causes the difference between market value on the date of issue (or the value at disposition if that is less) and the issue price to become taxable as income. Prior to 1964 such gains were taxable as capital gains (see Internal Revenue Code, Section 424).

Conversion of Income by Excessive Deductions from Basis

The over-depreciation of real estate produces artificial capital gains when the asset is sold. Similarly, the expensing of oil exploration and drilling costs and the costs of raising livestock for breeding and dairy herds (capital costs) permits the realization of excessive capital gains at the time of a sale. There have been abuses in all of these areas.[15]

Real estate presents the most perplexing problem of this type. Present depreciation formulas under Section 167 of the Internal Revenue Code do not reflect the peculiar elements of obsolescence and reduction in market value that are associated with the change in value of a particular property over a period of time. Consequently there is a substantial danger that an average rate of depreciation applied to a property will result in excessive deductions. Whenever this occurs, taxes on ordinary income are deferred and are converted to capital gains taxes when the asset is disposed of.

Treating real estate in a way that is directly parallel to the treatment of business depreciable personal property under Section 1245 would eliminate this major opportunity for tax avoidance. Capital gains treatment of gains in excess of the initial basis could still be used to provide preferential taxation for shifts in the market value of such property that are associated with general changes in price levels, growth, and other aggregate forces.

The Revenue Act of 1964 included a compromise for the recapture of income corresponding to excessive depreciation. Only the excess over straight-line depreciation is deducted from the gain on property held for more than twelve months to determine the amount eligible for capital gains treatment. Moreover, this deduction is reduced by 1 percent for each month that the property has been held beyond twenty months.

While the present treatment is superior to that before 1964, an avenue for some conversion of income into capital gains remains. The question that must be answered by experience under the 1964 Act is whether the restrictions are adequate to discourage the use of real estate as a means of escaping taxation. At a minimum, revisions

[15] *President's 1963 Tax Message*, Hearings, cited in note 13 above, pp. 278-350 (taxation of mineral industries); pp. 420-50 (taxation of real estate); pp. 451-58 (taxation of livestock).

should probably be made to require identical treatment of real estate and other business depreciable property under Section 1245.

The denial of capital gains treatment to gains from the sale of real estate that are in excess of the original cost may have merit if preferential treatment is confined to investment assets. Strictly speaking, real estate is not an investment asset as defined. Ownership in a particular property is unlikely to be widely marketed, and the owner's personal services may have a direct influence on the value of the property if he actively promotes a subdivision or buys a group of properties to create locational values that did not exist previously. On both of these counts, ownership of real estate may become a means for converting ordinary income into capital gains. At the same time, market forces substantially beyond the control of any individual operate on the value of particular properties. It might be argued that such forces dominate any value that attaches to owner-development of a particular parcel. In that case, the market for all parcels of a given general character may be broad enough to permit reasonable discounting of the possibilities for capital gains. If so, capital gains treatment of increments of value above the original cost would be appropriate under an investment asset definition.

Equitable tax treatment of areas in which capital expenditures can be currently expensed is as important as is appropriate treatment of depreciation taken on real estate. Arguments for taxing income corresponding to depreciation under ordinary rates apply even more to income corresponding to expensed costs of capital acquisition. Certainly deductions from income for the cost of raising livestock or developing oil properties ought not to create later gains taxable at capital gains rates. (Appendix D shows the mathematical similarities of these cases.)

The accounting and enforcement problems involved in reducing tax avoidance in this area are difficult. It is not always possible to determine the portion of deductible costs that represents investment in assets. For example, part of the feed of livestock goes for the maintenance of nondepreciable herds. Nevertheless, the expensing of costs that later create value in a capital asset ought to be controlled.

In 1963 the President proposed to deny capital gains treatment to gains on the sale of livestock to the extent that ordinary losses resulting from such expensed costs exceeded income from farming. An excess-deductions account would provide a cumulative balance of the excess of losses associated with farming over income from farming. The gain on the sale of livestock would be treated as ordinary gain up to the amount of the excess deductions account.[16]

To eliminate excessive deductions in connection with mineral properties, the President proposed that a gain on the sale of property be treated as ordinary gain to the extent of the original expensing of capital cost, depreciation, and depletion deductions. This would put depletable mineral property on the same basis as Section 1245 property. The "recapture" provisions enacted into law in 1962 for depreciable machinery and equipment suggest a general principle that ought to extend to all situations in which the adjusted basis of a property does not capture market values under present tax accounting rules.

Feasibility and Economic Impact of Definitional Reform

There are no legal barriers that would make it difficult to exclude these special situations from capital gains treatment. Indeed, Congress moved in the Revenue Acts of 1962 and 1964 to remove capital gains privileges from other special situations. The Acts limited the extent to which capital gains could be obtained when excessive depreciation had been charged on depreciable property and real estate.[17] Capital gains treatment for "issue" discounts on stock options was largely eliminated. Provisions were established for distinguishing gain from interest income in installment sales of assets.

Eliminating the remaining special situations and removing owner-manager investments from the area eligible for capital gains treatment would restrict capital gains tax privileges to gains on widely marketed assets. The fact that marketed investments would continue to enjoy some exemption from income taxation might be considered a compensation to investors for their risk-taking. In addition, investors would continue to receive the benefits of tax deferral and forgiveness at death under these proposed reforms.

The economic impact of these changes would not be of major significance. Appendix D indicates the relatively small role of capital

---

[16] *Ibid.*, pp. 144-46.

[17] Gains on the sale of Section 1245 property (depreciable business machinery and equipment) are considered ordinary income to the extent of depreciation claimed. Gains that can be attributed to the early turnover of real estate subjected to unrealistic accelerated depreciation are also treated as ordinary income. (See Chap. II.)

gains in the majority of business investment decisions. With the availability of capital gains treatment for special situations strictly limited, one can anticipate that the incentive for integrating natural resource ownership and the production of lumber and minerals might diminish. Agricultural price movements would quickly compensate for changes in the tax treatment of livestock and crops sold with the land; and small business would be largely unaffected, although a few taxpayers would find substantial increases in their tax liability. The revision would encourage the early distribution of ownership interests to the public, so that windfall elements in the formation and growth of new productive enterprises could be captured as capital gains under the investment asset definition. The reform might thus provide a useful stimulus for broadening the capital markets and widening the spectrum of risk and scale represented in national markets.

The overinvestment in livestock, timber growing, speculative real estate, and mineral development that is now encouraged would be reduced by narrowing the scope of capital gains. As a result one could expect greater efficiency in the economy and a better use of natural resources.

Narrowing the area eligible for capital gains taxation would also reduce compliance costs associated with the present law. Small businesses would not need to consider incorporating for tax avoidance reasons. Less legal advice and management time would be consumed in exploiting statutory gains and converting income into capital gains through the routes that are currently available.

In addition to these allocation effects, narrowing the scope of capital gains would generally increase the horizontal equity of the law, since preferential capital gains treatment would apply only to areas that are fairly accessible to the average investor, and would not apply to many special situations nor to owner-managed corporations, as it does under the present law.

Change in Holding Period Requirements

Under the present capital gains tax, the length of time that an eligible asset is held determines the degree of preferential treatment for the realized gain. Assets held for more than six months are entitled to taxation at the reduced rates implied by the partial inclusion of the gains in income and the alternative tax computation. Assets held until death are not taxable under the realization criterion, and thus the appreciation escapes taxation entirely.

The impact of holding period requirements on trading decisions and lock-in is examined below. Analysis indicates that there are three components to the effect of the holding period and of asset taxation on trading decisions. These components are first derived in general; then the results are summarized and discussed.

Effect on Decisions To Sell Assets

The capital gains deduction and the alternative tax treatment of gains on capital assets imply a differential between the tax rates on assets held for more than six months and those on assets held for a shorter period. The differential increases as the adjusted gross income and the marginal tax rate of the investor increase. Data from Hinrichs suggest that investors respond to this differential by holding an increasing proportion of their assets beyond the first six-month period, as their income rises. In fact, the investors respond to rising tax rates by realizing an ever larger increment of their capital gains as long-term gains.[18]

This empirical result might have been anticipated if an analysis had been made of the criteria on which investors base a rational decision concerning the timing of sales of securities. Disregarding the impact that the sale may have upon the diversification of the investor's portfolio, sale of a given security today creates proceeds of:[19]

$$(6.5) \qquad A_x = (P_{1x} - P_{0x})(1 - T[Y_1, H_1]) + P_{0x},$$

where:

$P_{0x}=$ the purchase price of the asset x, held in the portfolio today,

$P_{1x}=$ the price of asset x today, and

$T(Y_1, H_1)=$ the effective tax rate on the gain from sale, given current year income Y_1 and the holding period H_1 for asset x.

[18] The elasticity of response averages 1.3 for all investors and above 4.0 for investors with adjusted gross incomes greater than $200,000. These estimates are derived from income and behavior differences within a single cross-section and must be highly qualified, since fairly arbitrary assumptions about the uniformity of portfolios and the character of short-term sales were made in order to obtain the estimates. (See Harley H. Hinrichs, "An Empirical Measure of Investors' Responsiveness to Differentials in Capital Gains Tax Rates Among Income Groups," *National Tax Journal*, Vol. 16 (September 1963), pp. 224-29.)

[19] It is most convenient to think of nondividend-paying investments, although the argument holds more narrowly for the yield from appreciation of any investment.

If the asset is held for sale at some indefinite future time, the proceeds of the sale discounted to the present will be:

(6.6)
$$B_x = \frac{(P_{2x} - P_{0x})(1 - T[Y_2, \hat{H}_2]) + P_{0x}}{(1 + R)^{\hat{H}_2 - H_1}},$$

where:

R = the market rate of interest, and

P_{2x} = the price of the asset at the time of sale in the future.

If the investor anticipates that the present value of the return from holding the asset presently owned until some optimum future date, $\hat{H}_2$, exceeds the value of selling today and holding an alternative asset, he will not dispose of the asset.

If the asset x is sold, the capital gains treatment of the proceeds affects the choice of an alternative asset. Holding period requirements influence the perceived present value of the alternative assets held to any fixed date; expected appreciation at various future dates interacts with those holding period requirements to determine the optimum dates of sale for an alternative investment. If y is an alternative asset, the proceeds of an optimum sale of Y will be:

(6.7)
$$B_y = \frac{(P_{3y} - P_{1y})(1 - T[Y_3, \hat{H}_3]) + P_{1y}}{(1 + R)^{\hat{H}_3}}.$$

Since the optimum time of sale of the assets x and y are not necessarily the same, the present values of the proceeds are also not comparable. This can be remedied if it is assumed that the investor can reinvest his funds at the present market rate of return after the sale of x. Then the "hold x" investment alternative has a present value:

(6.8)
$$B_x{}^* = \left[\frac{(P_{2x} - P_{0x})(1 - T[Y_2, \hat{H}_2]) + P_{0x}}{(1 + R)^{\hat{H}_3}} \right] M,$$

where M is the after-tax amount of a dollar invested at the market rate for the period from $\hat{H}_2$ to $\hat{H}_3$, if $(\hat{H}_3 - \hat{H}_2) \geq 0$.[20] If $\hat{H}_2 > \hat{H}_3$, then M represents a short sale at the discount determined by the market rate of interest.

The "sell x; buy y" investment alternative has a present value:

[20] In fact, the tax on the investment M need not be paid at $\hat{H}_{3y}$ if the investor wants to keep the security in his portfolio beyond that date. Use of M causes the actual present value of this alternative to be understated.

$$(6.9) \qquad B_y{}^* = \left(\frac{B_y}{P_{1y}} \right) A_x,$$

since taxes preempt a portion of the proceeds from the sale of x.

Under the present law, $T(Y, H)$ is constant with respect to holding period except for discrete steps at death $(H = H_D)$, and at H equals six months. If six months $< \hat{H}_x, \hat{H}_y < H_D$ or $\hat{H}_x, \hat{H}_y > H_D$, a lock-in effect of capital gains taxation arises from the tax bite on the appreciated investment in the portfolio. (See the section on owner-management investments above.) If the optimum holding periods for the two assets lie on opposite sides of either the six-month discontinuity or the discontinuity at death, there may be further disincentives to sales. That is, the tax treatment of the alternative asset at $\hat{H}_3$ may differ from the tax treatment of the presently held asset at $\hat{H}_2$.[21] In this case, the ratio of after-tax rates of return on the two investments is not proportional to the ratio of pre-tax returns.

Finally, it should be noted that the "optimum" holding periods for the two assets cannot be determined independently of the tax law. Investors who are sensitive to after-tax trends in prices will be less apt to sell in response to a specified amount of price fluctuation if the marginal capital gains tax rate is high than if it is low. The tax effect on the comparison of investments may thus be resolved into three components:

1. The decrease in present value of the portfolio occasioned by the tax on gains realized now rather than at a later date.

2. The difference in present value of the investment alternatives that can be attributed to differences in the tax treatment of investments held for different optimum holding periods.

3. Changes in the expected holding period induced by interaction of investor's sensitivity to after-tax return and price anticipations.

These concepts are illustrated in Figures 6-1 and 6-2. Figure 6-1 indicates the relationship between market appreciation and after-tax appreciation under the present holding period requirements. Figure 6-2 illustrates how an investor might use expected prices and tax provisions to arrive at a likely "optimum" holding period for an investment.

---

[21] Charles C. Holt and John P. Shelton discuss aspects of both effects. (See "The Lock-in Effect of the Capital Gains Tax," *National Tax Journal*, Vol. 15 [December 1962], pp. 337-52.)

FIGURE 6-1. Present Value of an Investment Under Present Holding Period Requirements

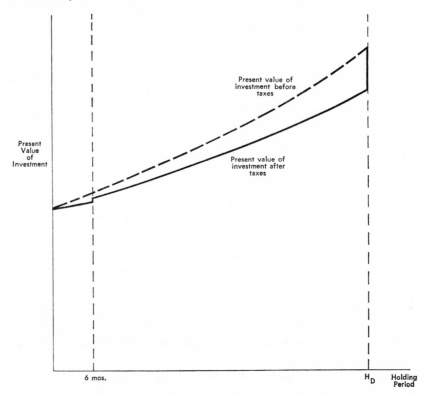

H_D Holding period at death

Figure 6-3 illustrates price expectations that might induce trading before the end of the six-month holding period required for long-term capital gains. Figure 6-4 shows the after-tax present value of two equal investments, B^*_x and B^*_y . B^*_x is currently in the portfolio; B^*_y is not. Clearly B^*_y has a greater present value after taxes if it is held to the "optimum" date. Figure 6-5 shows how the "tax bite" from realization may induce deferment of sale past an optimum that obtains in the absence of taxes. Figure 6-6 demonstrates an alternative form of lock-in. In this case, the application of a somewhat lower rate of appreciation to the investment held in the portfolio produces the greater optimum present value since appreciation can be realized on the deferred tax liability.

FIGURE 6-2. The Optimum Holding Period As Determined by the Investor's Expectations of Future Appreciation and Market Conditions

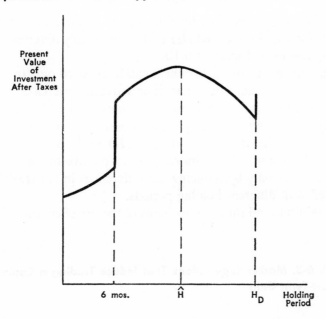

H_D Holding period at death

$\hat{H}$ Optimum holding period

The components listed above can be seen more clearly by computing the ratio B_x^* / B_y^*. Let Γ_{uij} be the percentage appreciation of the uth asset from period j to period i. Then:

$$(6.10) \quad \frac{B_x^*}{B_y^*} = \frac{(\Gamma_{x20}[1 - T(Y_2, \hat{H}_2)] + 1)M}{(\Gamma_{y31}[1 - T(Y_3, \hat{H}_3)] + 1) + (\Gamma_{x10}[1 - T(Y_1, H_1)] + 1)}.$$

A comparison of B_x^* / B_y^* with the Holt-Shelton "tax bite" factor shows that component (1) of the tax effect is smaller than their "tax bite" factor by the amount of taxes that must be paid on liquidation of the investment represented by M. Component (2) of the tax effect may be thought of as the effect of $T(Y_2, \hat{H}_2) \neq T(Y_3, \hat{H}_3)$ on B_x^* / B_y^*. The third tax component results from the dependence of $\hat{H}_2$, $\hat{H}_3$ on the interaction of tax rates and appreciation. This effect can be seen most clearly by assuming $T(Y, H) \equiv 0$. Then:

$$(6.11) \qquad \frac{B_x^*}{B_y^*} = \frac{(\Gamma_{x40} + 1)M}{(\Gamma_{y51} + 1)(\Gamma_{x10} + 1)}.$$

By optimizing choices, the investor selects no-tax optimum holding periods for x and y ($\hat{H}_4$ and $\hat{H}_5$) that are generally different from the periods shown in Equation 6.10.

Component (1) of the tax effect can be reduced only by reducing the capital gains tax rate. That same reduction increases the probability that taxes affect investment comparisons by (2) or (3). Under the present law, for example, the discontinuity in tax treatment at six months implies differences in $T(Y_2, \hat{H}_2)$ and $T(Y_3, \hat{H}_3)$ that could be very significant. These distorting effects on investment choices can be eliminated only by reducing the differences in tax treatment associated with different holding periods.

To minimize all three components of the tax effect on investment

FIGURE 6-3. Market Expectations That Induce Trading a Capital Asset for Short-Term Gain

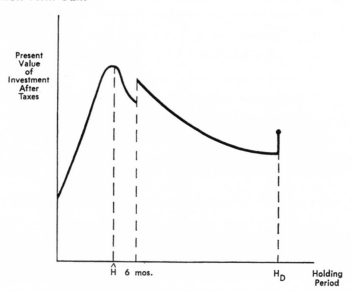

H_D Holding period at death

$\hat{H}$ Optimum holding period

FIGURE 6-4. Portfolio Choice: The Alternative Investment Should Be Purchased by the Rational Investor

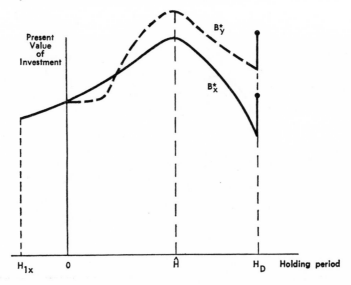

B_x^* Present value of investment currently in portfolio after taxes

B_y^* Present value of alternative investment after taxes

H_D Holding period at death

H_{1x} Date of purchase of asset x

$\hat{H}$ Optimum holding period for assets x and y

(i.e., $H_{2x} = H_{3y} = \hat{H}$)

choice, continuous downward gradation of tax rates according to holding period might be the appropriate solution. For example, the present capital gains deduction and alternative tax could be replaced by a capital gains deduction that would be zero for assets held less than a year and would increase by 1 percent for each month that the asset was held beyond one year until a desired maximum deduction had been reached. The exact rate of increase of such a deduction and the maximum rate could be varied to increase or reduce the lock-in resulting under the present system.

The choice of optimum holding periods would not be strongly influenced by a graduated system; investments with similar maturities would receive nearly similar tax treatment; and the increase in the

FIGURE 6-5. Lock-in Associated with the Six-Month Holding Period

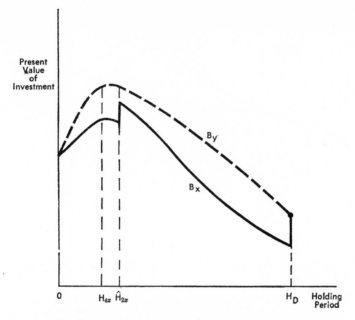

B_x Present value of investment after taxes

B_y Present value of investment before taxes

H_D Holding period at death

$\hat{H}_{2x}$ Optimum holding period after taxes ($H_{2x} = 6$ months for investment x)

$\hat{H}_{1x}$ Optimum holding period in the absence of taxes

present value of tax liabilities for most investments would not need to rise above present levels.[22]

Unfortunately, to the extent that any gradation of the holding period would mean that taxpayers would have to pay a greater average tax rate on assets held for an optimum period, the tax effect of component (1) would be increased. Clearly, there is some optimum gradation of the present tax differential that would have less disincentive effect than the present law. The argument here is that the lock-in

[22] Some aspects of the effect of capital gains taxes on the supply of and demand for securities are explored by Somers and Richman. See Harold M. Somers, "Reconsideration of the Capital Gains Tax," *National Tax Journal*, Vol. 13 (December 1960), pp. 289-309; and Raymond L. Richman, "Reconsideration of the Capital Gains Tax—A Comment," *National Tax Journal*, Vol. 14 (December 1961), pp. 402-4.

FIGURE 6-6. Lock-in Associated with the Present Value of Deferred Tax Liability: The Investor Should Defer Sale of x in Spite of a Superior Market Alternative

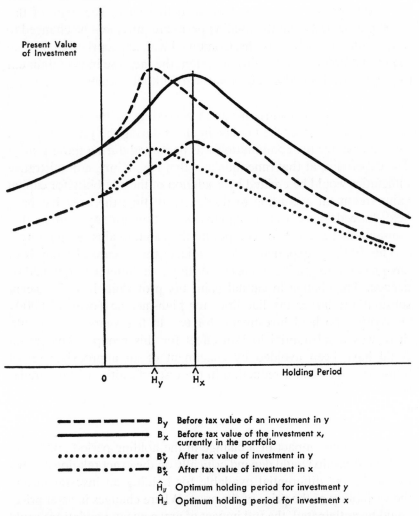

B_y Before tax value of an investment in y

B_x Before tax value of the investment x, currently in the portfolio

B_y^t After tax value of investment in y

B_x^t After tax value of investment in x

$\hat{H}_y$ Optimum holding period for investment y

$\hat{H}_x$ Optimum holding period for investment x

effect of any increase in capital gains tax rates could be greatly reduced by an appropriate gradation of the preferential rates with the length of the holding period.

The present system creates important incentives for holding assets through the minimum holding period of six months. During that period, market forces must be extremely strong if they are to precipitate a sale. There is no logical reason for taxing the income earned from the sale of assets held for less than a year any differently than any other form of casual income.[23] Accounting principles require that the proceeds of any sale of an asset purchased within an accounting year be recognized as income attributed to that year. The logic of this principle suggests that the holding period requirement be changed to a minimum of twelve months. Combined with appropriate changes in the gradation of capital gains inclusion, the increase in the minimum holding period could be accomplished without extreme disincentive effects.

The percentage inclusion varied according to the length of the holding period under the tax law in effect during the years 1934-37. (No alternative tax computation was permitted during those years.) The experience at that time indicates that few, if any, administrative difficulties would be created by gradation of the eligibility for capital gains treatment according to the length of time the asset has been held. Indeed, present capital gains accounting already requires that transactions be dated for computing the capital gains tax liability.

The 1934-37 experience does indicate that a careful analysis of any proposal to graduate rates according to holding period would be needed. The change in capital gains tax provisions in 1934 meant substantially larger tax liabilities for high-income (over $50,000) taxpayers who held investments for two to five years. As a result, there was a substantial lock-in effect for this group.[24] That result could have been avoided by enactment of an appropriate set of transition rules and a reduction in the discontinuities of that gradation.

Revenue Effect

The revenue impact of a change in the holding period and inclusion relationship would depend critically on the exact relationship between the tax differential available for holding an investment and the variability of the price of the asset. Where changes in asset prices could be anticipated, the full impact of any new tax regulations could

[23] The President's 1963 Tax Message proposed extending the holding period to one year. (See Hearings cited in note 13 to this chapter.)

[24] For a discussion of the experience provided by graduated rates, see Seltzer, *op. cit.*, pp. 167-72. He points out that gradation implies an increasing return to holding an asset as the marginal rate increases. That is, the gradation of rates means a reduction in the tax rate from 4 to 1.2 percent for a taxpayer with $5,000 of income and from 54 to 16.2 percent for one with a $100,000 income.

be discounted in the purchase price. The asset would then be held so as to get the maximum preferential tax treatment. Greater lock-in results the longer the average holding period required to obtain a given tax benefit. However, if future changes in asset prices could not easily be predicted, the gradation of preferential rates would cause the market to respond more readily to current changes in prices, reducing the lock-in of particular gradations in rate, such as occurs with the shift from ordinary to capital gains rates at six months. Revenue realized in the short run would depend on a balancing of these two effects. In the long run, however, more revenue would be realized in proportion to any increase in the average percentage inclusion of capital gains in income, provided that the change in holding period requirements did not precipitate a large-scale increase in the holding of assets to death (an unlikely possibility).

McClung has made estimates of the distribution of unrealized capital gains according to the length of the period held.[25] Although the estimates are based on broad assumptions concerning the stochastic process determining market sales and the turnover of assets eligible for capital gains treatment, they are quite relevant for a discussion of change in holding period requirements. McClung estimates that out of $233 billion of unrealized capital gains, one-tenth accrues on assets that have been held for seven years or less. The aggregate effect of graduating holding period requirements on investors' decisions could not be large, since the majority of investments are held for substantially longer periods.

A change in the holding period requirements would affect a larger number of investors than would limiting the areas eligible for gains. Potentially all owners of property rights could be affected, although one suspects that the change in holding period requirements would affect chiefly a limited number of traders whose primary occupation is closely related to the financial sector.[26] The long average holding period for common stocks suggested by McClung indicates that a sizable group of investors are insensitive to short-term market fluctua-

[25] Nelson McClung, "The Distribution of Capital Gain on Corporate Shares by Holding Time," *Review of Economics and Statistics,* Vol. 48 (February 1966), Table 5, p. 48.

[26] Robin Barlow, Harvey E. Brazer, and James N. Morgan have found that such persons are likely to have greater tax consciousness and engage more frequently in tax avoidance behavior. (See *Economic Behavior of the Affluent* [Brookings Institution, 1966].)

tions and would not find an extension of the minimum holding period required for capital gains treatment onerous, nor would it cause them to defer sales to any great extent. The same investors would find it advantageous to liquidate a part of their portfolios before death if the gradation of rates on investments should decline to less than the 25 percent minimum rate now available.

In 1963 the United States Treasury estimated that extension of the holding period to twelve months would increase revenues by about $180 million after allowing for any deferment of sales that might result.[27] A comparison of that figure with the estimated overall yield from the capital gains tax of $3.0 billion in 1963 suggests that a change in holding period requirements would, in the aggregate, have a negligible effect.

Treatment of Capital Losses

While net long-term capital gains in excess of short-term losses receive preferential tax treatment, net capital losses are deductible at ordinary income rates, up to $1,000. This asymmetric treatment encourages realization of losses in early tax years and gains in later tax years to reduce and defer tax liability. In fact, tax liability can be reduced over a period of time without extensive deferment of gains if the investor realizes gains and losses in alternate tax years.

The limitation on deductibility of net capital losses has been viewed as a necessary safeguard against tax avoidance by this means.[28] A further safeguard enacted in the Revenue Act of 1964 is the requirement that losses carried forward be used to offset gains of a like kind in future years. (See Chapter II.) While the present system reduces the possible deductions from ordinary income that arise from the sale of assets with capital losses, it does nothing to recognize the differential rate treatment of net long-term gains and net capital losses. Some recognition is required in the interest of equity.

In addition, the deductibility of losses has a profound effect on the willingness of private investors to undertake risky investments. Musgrave and Domar show that income taxation with 100 percent deductibility of losses would encourage risk-taking beyond that

[27] Hearings cited in note 13 to this chapter, p. 708.
[28] Barlow, Brazer, and Morgan show that realization of losses is associated with recent realizations of gains (*op. cit.*, Chap. 9).

which would occur without a tax. If losses were not deductible, this would not necessarily be the effect.[29]

There is a possible capital gains tax system that would be no more complex than the present one, yet would result in more immediate recognition of losses and more appropriate rate treatment. Three changes would be needed: (1) Liberalize the present $1,000 limitation on net capital losses, (2) cumulate net capital losses in a capital loss reserve, and (3) require that any capital gains be taxed as ordinary income to the extent of the capital loss reserve.[30]

In practice, this amendment would require computation of accumulated net capital losses in a capital loss reserve. In any year when such losses were deducted from ordinary income, a like amount would be added to the reserve. Gains up to the amount of the accumulated losses deducted from income would be taxable at ordinary income tax rates. Those gains would also be subtracted from the capital loss reserve. Gains in excess of the capital loss reserve could receive preferential rate treatment.

Adoption of such a system would mean that no taxpayer could expect preferential rate treatment on more than the average rate of appreciation of his portfolio. A reduction of current ordinary income by judicious culling of losses out of the portfolio would still be possible; however, a future increase in tax liability on any gains remaining in the portfolio would also be incurred. Only the present value implicit in the deferral of taxation would offer an incentive for such judicious culling. At present, asymmetric rate treatment provides an additional incentive. The incentive for tax deferment would thus be much smaller under the proposed system.[31]

Under the present system of capital gains taxation, the individual may ultimately offset all capital losses against ordinary income (unless he dies first). However, this is limited to a maximum of $1,000 a year. Under the proposed system, losses would more generally be

[29] See Evsey D. Domar and Richard A. Musgrave, "Proportional Income Taxation and Risk-Taking," American Economic Association, *Readings in the Economics of Taxation* (Richard D. Irwin, Inc., 1959), pp. 493-524.

[30] The extent of deductibility is contingent on the ability to capture unrealized gains during the lifetime of the investor. If, in addition, gains were presumptively realized as they passed into the estate, the limitation on loss offsets could probably be removed.

[31] The conference participants favored such an amendment and expressed some concern over the highly asymmetric treatment of gains and losses under the present tax. (See Chap. X, pp. 223-24).

fully deductible in the current year. An immediate loss offset would result unless current losses exceeded all income or the higher statutory limitation. In that case, carry-forward of losses in excess of income from other sources would reduce future tax liabilities.

More current availability of loss offsets and a somewhat higher rate of tax on appreciation due to symmetrical treatment of gains corresponding to losses would encourage aggregate risk-taking. The variation in probable gains and losses would be reduced as the effective rate of tax on appreciation rose. Gains corresponding to losses taken against ordinary income would be taxed more heavily, since they would be taxed at ordinary rates, while the possibility of losses that do not lead to tax reductions in the current year would be largely eliminated.

In the same way that a possible variation in the yield of a single asset would be reduced by heavier taxation, the possibilities for diversifying a portfolio to minimize risk would be altered. Investment in speculative, nondividend-paying securities would require less complementary investment in alternative areas, with independent (or inversely related) price movements to give the portfolio a desired degree of stability.

Domar and Musgrave conclude that under equilibrium conditions: (1) a lower average tax rate reduces risk-taking; and (2) limitations on loss offset reduce risk-taking.[32] The present law thus encourages savers to invest in lower-risk assets in the aggregate than would the proposed system of capital loss reserves. Heavier uniform taxation of an investor's income, plus increased government participation in losses, would encourage the private investor to find a portfolio that involved somewhat less after-tax risk for himself. But that risk, combined with government credits against deductible losses, implies a greater aggregate risk-taking in the economy as a whole. That is, a uniform tax at current effective rates would probably increase the *total demand* for risk-taking in the economy over that under the present system. While this effect might not be very large, such a change would probably be a desirable step toward increasing the responsiveness of the economy to innovation.

Unfortunately, the desirable effects on risk-taking would be partially offset by increased lock-in. Investors who realize losses and

---

[32] See Domar and Musgrave, *op. cit.*, and Richard A. Musgrave, *The Theory of Public Finance* (McGraw-Hill, 1959), pp. 312-36.

defer gains would find that the early recognition of losses would mean a higher average tax rate on the remaining assets. The net effect would be beneficial to the taxpayer, but his incentive to hold onto his existing portfolio in the future would be increased in proportion to the loss deductions already taken.

Summary

A number of proposals have been discussed in this chapter to deal with definitional problems created by the present capital gains tax structure. Each could be enacted piecemeal, or they could be combined to produce a substantially more equitable and uniform tax. Limiting preferential tax rate treatment to investment assets would reduce the element of remuneration to personal services that is currently treated as capital gains. And eliminating special provisions concerning patents, crops sold with land, livestock, real estate, mineral properties, and lump-sum distributions would reduce the extent to which ordinary profits could be taxed as capital gains.

Preferential treatment would be available primarily for assets that are widely marketed. Thus, the average investor would find that tax avoidance possibilities would be discounted by the operation of the market. Investment would be less likely to migrate to certain activities favored by tax arrangements and would be more efficiently used. In addition, compliance costs associated with the current law would be reduced as the type of transaction or business activity became less important for determining tax liability.

Graduating the average holding period would increase the equity of taxation on investments held for periods of slightly differing lengths, and might reduce some present disincentive in the law. More appropriate treatment of capital losses deducted from ordinary income could reduce the extent to which tax avoidance through judicious timing of asset sales is possible under the present law at the same time that loss offsets for persons with large capital losses that were not tax motivated are restricted.

Changing the minimum holding period, graduating the rate of inclusion, and adjusting the rate treatment of capital gains corresponding to net capital losses in other years would probably not have a major effect on incentives or asset markets. Gradation of the holding period might reduce the extent to which the optimum date of sale is tax-determined. These adjustments can be defended largely on equity grounds and would eliminate certain arbitrary features of the current law.

Some of the reforms suggested above were proposed in the President's Tax Message of 1963. The arguments used then are equally valid today. All the proposed changes seek to repair the rents in the capital asset definition made under pressure from special interests over the past generation.[33]

[33] Unfortunately, problems of definition remain; they will be discussed in Chap. VIII.

CHAPTER VII

Transfers by Gift or Bequest

If property is acquired through bequest, devise, or inheritance, the basis for computing the amount of gain or loss upon sale is the fair market value of the asset at the date of death or twelve months later.[1] This is perhaps the least acceptable provision applying to capital gains. Estimates given above suggest that at least three-fourths of the gains on stocks are unrealized during the lifetime of the investor. This appreciation passes into the hands of the succeeding generation with the appreciated fair market value as a basis for taxation.[2] This difference in treatment could be eliminated in either of two ways:

1. Property transmitted at death could be taxed on the presumption that passage into the estate constitutes a realization of taxable income (*presumptive realization*).

2. The heirs could be required to consider the decedent's basis as their basis for computing in the future the capital gains tax owing on the transferred property (*carry-over of basis*). This method is now applied to gifts.

[1] The choice is made by the executor of the estate (Internal Revenue Code, Sections 1014 and 2032).
[2] See pp. 99-100, above.

Either method would ultimately subject assets to capital gains taxation. The merits of each approach are outlined below.

Legal and Administrative Aspects of Presumptive Realization

If the principle of presumptive realization were followed, gains would have to be subjected to tax prior to the bequest. The only incentives to hold assets beyond an optimum time of sale would arise from the deferral of taxes that is possible if realization is postponed until the death of the taxpayer.[3] Faced with a situation in which taxes must ultimately be paid on all appreciation in the portfolio, the investor would find that he would maximize his estate by trading securities in his portfolio that are not profitable to sell under the present law.[4] The present discrete increase in value of the portfolio at death

---

[3] Of course, for corporations the ability to defer tax liabilities would still be a substantial boon. For individuals the deferral would be more limited in time, and its value would not be great at capital gains rates. See Table 8-1, below, where the value of deferral has been calculated for various holding periods and various marginal tax rates.

[4] Under the present law the advantage of switching portfolios can be shown to be:

$$\sum_{n=1}^{N} [(1 - T)(1 + S)^N - (1 + H)^{(n-0.5)}(1 + S)^{(N-n+0.5)}] P(A, n)$$

$$+ (1 - T)[(1 + S)^N - (1 + H)^N] \left[1 - \sum_{n=1}^{N} P(A, n) \right].$$

H represents the return on the present portfolio, T the proportion of the portfolio that must be paid in taxes if gains are realized, S the return on the alternative portfolio, and $P(A, n)$ the probability that the investor will die in the nth year from the present, given that he is now age A. N is a maximum holding period representing a horizon at which the entire portfolio is liquidated. The above result applies if there is no tax at death and if both investments are held for the period required to be eligible for capital gains treatment. A similar expression could be obtained for any tax formula that favors unrealized gains as opposed to realized gains. The result here is derived on the assumption that the investor wishes to maximize the expected value of his portfolio at the horizon N.

If only loss in current yield were considered, as would presumably be the case if gains were taxed at death, the advantage of switching portfolios would be:

$$(1 + S)(1 - T) - (1 + H).$$

(See Charles C. Holt and John P. Shelton, "The Lock-in Effect of the Capital Gains Tax," *National Tax Journal*, Vol. 15 [December 1962], p. 347). A parallel analysis appears in Beryl W. Sprinkel and B. Kenneth West, "Effects of Capital Gains Taxes on Investment Decisions," *Journal of Business*, Vol. 35 (April 1962), pp. 122-34.

would be removed. Presumptive realization would create some incentive for taxpayers to realize gains prior to death. And since a portion of the appreciation in an estate would have to be paid in the form of capital gains taxes, early disposition of some assets to provide enough liquidity for tax payment at the time of death might prevent unfavorable sales at death.[5]

Presumptive realization would create some administrative and legal problems. It might entail difficulties of valuation and tax payment if closely held business investments were included in the inheritance. However, these problems are already present in estate tax computation and compliance. Payment of estate taxes in installments, which is used to minimize the dislocation of investments caused by large cash liabilities, could well be extended to the terminal capital gains taxes owing on the decedent's estate.[6] Presumptive realization of capital gains would require that substantially more estates be reported than now have to be for inheritance and estate tax purposes. Even a small investor would presumably have some appreciated asset requiring declaration and valuation. This additional reporting would not prove an onerous problem for the majority of small estates, as terminal tax returns are required in any case. In fact, more effective compliance and reporting on the income tax return filed in the year of the taxpayer's death might facilitate administration of the estate tax.

Presumptive realization at death could be modified to provide

[5] In their investigation of high-income investors, Barlow *et al.* discovered little evidence that liquidity is a factor motivating sales prior to death. (See Robin Barlow, Harvey E. Brazer, and James N. Morgan, *Economic Behavior of the Affluent* [Brookings Institution, 1966], Chap. VIII.)

While liquidity has not been a significant motivation in the past, if the capital gains tax were applied extensively to appreciation passing into the estate, this might bring the problem to the attention of those taxpayers who are not now taxable to any appreciable degree under the federal estate tax.

[6] The only new problem that presumptive realization would bring is that a basis would have to be determined for every asset passing into the estate. At present that information is required only when the property passing into the estate was given to the decedent.

In fact, the installment provisions of the present law are not as effective as they might be. The executor is fully liable for the estate tax due, regardless of any diminution in value of the closely held business or other assets on which installment payment of taxes would appear appropriate. If the business becomes worthless, for example, present law holds the executor personally liable for any unpaid estate taxes. The American Law Institute proposals attempt to remedy this situation (*Unified Transfer Tax,* American Law Institute Study Draft No. 1, 1965).

some exemptions designed to alleviate the economic problems of survivors, parallel to those in the estate tax. Thus, some exemption might be provided for the widow and dependent children.[7]

A more serious difficulty would arise if the accrued value of gains led to a net loss for the assets passing into estate. In ordinary transactions the deductibility of the loss is limited; and losses not deducted from income may be used to offset capital gains and income of future years. In the case of presumptive realization this formula could not carry over without modifications. As death cannot be anticipated, full offset could be granted for losses up to the amount of income in the year of the taxpayer's death. This might not be sufficient, and adequate allowance for excessive losses would require further provisions. Permitting carry-back of losses to income earned by the taxpayer in previous years would also take care of the problem. The taxes for earlier years would have to be recomputed.[8] Administrative convenience appears to favor unlimited offset of losses against income in the year of the death of the taxpayer, combined with a recomputation of taxes in prior years. Since capital gains are not fully included in income, losses should receive parallel treatment and lead to fractional reductions in income rather than the 100 percent reduction presently permitted for lifetime losses amounting to less than $1,000.

Equitable taxation under presumptive realization also would call for changes in the estate and gift taxes. If the value of estate or gifts subject to tax remained unchanged, the taxable value would include the capital gains tax liability. Estate taxes would be paid on value that actually did not pass to the estate. The value of any capital gains taxes paid on estates and gifts thus should be deducted from the value

[7] Such exemptions would be tantamount to a tax subsidy to widows and dependents. On welfare grounds it would be more desirable to apply such subsidies in all cases, not merely in those where the decedent has left an appreciated estate.

Proposals for exemptions for personal and household effects, a marital exclusion, and a fixed minimum amount of gains were included in the President's 1963 Tax Message. (See testimony by C. Douglas Dillon in *President's 1963 Tax Message*, Hearings before the House Committee on Ways and Means, 88 Cong. 1 sess. [1963], Pt. 1, pp. 129-37.)

[8] This was the technique favored by the Treasury in the 1963 tax reform proposals. Capital losses could be used to offset income in the three prior taxable years to the extent that gains were includable in income. Under the proposals each dollar of loss would thus generate $0.30 of reduction in the prior years' income. (See Hearings cited in note 7, above, pp. 128-29).

Alternatively, losses could be carried forward to income of the heirs. However, it might be difficult to allocate losses among heirs.

subject to those transfer taxes, just as final tax liability is now deducted from taxable value of the estate. Otherwise there would be incentives for the taxpayer to convert property into cash prior to transfer, which would not be desirable.

The legal basis for presumptive realization of appreciated assets at death appears reasonably sound. Bequests are now clearly excluded from income realizations, while numerous other transactions that do not involve actual receipts of cash are considered taxable realizations.[9] (For example, in *Helvering v. Bruun,* default on a lease was considered the occasion for recognizing gain.) Thus legal scholars give little weight to the earlier view expressed in *Eisner v. Macomber* that income may be taxed only when realized as cash.[10] (The Supreme Court held in the latter case that stock dividends are not taxable until realized in cash.) If presumptive realization were enacted into law, the clear intent of Congress to recognize such gains and its unchallenged power to tax gifts and estates would constitute a powerful argument against any litigation seeking to invalidate the reform. This is reflected in an opinion of the General Counsel of the Treasury supporting the constitutionality of presumptive realization proposals incorporated in the 1963 Tax Message.[11]

The extensive change in capital gains taxation that would be associated with presumptive realization might require some transitional rule that would permit investors to accommodate themselves to the new structure. The choice of a transitional rule ought to be governed by two criteria: (1) The rule ought not to delay application of constructive realization for an unduly long period—not more than three to five years; and (2) it should not create compliance problems that are not inherent in the system when it is fully operative.

Under both criteria it does not appear desirable to apply constructive realization only to appreciation that occurs after an effective date. Whether the effective date is the date of passage of the new law or whether it is some time in the past, use of a transitional rule would demand valuation of the portfolio on the effective date. The valuation of closely held corporations, land, and small business interests

[9] Lawrence H. Seltzer, *The Nature and Tax Treatment of Captial Gains and Losses* (National Bureau of Economic Research, 1951), pp. 41-42.

[10] Stanley S. Surrey, "The Supreme Court and the Federal Income Tax," *Illinois Law Review,* Vol. 35 (March 1941), pp. 779 ff.

[11] Hearings, cited in note 7 above, Pt. 1, pp. 596-602.

on a given effective date might be a difficult problem. Moreover an effective date rule would mean that some appreciation would be exempt from constructive realization for many years to come.

A simple though somewhat arbitrary transition rule would require that an increasing percentage of the tax attributed to presumptive realization be paid in each year after the effective date. For example, transition could be accomplished by the following rule: one-third of the capital gains tax owing when the system was fully operative could be levied on gains presumed realized in the first year of transition; two-thirds of the tax could be levied on gains presumed realized in the second year; and the principle of constructive realization could become fully operative in the third year after the effective date.[12]

Economic Impact of Presumptive Realization

The economic impact of presumptive realization would be significant. A reduction in the tax avoidance possible at death would (1) raise substantial revenues if tax rates were held constant; (2) discourage the lock-in of investments in portfolios held by persons with short life expectancies; (3) stimulate saving by households with explicit objectives for leaving a bequest; and (4) shift the demand for marketable securities toward those paying current dividends.

The revenue yields of such a proposal were suggested in Chapter IV. The appreciation in decedents' estates is currently of equal or somewhat greater magnitude than the appreciation realized in the sales of capital assets. About $2 billion could thus be obtained annually from the taxation of gains included in decedents' wealth. (See Tables 4-26 and 4-30.) Clearly, if constructive realization were adopted, some compensating shift in tax rates would have to be initiated if constant revenue yields were to be maintained.[13] In the following discussion it is assumed that the new rate structure would provide an equal yield from each income bracket. That is, new bracket rates are set so that taxation of gains in decedents' estates would exactly offset the reduction in ordinary income tax rates for the remaining taxpayers in the bracket.

[12] Considerable discussion of possible transition rules and their relative merits occurred during the conference. The conferees agreed that a transition rule exempting gains prior to a given effective date would be cumbersome and inequitable. (See Chap. X, pp. 222-23.)

[13] It is assumed that equal revenue yields would mean approximately the same aggregative economic effects under both tax structures.

It is not known just what effect presumptive realization might have on saving. Theoretically, increased taxation on portfolios would tend to increase saving. Investors with a desire to leave a fixed amount of wealth to their heirs would need to accumulate a larger estate in order to leave the same after-tax bequest. Investors with no particular desire to leave a bequest would also save more. They would anticipate paying capital gains taxes during their lifetime whether or not the law were revised.[14] However, they would find their marginal tax rates reduced as a result of increased yields from the taxation of decedents' wealth. Their increased disposable income would produce increased savings.[15]

Investors whose bequest motives are not fixed in dollar amounts would find the return to saving reduced by the taxation of bequests and increased by the tax reduction on lifetime savings. The net effect on their aggregate savings would depend on their relative preferences for bequests and lifetime savings. It is assumed here that lifetime savings dominate preferences and that most investors are either lifetime savers or savers with limited, fixed targets such as bequests to be made to immediate heirs. If this is so, savings would rise in response to presumptive realization.

A redistribution of the burden of taxation from present nonholders of appreciated assets to present holders would somewhat offset these increased savings. Present holders of capital gains-yielding assets are highly motivated investors. If the tax structure were altered to tax them more heavily and distribute the benefits to others (in the same income brackets), one suspects that tax liability would be redistributed to a group with somewhat lower savings aspirations.

The effect of presumptive realization on portfolio selection may be seen by analyzing the investors' motives. A portfolio bearing a stream of income assures some money yield without the inconvenience, uncertainty, or transactions costs associated with the trading

---

[14] Such persons might still leave bequests by the accident of not living out their life expectancy or by the intentional accumulation of enough wealth to support their consumption to a date substantially beyond their life expectancy. M. E. Yaari has treated this problem for the no-tax case in "Consumption-Savings Decisions When the Horizon is Random," Cowles Foundation Discussion Paper No. 156 (Mar. 8, 1963) and in "On the Consumer's Lifetime Allocation Process," *International Economic Review*, Vol. 5 (September 1964), pp. 304-17.

[15] This result was generally proved for the case in which the utility function is homogeneous. (See Albert Ando and Franco Modigliani, "The 'Life Cycle' Hypothesis of Saving: Aggregate Implications and Tests," *American Economic Review*, Vol. 53 [March 1963], pp. 55-84, and references therein.)

of capital assets to derive that money yield. Cash flows are available for consumption or for manipulating the balance and size of the portfolio. To the extent that the investor wants to enlarge his portfolio by buying more of the types of securities that he already has, it is clearly not important that current investments yield income. Indeed, it may be a convenience to have the funds automatically reinvested by the corporation without flowing through the hands of the investor for his personal allocation. Investors place varying emphasis on income in their portfolios depending on the balance of these two motives. Selection of an optimum portfolio from this point of view appears to be a matter of convenience. This convenience may not be of great importance in portfolio selection, although a general lack of delegation of portfolio management to professionals indicates that it is of concern to some investors.[16]

The need for current income derived from investments would appear to have definite limits for most investors. The preferences for current income might thus be reflected in the situations represented in Figure 7-1, in which ρ indicates the proportion of earnings in current income and μ indicates the rate of return of the portfolio.

The tax treatment of capital gains establishes differential rates of return for different payout ratios. Current income is taxable at a rate t. Capital gains associated with corporate retentions are taxed preferentially on realization, giving rise to an effective present value of the tax rate of g.[17] The net return as a function of payout is μ_t:

$$\mu_t = 1 - [\rho t + (1 - \rho)g]\mu$$

[16] Barlow, Brazer, and Morgan indicate that 8 percent of income (over $10,000) is received by persons who had delegated some authority for investment management to professionals. Even where management is not delegated formally, the extensive reinvestment of corporate funds accomplishes somewhat the same function for the investor who holds largely growth securities. (*Op. cit.*, Chap III.)

While the reinvestment of corporate savings is likely to be concentrated in risks similar to those in which the corporation already has a stake, the growth of diversified enterprises makes many corporate stocks similar to a diversified portfolio. Thus investment in growth stocks may substitute to a limited extent for professional portfolio management.

[17] Bailey discusses this feature in some detail:

$$g = \frac{r - s}{r}, \quad \text{where}$$

$$s = \sqrt[T]{C_T} - 1 \quad \text{and} \quad C_T = [1 - t_g](1 + r)^T + t_g.$$

That is, C_T is the net value of an asset appreciating at r percent a year for T years;

FIGURE 7-1. Investor Preferences for Dividend Payout

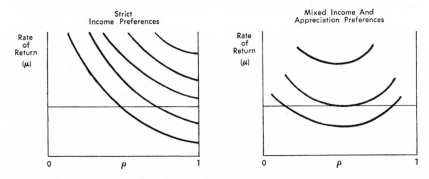

μ   Rate of return of the portfolio
ρ   Payout ratio

This formula is analogous to that discussed in connection with tax avoidance and incorporation (Chapter VI, Equation 6.1). The equation holds if corporate retentions are reflected dollar-for-dollar in increments to the value of securities and ρ is the rate of dividend payout.

Under the present law, the difference between the rate of tax on earned income and that on capital gains is at least $t/2$ and may be substantially larger. Forgiveness of the tax at death, the interest advantage of tax postponement, and the limitation on g implied by the alternative tax computation all mean a differential between t and g greater than $t/2$. Clearly it is to the advantage of the taxpayer with a high t and low life expectancy to bid actively for those stocks with low ρ. Figure 7-2 shows how the differing taxability of current income and capital gains shifts portfolio composition in the direction of appreciation (even for an investor whose preferences under uniform taxation would be for income-earning assets).

Eliminating forgiveness of tax at death would significantly reduce the differential between t and g. The reduction is suggested by the line extending to the point $μ (1-g^*)$ in Figure 7-2. The increased taxation of appreciation would mean an increased demand for securities of corporations that pay out their earnings as dividends.

As an adaptation to increased household demand for current in-

s is the equivalent tax-free rate of growth; and t_g is the statutory tax rate applicable to capital gains (*op. cit.*).

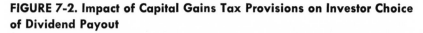

FIGURE 7-2. Impact of Capital Gains Tax Provisions on Investor Choice of Dividend Payout

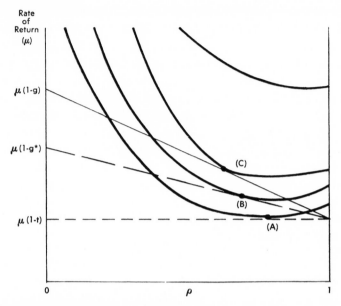

(A) Optimum portfolio under uniform taxation

(B) Optimum portfolio with preferential treatment of capital gains at realization or death

(C) Optimum portfolio with appreciation not taxable at death

μ Rate of return of the portfolio

ρ Payout ratio

come under the new tax structure, corporations would increase their dividend payout ratios. The payout ratio generally demanded by individual investors would have shifted in the direction of greater payout; consequently capital costs on new issues would be reduced if dividends were increased. An increase in payouts would produce a concomitant increase in new issues to raise funds for new investment. Fewer internal funds would be available for corporate investment. Thus presumptive realization would increase the breadth of new issues and reduce the amount of corporate retentions. When that effect is coupled with the hypothesized increase in household savings and a possible increase in turnover associated with investors' desire for increased liquidity, it becomes clear that presumptive realization would increase the depth and breadth of the economy's asset markets.[18]

Risk-taking would be affected by the change in taxation to the extent that the bequest motive is important in investors' decision-making. Increased taxes payable at death would cause some reallocation of resources between lifetime consumption and bequests. If the bequest motive were strong, lifetime consumption would be reduced, and the utility of income in all uses would rise. Thus incremental gains in income that could be obtained from investments with slightly higher risk would appear more desirable, and the investor would be likely to take on a higher degree of risk in his portfolio. The income effect of the increased taxes would create pressures for a level of risk-holding that would mean greater total risk than under the present law.[19] If bequests were the unintentional outcome of allocations of income over an uncertain lifetime, no additional risk-taking would be generated.

Carry-over of Basis

The legal standing of carry-over of basis is more certain than that of presumptive realization, since it already applies under the present law in the case of *inter vivos* gifts.[20] If carry-over of basis were applied to bequests, no new problems of liquidity or loss credits would arise as in the case of presumptive realization, since the tax could be spread out by the judicious timing of the disposal of appreciated assets. The heirs would always have the option of retaining assets rather than paying taxes; this is the same option that any owner of an appreciated asset has. Moreover, the beneficiary could be expected to live long enough to make use of loss carryovers.

In spite of these advantages, carry-over of basis would entail substantial difficulties. Providing exemptions for widows and dependents would be cumbersome, since the value of the exemption would have to be allocated to particular assets. If any part of the appreciation in an estate were exempted, reporting of capital gains would be re-

---

[18] This hypothesis is supported by empirical data on factors affecting dividend payout. See John A. Brittain, *Corporate Dividend Policy* (Brookings Institution, 1966).

[19] The argument for this effect is identical to that cited earlier in connection with a change in the treatment of losses. See Chap. VI, pp. 140-43.

[20] Internal Revenue Code, Section 1015. See Figure 2-1, p. 14.

quired both at the time of death and later upon disposition of the asset. Thus carry-over of basis would combine at least a portion of the problem of reporting at death, which would be necessary under presumptive realization, with the defects of nonrecognition of gains on any assets that were not sold during the lifetime of the beneficiary.

Carry-over of basis would aggravate the existing use of voluntary realization to defer tax liability. The investor could choose to realize losses during his lifetime, while being legally assured that gains would not have to be realized, even by his heirs, unless they so desired. Thus carry-over would accentuate the problems already discussed in Chapter VI in connection with the deductibility of losses from ordinary income.

Carry-over of basis would also create administrative difficulties in allocating basis. At present the estate can be distributed according to a testamentary formula on the basis of the value of the estate alone. If carry-over of basis were adopted, each asset in the estate would also carry with it a basis value that could mean tax liabilities or benefits to the heir. To avoid inequities, the benefits and liabilities inherent in the decedent's basis would also have to be apportioned among the heirs according to the testamentary formula. This could prove burdensome. For example, ten shares purchased in two lots of three and one of four at different times can easily be transferred to two heirs by issuing two new certificates for five shares, if the basis of the shares can be ignored. If the basis must be carried over, it may be easier for the executor to sell the shares and realize past gains than to distribute the basis equally among the heirs.

Unlike presumptive realization, carry-over of basis would not require any special transition rule, since each taxpayer could time the payment of taxes to suit his own convenience.

Carry-over of basis would require each taxpayer to maintain records of the basis of property acquired by gift or bequest. Although knowledge of basis would also be required under presumptive realization, the record-keeping problem would be less difficult. Under presumptive realization the basis would always be the market value of the asset on the date acquired, regardless of how it was acquired. Furthermore, only the ownership of the present holder of the asset would have to be considered. Under carry-over, the basis could be substantially different from market value on the date of acquisition by the present owner; it might be necessary to trace the ownership of the asset through several previous owners, including trusts, to determine its basis value. Any break in the chain of records required would make it difficult to assess capital gains taxes properly when the asset was ultimately sold.

Carry-over of basis would create less incentive to dispose of assets at the optimum time of sale than would presumptive realization. Assets could still be held indefinitely without being subject to tax. Any potential tax liability acquired by the heirs of an estate, when discounted at market rates of interest, would be less than the present value of the liability associated with presumptive realization. (Both the difference in time of tax payment and the likely lower marginal tax rates of heirs would reduce the present value of the tax liability below the level associated with presumptive realization.) The incentive to dispose of assets during the lifetime of the present taxpayer would therefore be that much smaller. In addition, the present owner of appreciated assets would not have an incentive to provide adequate liquidity for payment of capital gains tax at death; this would eliminate another consideration that might encourage early realizations.

Since the decision to realize would remain voluntary, one would not anticipate an important economic impact. Only the needy heir would be forced by immediate consumption requirements to liquidate a part of the bequest. While some widows might be in this group, the holders of the major share of appreciated wealth would probably not feel any particular pressure to liquidate.[21] A substantial portion of inherited assets could escape taxation if the basis were carried over. The inherited property could provide collateral for loans in preference to outright sale, or it could be used for further bequests. Moreover, the heir could sell noninherited assets involving less appreciation to avoid realizing appreciation on inherited wealth.

At best, only a modest increase in tax yields could be expected with carry-over of basis. In proportion to that increase, one might expect slight increases in savings to maintain a given level of bequest.

Pressures for voluntary deferral of taxation would be altered by a

---

[21] Taxpayers with enough wealth could anticipate their widows' needs by leaving a lifetime income interest in trust and the remainder interest to the succeeding generation. This technique has the advantage of avoiding application of the estate tax both on the decedent and on his widow.

carry-over of basis. Lock-in associated with present anticipation of tax forgiveness at death would be eliminated. A new form of lock-in would take its place. Taxpayers with short life expectancies could be expected to trade their assets with the same ease as those with long life expectancies if they anticipated that their heirs would face tax burdens similar to those resulting from current realization of gains. But to the extent that heirs would pay less tax, there would still be a lock-in effect. Since anticipation of death theoretically accounts for a large part of the present lock-in in investor choices, one would expect some increase in trading by the original owners under a carry-over system. However, the behavior of the heirs must also be considered.

Under carry-over of basis, the heir would acquire the basis of the decedent and would be inhibited from selling by past appreciation. Disincentives to trading, which would not exist under presumptive realization, would be created. Under presumptive realization, as under the present law, the heirs to a bequest would not be encumbered by the basis of the decedent and would acquire a basis at market value on the day of bequest, or the alternative valuation date. No disincentive to the immediate sale of a bequest would arise from the tax treatment of appreciation.

Under carry-over of basis the incentive for the heirs to defer sales would be strong to the extent that the bequests were received by young persons who could obtain substantial economic power from a large interest-free loan. Disincentives could be as great as they now are as a result of forgiveness of tax at death. (The actual magnitude of each of these disincentives is speculative and should be ascertained by careful empirical analysis.[22]) To the extent that bequests generally pass from high-income taxpayers in high tax brackets to heirs with less current income and in lower marginal tax brackets, some moderation of lock-in would occur. The heir could realize gain at a lower tax cost than the decedent could have.

[22] Studies by the New York Stock Exchange that seek to measure the increase in turnover associated with a reduction in tax rates were developed from questions in which taxation of gains was explicitly mentioned. (See *A New Look at the Capital Gains Tax Rate* [New York Stock Exchange, October 1965].)

Inquiries by Barlow, Brazer, and Morgan avoided mention of tax motivations and showed substantially less behavior response to tax avoidance. Neither study reveals regularities in investor behavior from which an analytical model of investors' reactions can easily be inferred. (See *Economic Behavior of the Affluent* [Brookings Institution, 1966].)

Thus, carry-over of basis is not likely to produce significant economic effects, and it is likely to create disincentives to realization that might be large in comparison with the disincentives it removed. Presumptive realization would be a more effective instrument for applying taxes to appreciated assets. It would increase incentives to save, to hold riskier assets, and to receive more income from portfolio investments. These effects would cumulate to make financial asset markets a more important element in the transfer of savings to corporations with new investment demand.

Inter Vivos Transfers

The treatment of transfers between living individuals should correspond with the treatment of property passing to new ownership at death. Otherwise property donated in anticipation of death would be taxed differently from bequests, thus creating needless and inefficient tax-avoidance behavior. Moreover, it could create difficult problems of intent, such as are already encountered in the gift tax.

If gains should be presumed to be realized at death, gifts between living individuals ought also to bring about realization for tax purposes. Present regulations affecting the basis of assets received in the form of gifts would have to be altered. No special provisions would be needed to facilitate tax payment on gifts, since the taxpayer could always anticipate the liability owing and provide the necessary cash for tax payment by judicious timing. Loss carry-over would operate as effectively on *inter vivos* transfers as for any other form of realization, since the taxpayer could continue to deduct unused loss credits from income earned in future years.

While the present law provides for the carry-over of basis where the donated asset has a net gain, gifts of assets with a loss to the donor do not generate loss deductions for the donee. The donor's basis or fair market value, whichever is lower, becomes the donee's basis. This asymmetrical treatment of gains and losses results from the fact that the judicious distribution of securities with losses among members of a family can be used to circumvent the $1,000 limitation on the extent to which losses can be deducted from ordinary income in the year of their receipt.[23] The ability to time gifts optimally and re-

[23] See Chap. II, pp. 33-35. If the treatment of losses recommended in Chap. VI, pp. 140-43, wese adopted, the point would be moot, as the donor of the loss-producing property would increase his net capital loss reserve proportionately.

peat gifts over a large number of tax years, perhaps even to the point where the same asset passes between the same family members more than once, requires asymmetric tax treatment of *inter vivos* gifts, so long as carry-over of basis is the principle applied. Presumptive realization of gain or loss would obviate the need for this asymmetry.

One other feature of the present law should be noted. Gifts of property to charitable institutions are deductible from income to the amount of their current market value. Any unrealized increase in value of the property is not recognized as income.

Prior to the Revenue Act of 1964, the tax reduction associated with the donation of appreciated property could exceed the net cash realizable from sale for taxpayers in high marginal tax brackets.

If $t=$ the marginal tax rate,
$g=$ the rate on capital gains,
$y=$ the market value of an asset, and
$x=$ its basis, then
$ty=$ the tax reduction associated with charitable contribution of the property, and
$y-(y-x)g=$ the net cash proceeds of the sale of the property.

For a donation to be more profitable than a cash sale:

(7.1) $$ty > y - (y - x)g.$$

Dividing by y and g,

$$\frac{1-t}{g} < \frac{y-x}{y}.$$

Since the ratio of appreciation to current value is necessarily less than 1,

$$\frac{y-x}{y} < 1.$$

Combining this with Equation 7.1,

(7.2) $$1 \geq \frac{1-t}{g}.$$

Equation 7.2 is a necessary condition for a donation to be more profitable than a cash sale. Under the present law, $g = 0.25$, when $t \geq 0.50$, and Equation 7.2 holds when $t \geq 0.75$.

Before 1964, t ranged as high as 0.91, giving rise to opportunities for tax avoidance by this route. As long as the condition in Equation 7.1 is satisfied, the taxpayer would earn a net profit from realizing gains circuitously through charitable donations. This would be profitable whenever the market is such that selling current holdings is desirable. If capital gains tax rates were increased relative to ordinary rates, such opportunities for tax avoidance would once more become profitable.

Even under present lower rates of taxation, the lack of presumptive realization of gains at the time of gift confers a tax advantage on persons who are otherwise committed to supporting charitable organizations and who want to sell a part of their current holdings. The federal government subsidizes such contributions, not only to the extent of the reduction in tax on ordinary income because of the deductibility of contributions, but also to the extent of the capital gains taxes that would otherwise be paid at the time of asset sale. Thus under present law, contributions of property no longer generate a net profit for the taxpayer, but they do offer a way to avoid the tax on appreciation on property.[24]

Of course, the high-income taxpayer can avoid taxes altogether by retaining the asset until death. This is precisely the area of tax avoidance that presumptive realization would eliminate.

Relation Between Capital Gains and Transfer Taxation

Taxing appreciation at the time when assets are transferred by gift or bequest would add a new dimension to transfer taxation and raise some difficult questions as to how the two taxes should be structured to avoid inequities, administrative difficulties, and compliance problems. Although a discussion of the structure of transfer taxes is outside the area of this book, an understanding of the interdependence of transfer and capital gains taxes at gift and at death is indispensable in formulating a revised capital gains tax.[25]

Capital gains taxes become linked to transfer taxes in two ways: First, transfer taxes may be considered as a supplement (an alternative) to a progressive income tax in limiting the accumulation of large stocks of wealth over several generations. If the present income

---

[24] The conference participants were unable to agree that gains on charitable donations should be presumptively realized. See Chap. X, pp. 221-22.

[25] The studies by Carl S. Shoup and the American Law Institute provide a foundation for the reform of the federal estate and gift taxes. See Carl S. Shoup, *Federal Estate and Gift Taxes* (Brookings Institution, 1966), and the American Law Institute Study Draft No. 1, *Unified Transfer Tax* (1965).

and transfer taxes achieve a satisfactory balance, the increased income taxation associated with the presumptive realization of gains at gift or death would have to be offset by reduced transfer taxation. (If the two tax structures are *not* now in balance, presumptive realization should be considered as part of a larger reform program to achieve an equitable distribution of taxation.)

Also, if increasing transfer taxes above their present levels would create dislocations in the operation of small businesses or radical changes in consumption by a surviving spouse, it would be desirable to limit (through a reduction in transfer taxation) the increase in tax burden resulting from presumptive realization of capital gains.

Second, it may be convenient for both the government and the taxpayer to limit presumptive realization to those who are required to file estate tax returns. That population holds the bulk of personal wealth, and the machinery for establishing the value of assets transferred already exists for them. Considerations of need and justice that justify exempting small estates from taxation may also justify exemption from the capital gains tax of any appreciation inherent in those estates.

One conflict arises between the two taxes. Transfer taxes apply to individuals, while the income and capital gains taxes may electively be applied to a marital unit that includes both husband and wife. The difference in taxpaying unit makes it administratively awkward to apply presumptive realization to the appreciation inherent in the estate of one spouse only. Indeed any tax applied on the death of one spouse may appear inequitable to the surviving spouse, who has come to think of the wealth of the marital unit as a common holding. Both the administrative problem and the apparent inequities would be avoided, however, if: (1) interspousal transfers were exempted from transfer taxes, (2) carry-over of basis were applied to transfers between spouses, and (3) presumptive realization were applied on transfers outside the marital unit. While this would be somewhat more complex than applying presumptive realization to all transfers, it would succeed in effectively linking the capital gains taxes and the transfer tax system.

With rare exceptions, transfers outside the marital unit need not be exempted from transfer taxation on equity grounds.[26] The population

---

[26] An additional exemption could be geared to the number of minor children and the length of time that they must be supported until maturity. This general approach was adopted by the American Law Institute (*op. cit.* in note 25 above).

subject to the estate tax would account for nearly all the appreciation in capital assets. The administrative mechanism applied to estate taxation could easily be extended to presumptive realization of capital gains on all such transfers. At the same time, exemption of interspousal transfers from estate taxation, with carry-over of basis, would mean that the surviving spouse would remain liable for taxes on capital gains accrued during the lifetime of the decedent. No problem of allocation of basis would arise, as only the spouse would be entitled to the exemption from transfer taxation. No additional exemptions would need to be granted in capital gains taxation beyond those permitted by the transfer taxes.

The foregoing discussion makes clear that it may be necessary to consider applying capital gains taxes at the time of transfer as part of the transfer tax system. Both administrative convenience and psychological barriers to increased taxes assessed at death suggest that some balance in the income and transfer tax systems must be achieved. At the same time, it appears that presumptive realization can readily be integrated with transfer taxation in such a way as to minimize differences in the taxpaying unit and the tax base as between the transfer tax and the income tax.[27]

Revision of Capital Gains Taxation

Within the framework of the present law, presumptive realization combined with the proposed changes in the capital gains tax outlined in Chapter VI would provide an integrated solution to the major incentive and equity problems created by the present tax treatment of capital gains. Taken together, narrowing the base of eligible transactions, grading the tax differential to holding periods in excess of one year, establishing a capital loss reserve, and providing for presumptive realization of gains upon the transfer of assets would eliminate

[27] Investment counsellors and lawyers participating in the conference felt strongly that presumptive realization should be considered as part of a general reform of transfer taxation. Moreover, general sentiment among the conferees appeared to favor tax revision that would not increase substantially the yield of taxes levied at death. Exactly what the latter view implies for presumptive realization is not clear. Rules to eliminate step-up of basis at death would unlock portfolios and would mean substantially greater tax yields from lifetime realizations. The yield of a provision for presumptive realization at death remains uncertain. For an elaboration of these views, see the conference summary, Chap. X, pp. 220-23.

the most inequitable tax advantages that arise from the present capital gains tax. The revenue obtained could be used to reduce substantially the tax rates on upper-income groups.

Presumptive realization would have the widest application of the four suggested revisions, since it would influence all investors, while the other changes would probably be of particular significance only to certain types of investors. Investment activity motivated by a desire for lifetime consumption would be affected indirectly. The differential tax on income saved in the form of appreciated assets would continue as before, but revenues realized by unlocking portfolios and taxing assets passing into estates would finance a considerable reduction in the marginal tax rates applied to income generally. Reducing the incentive to hold assets until death would increase turnover, risk-taking, and breadth of capital markets.

Other changes in the present treatment of capital gains might be added to those suggested above, according to the objectives sought. If the present system is considered to create excessive or discriminatory exemption of savings from income taxation, the percentage inclusion of capital gains in income and the alternative tax should also be modified. So long as the philosophy underlying capital gains taxation is not changed and gains continue to receive some exemption from income taxation, the major goal of revision legislation would be to make the treatment of gains as uniform, and as uniformly available to all taxpayers, as possible. The tax structure should minimize tax avoidance possibilities that are available to only a few individuals. The four types of changes discussed would go a long way in that direction. However, problems in defining the area eligible for gains will continue to create litigation and raise questions concerning the equity of the system.

Continuing problems of definition can be eliminated only by construing the objective of capital gains tax revision more broadly. Revision must eliminate both the arbitrary differences among different individuals in the taxation of capital gains and the differential between income received in the form of capital gains and income received from other sources. Chapter VIII suggests alternative approaches to this broader problem.

Revision of the Underlying Framework

ONE OF THE PRIMARY arguments for special treatment of income from capital gains is that such income may be derived from activity that has taken place over several tax years. Full taxation in the year of realization of the gain would create undue progression on the resulting income. This could be avoided, without excluding a part of capital gains from the tax base, if provision were made to average the fluctuations in reported income that are created by the irregular realization of gains and losses on capital assets.

A variety of alternatives can be considered. Capital gains and losses could be treated under an averaging system that does not extend to other income sources, or all forms of income could be averaged under the same heading. Averaging could be used primarily as a device to avoid rate progression, or it could be extended to equalizing the base on which taxes are levied. The former objective is considered first below.

One way to limit rate progression would be to add a proration device for capital gains to the present law. Since averaging provisions now exclude net long-term capital gains from averageable income, an independent system could be applied to such gains, although the result would undoubtedly be rather complicated.[1]

---

[1] The present averaging form is incomprehensible to most taxpayers. Addition of an independent proration scheme for capital gains would make matters worse.

Proration of Capital Gains

The proration of capital gains is basically a device to limit the inclusion of gain and loss in establishing the marginal tax rate. A number of alternative methods (limited to capital gains) could be devised to prorate gains and provide the benefits of averaging. The method described here has several features that distinguish it from more general averaging schemes. The proration computation could reduce the marginal tax rate at which capital gains are taxed. The amount of prorated capital gains would be used to find a suitable rate of taxation to apply to capital gains. The entire gain or loss would then be taxed at that rate. No information from prior tax years would be required, and proration in one year would not affect the tax rates on liabilities in other years. Capital gains and losses would need to be distinguished from other income. Proration would be accomplished as follows: (1) The tax on ordinary income, less exemptions and deductions, would be calculated.[2] (2) The tax on ordinary income plus the capital gains taxable by law in that year would then be calculated. (3) The difference between (1) and (2) would be multiplied by a proration factor (see pages 170-72) and added to the tax on ordinary income. Thus, the full gain or loss would be included in the tax computation at a reduced marginal rate.[3] The present percentage inclusion and alternative tax would, of course, be omitted.

Using the sum of prorated capital gains and ordinary income in the current year to determine the rate at which marginal tax liability or tax credits are granted would be a narrow and logically consistent form of averaging. In years when there are net losses, the taxpayer would receive credits on the full amount of the losses at the rate determined by the proration calculation; in years of net gains the full gain would be taxable at the single rate determined by the proration calculation. No further progression would be induced by irregular

[2] If a portion of the income (excluding income from capital gains) were deemed averageable, provisions similar to those of the Revenue Act of 1964 could be applied.

[3] If Y is ordinary income less exemptions and deductions, G net capital gains or losses, $T(Y)$ the tax function, and $1/A$ the proration factor, the tax liability would be:

$$T^* = T(Y) + A \left[T \left(Y + \frac{1}{A} G \right) - T(Y) \right].$$

realizations. This procedure would provide appropriate net capital loss offsets against ordinary income, while at the same time, taxation of income would be basically on an annual basis. Taxes paid in other years would not be affected by computation of the current year's tax liability; the amount of ordinary income in the current year would remain a major determinant of the marginal tax rate, just as it is under a system with no averaging provisions.[4]

Any basis could be chosen for the prorating factor. The average holding period of investment assets, an arbitrary factor of 5 or 10, or a factor equal to the averaging period for ordinary income could be used. Proration would have the same result as simple income averaging when ordinary income remains constant for a period equal to the proration factor and capital gains are realized only in the last period. To the extent that capital gains are realized under such circumstances, the proration factor could be chosen by standards that determine an appropriate averaging period. However, proration could provide favorable treatment for capital gains in circumstances where averaging offers no advantage. That is, constant large realizations of gains over a period of time would not yield any tax benefits under an averaging scheme. Proration (as it is defined here) would effectively reduce the progression on those large realizations, year in and year out.

Proration to determine the marginal rate of tax on capital gains would eliminate much of the tax avoidance inherent in the present system. Full taxation of gains upon realization would eliminate the tax avoidance that is possible today because different rates apply to ordinary income than to capital gains. Narrowing the scope of capital gains transactions, as was proposed in Chapter VI, would still be required to avoid the conversion of compensation into income that could be prorated as capital gains. The advantages of such conver-

[4] The conferees were favorably disposed toward proration as a device for limiting the progression of tax rates on capital gains. (See Chap. X, pp. 218-19.) The proposed system of rate averaging would differ from the system of averaging introduced for ordinary income in the Revenue Act of 1964. Capital gains received in the current year would be taxed at the rate determined by the proration, regardless of the amounts of such gains in other years. At present, only the amount of income exceeding average income of the four prior years by more than one-third and $3,000 benefits by averaging. If proration to determine the rate applicable to gains were adopted, the averaging provisions already in effect could be continued, since current averaging could be applied only to income from sources other than capital gains.

sion would be much smaller than under the present differential rates. However, the premium for deferring taxes by postponing realization would be substantially greater than under the present system. For this or any other averaging proposal to be effective, it would have to be combined with presumptive realization of gains at death; otherwise taxes could still be avoided on a large scale.

If a combination of presumptive realization and proration were enacted, little importance would attach to defining capital gains transactions. Deferral of tax liability would be the only incentive distorting investor choices and the timing of asset transactions. For short-term and intermediate-term investments, this factor would be small relative to changes in the yield of optimum portfolios.

Depending on the expected holding period T, the present value of tax deferral per dollar of investment would approximate:[5]

$$d(\tau, T, R) = \tau \left(\frac{R[T - 1] - 1}{1 + R} + \frac{1}{(1 + R)^T} \right),$$

where:

$\tau =$ the uniform marginal tax rate on income in the period T, and
$R =$ the market rate of interest and the assumed rate of growth of asset prices.

[5] If the rate of growth of asset prices is R,

$$P_T = P_0(1 + R)^T, \quad \text{and}$$
$$P_t - P_{t-1} = RP_{t-1}.$$

Taxation of gains on accrual would amount to τRP_{t-1} in the tth period. Cumulatively, the present value of the tax liability is:

$$\sum_{k=1}^{T} \frac{\tau RP_{t-1}}{(1 + R)^k} = \frac{\tau RP_0}{1 + R} T.$$

Taxation of gains on realization implies a present value of tax liability equal to:

$$\tau \frac{([1 + R]^T P_0 - P_0)}{(1 + R)^T}.$$

The present value of the difference is:

$$\tau P_0 \left[\frac{RT}{1 + R} - 1 + \frac{1}{(1 + R)^T} \right],$$

or

$$\tau \left[\frac{R(T - 1) - 1}{1 + R} + \frac{1}{(1 + R)^T} \right]$$

per dollar of initial investment.

An elaboration of the formula makes it possible to consider the value of tax deferral when securities appreciate at a rate $R > M$, the market rate of interest:

$$d(\tau, T, R, M) = \tau \left(\left[\frac{1 + R}{1 + M} \right]^T - \frac{1}{(1 + M)^T} - \frac{R}{1 + M} \sum_{k=1}^{T} \left[\frac{1 + R}{1 + M} \right]^{k-1} \right).$$

If a true picture of the importance of deferral as a consideration motivating the time of sale is to be obtained, the present value of tax deferral must be related to the present value of the appreciation of the asset net of taxes. Some typical ratios of the tax saving to the net present value of the asset are shown in Table 8-1.

Using the distribution of holding periods derived by McClung,[6] a 7 percent rate of appreciation, and a marginal tax rate of 0.25 indicate that the average value of deferral is about 4 percent of the present value of an asset, net of taxes. Increasing the marginal rate to

TABLE 8-1. Ratio of Present Value of Tax Deferral to Present Value of an Appreciating Asset[a]

Holding period (years)	Tax rate of 25% and Rate of growth of			Tax rate of 40% and Rate of growth of			Tax rate of 65% and Rate of growth of		
	3%	5%	7%	3%	5%	7%	3%	5%	7%
5	0.002	0.006	0.011	0.003	0.009	0.018	0.006	0.016	0.032
10	0.009	0.025	0.046	0.016	0.043	0.081	0.028	0.078	0.115
15	0.022	0.056	0.102	0.037	0.099	0.185	0.067	0.192	0.382
20	0.038	0.098	0.174	0.066	0.175	0.360	0.125	0.360	0.745
30	0.084	0.186	0.350	0.149	0.381	0.671	0.301	0.857	1.633

[a] Net of capital gains taxes, for selected rates of appreciation, marginal tax rates, and holding periods. Calculated from the formula:

$$\tau\left(\frac{R[T-1]-1}{1+R} + \frac{1}{[1+R]^T}\right)\left(1 - \tau\left[1 - \frac{1}{[1+R]^T}\right]\right)^{-1}.$$

0.40 would increase the value of deferral to 7 percent of the net asset value.

Although Table 8-1 indicates a substantial incentive for heavily taxed individuals to defer sales of long-term investments, if tax rates remain the same, a major part of the disincentive to sell could be offset by using the additional revenue produced by heavier taxation of capital gains to reduce the level of tax rates now in effect.

Proration would increase the taxpayer's incentive to use the voluntary timing of realizations that is possible under the capital gains tax to offset tax liability owing on ordinary income. Large losses incurred in early years could offset the taxes due on ordinary current income, while gains would be taxable in future years. To minimize

[6] Nelson McClung, "The Distribution of Capital Gain on Corporate Shares by Holding Time," *Review of Economics and Statistics,* Vol. 48 (February 1966), pp. 40-50.

the tax avoidance that would be possible by this means, the amendment of loss carry-over suggested in Chapter VI might be enacted. That is, gains corresponding to the accumulated capital losses (prior losses deducted from ordinary income) would have to be treated as ordinary income and would be excluded from proration privileges. As a consequence, deferral of income by selective realization of losses would mean greater progression on future income, other things being equal.

No major transitional or administrative problems would arise from introducing a proration scheme of this type. The closely parallel averaging provisions already in the law and the independence of the averaging calculation from tax calculations in other years are desirable and would limit the need for administrative changes. The system could be put into effect immediately without any special transitional arrangements.

The Proration Factor

There has been considerable discussion and analysis of the effect of alternative proration factors.[7] The considerations most important for capital gains taxation will be outlined below.

Under some circumstances, proration could result in extremely high effective marginal rates on ordinary income, sometimes exceeding 100 percent. It could be to the taxpayer's advantage to reduce his ordinary income, in a year in which large capital gains are to be realized, in order to reduce the rate of tax to be applied on the prorated basis to his capital gain. For example, A has ordinary income of $50,000, on which the tax is $15,000. In addition, in a particular year he has a capital gain of $250,000, prorated by a factor of 5. If the tax on $100,000 is $40,000, each $50,000 of capital gain will pay $25,000 in tax, or a total tax of 5 × $25,000 + $15,000, or $140,000; net disposable income after tax will be $160,000. If A offers to work for no salary in the year of his gain, his ordinary income will be zero. The tax on the capital gain will then be 5 × $15,000, or $75,000, and his net income will be $175,000, exclusive of any future benefits he may have been able to obtain in lieu of the salary given up.

[7] For example, U.S. Treasury Department, Tax Advisory Staff, *Federal Income Tax Treatment of Capital Gains and Losses* (1951); Wilbur A. Steger, "Averaging of Income for Income Tax Purposes" (Doctoral thesis, Harvard University, 1956); William S. Vickrey, *Agenda for Progressive Taxation* (Ronald Press, 1947).

Even though a taxpayer might not ordinarily plan to realize such a large amount of capital gains, the opportunity to increase his after-tax income might be attractive enough to induce him to do so. Indeed, it seems that proration would leave the door wide open to tax avoidance through extensive realization of gains in years of low ordinary income. The lock-in effect of waiting for such a year of low ordinary income might be substantial.

To the extent that proration is viewed as an averaging device for occasional capital gains, the proration factor ought to correspond to the period over which capital gains and losses have accrued. In practice, prorating gains resulting from each realization over different periods could prove an annoying detail for the bulk of capital assets transactions. Since proration would affect only the degree of progression and not the income base subject to tax under the proposed averaging scheme (averaging to determine marginal rates), discrepancies between the period of accrual and the proration factor could not produce gross inequities in most instances. A suitable proration factor would be one that corresponded roughly to the mode of the holding period.

Proration by a constant factor would create incentives for the taxpayer to sell an asset at the earliest date for which proration treatment is available. If G were an isolated gain realized at the end of T periods and A were the proration factor, G/A would be the prorated increment to income, and G/T would be the true annual increment that would have produced the gain G. The difference per dollar of gain $F = (1/A - 1/T)$ would increase as T increases for $T > 0$. For $T < A, F < 0$, implying that the arbitrary proration factor would understate the average contributions to income from the appreciating asset. (See Table 8-2.) The resulting incentive to early realization would partially offset disincentives arising from the increased value of avoiding tax by deferring realizations that would be subject to tax rates substantially larger than the present capital gains rate.

Another consideration in choosing a proration period is the structure of surtax rates. Each surtax rate p_i would apply to an interval of income $\Delta y_i = y_i - y_{i-1}$. Prorating gains by some factor A would mean that the marginal rate p_i would apply effectively to an interval $A \Delta y_i = A y_i - A y_{i-1}$. That is, capital gains less than, or equal to, $A \Delta y_i$ would be taxed at the rate p_i if ordinary income were y_{i-1}. If the factor A were sufficiently large that a majority of realized gains would not increase the initial income beyond the limit Ay_i, proration would have served the purpose of eliminating undue progression associated with the realization of capital gains.

Indeed, A could be indefinitely large. That would be equivalent to taxing all capital gains at the marginal rates applicable to the last dollar of ordinary income. Losses would yield tax credits at the marginal rate determined by ordinary income. If the scope of transactions receiving capital gains treatment were sufficiently narrow, this treatment would not create undue tax avoidance and would have the merit of somewhat greater simplicity than the above computation.

However, where capital gains are recurrently realized, this argument must be modified. Proration of a steady flow of gains would provide continuously favorable marginal tax rates for capital gains as opposed to ordinary income. The proration factor chosen thus would determine whether, and to what extent, progression is to apply to capital gains. If an indefinitely large proration factor were chosen, a regular flow of capital gains would not increase the progression of taxation in spite of the fact that no fluctuation occurred.

TABLE 8-2. Difference Between Average Accrued Gain and Amount of Gain Used in a Proration Computation (F)[a] and Distortion of Income Associated with an Arbitrary Proration Factor (FT)[b]

Proration factor (A)		Period of accrual (T) in years						
		1	2	5	10	20	40	50
1	F	0	0.500	0.800	0.900	0.950	0.975	0.980
	FT	0	1.000	4.000	9.000	19.000	39.000	49.000
3	F	−0.667	−0.167	0.133	0.233	0.283	0.308	0.313
	FT	−0.667	−0.333	0.667	2.333	5.667	12.332	15.667
5	F	−0.800	−0.300	0	0.100	0.150	0.175	0.180
	FT	−0.800	−0.600	0	1.000	3.000	7.000	9.000
10	F	−0.900	−0.400	−0.100	0	0.050	0.075	0.080
	FT	−0.900	−0.800	−0.500	0	1.000	3.000	4.000

[a] F = the difference in the proportion of income to be added to ordinary income under an arbitrary proration factor, A, and the true period of accrual $(F = 1/A - 1/T)$.

[b] FT = the ratio of the difference F and the true average income obtained by prorating increments over the period T. FT indicates the extent of distortion in income produced by the arbitrary proration factor A.

Other Limited Averaging Devices

As an alternative to the proration scheme discussed above, capital gains could be averaged to determine the applicable tax, or some system of income averaging by source could be applied on an elective basis.[8] The chief advantage of a limited averaging scheme is also its major weakness. Some data on capital gains realized in previous years would be needed to compute the tax on gains in the current year. Unlike under proration, no preference would be given to capital gains except insofar as average gains deviated from actual gains realized in a particular year.

If limited averaging is applied, the averaging period should be chosen in such a way that the average of realized gains in some way reflects the underlying accrual of income. The correspondence can never be perfect, since assets may be held for periods differing greatly in length. However, choosing the mode of the holding periods as the averaging period would maximize the frequency with which the averaging calculation would produce a correct statement of the accruing income. Unlike the mean, the mode would be independent of the skewness of the distribution of holding periods. Assets held for a period longer than the modal holding period would contribute an increment to income for purposes of determining the tax that is somewhat larger than the increment based on actual holding periods. (See Table 8-2.)

Economic Effects of Proration

In combination with presumptive realization, the full inclusion of capital gains in income would produce some economic responses that are clearly desirable, some that are undesirable, and some situations in which the response cannot be predicted from available information. The economic effects can be seen most easily by viewing the incremental changes that would be induced by full inclusion in a tax system that called for presumptive realization of gains at pre-

---

[8] Such an elective plan was proposed by Harold M. Groves and Henry C. Simons. Taxpayers who found that their tax liability was reduced by more than a minimal amount when it was recomputed on the basis of a fixed average income could file for a refund. The average would cumulate to exactly the amount of income actually received over the averaging period so that only rate progression, not a difference in definition of the tax base, would create the need for a refund. See Vickrey, *op. cit.*

ferred rates at death (that is, by grafting full inclusion of gains on the argument presented on pages 150-55).

An increase in the rate of tax applicable to gains passing into the estate at death would provide substantial additional revenues. If proration produced an increase in average tax rates on decedents proportionate to the increase in tax rates observed when proration is simulated on realized gains in 1962 returns, the increased inclusion of gains associated with returns of deceased persons could run as high as $2 billion.[9] There would have to be offsetting legal rate reductions in order to maintain constant tax yields. It is assumed, as in Chapter VII, that tax rates on ordinary income would be reduced sufficiently to maintain present effective tax rates within each income bracket.

The resulting tax structure would increase saving, increase realization of gains prior to death, increase corporation dividend payout, and increase risk-taking, insofar as investors have a target bequest motive. (The argument is analogous to that used in Chapter VII.) The uncertainty of date of death and the certainty of ultimate death would combine to cause the bequest-minded investor to increase trading and saving.

One new element would enter the picture, however. Persons with no motive to save for bequests would face a higher rate of tax on their saving than they do under the present law. Saving for contingencies and for retirement consumption would be more heavily taxed. Asset appreciation could no longer be realized at preferential tax rates. A dollar of present saving in the form of appreciated assets would yield less future consumption. If maximization of lifetime consumption were the objective of the investor, his savings would fall in response to the reduced return for deferring consumption. If a particular level of future consumption during retirement were his objective, his savings would increase to offset the reduction in the return to savings. Either motive might predominate. Thus the substitution effects of the increased lifetime taxation of investors are uncertain.

The response of two polar groups—those with a bequest motive and those with no bequest motive—is indicated above. Few investors

[9] See Tables 4-26, 4-29, and 4-30. Proration over five years would produce an average tax on capital gains of 28 percent. A base of $13.6 billion of decedents' wealth then would imply yields close to $4 billion. Presumptive realization at present rates averaging 15 percent would produce about half that amount.

would behave in the manner suggested by either extreme. It is unlikely that the majority would increase their saving enough to completely recoup the reductions in estates brought about by the increased tax on appreciation. While some increase could be anticipated, it is unlikely that target saving would compensate for a large share of the tax on appreciation inherent in a bequest.[10] In addition, the burden of about $4 billion of additional asset taxation would be shifted from noninvestors to investors within each income bracket. That redistribution would also have a negative impact on savings. Combining these various effects suggests that household saving would be reduced by the increase in effective rates on appreciation.

The flow of savings into savings deposits and life insurance, on the one hand, and equity investments, on the other, would also be reallocated. To the extent that savings institutions and life insurance companies are more favorably taxed than is the average public corporation, there would be incentives to shift savings into new forms. This reallocation in the flow and level of savings would occur along with a shift in the valuation of current asset stocks and portfolio behavior.

The effect of proration on portfolio behavior would take three forms—longer holding periods, a shift in the desire for payout of dividends, and a change in flexibility of the market to receive new issues of high risk. The extent to which incentives to defer realization are increased by the increase in effective taxes on capital gains has already been discussed. How important such tax incentives are in relation to other market-determined considerations is hard to determine. Barlow, Brazer, and Morgan find that a relatively small proportion of high-income investors fail to sell appreciated investments for tax reasons; most retain their investments because no better opportunities appear to be available in the market.[11]

This finding is not easily reconciled with Hinrichs' observation that taxpayers at different income levels show different propensities to realize long-term gains, or with the New York Stock Exchange

[10] A reduction in estate taxation due to an adjustment of the value of the estate to account for terminal capital gains taxes would ameliorate the effect of full taxation of gains in the estate. The investor with a fixed bequest motive need not recover 100 percent of the increase in tax liability at death in order to maintain a fixed bequest after taxes.

[11] Robin Barlow, Harvey E. Brazer, and James N. Morgan, *Economic Behavior of the Affluent* (Brookings Institution, 1966), Chap. IX.

studies indicating that more-than-proportionate increases in realization of capital gains would follow reductions in the percentage inclusion of capital gains in income and the alternative tax.[12] Neither finding is fully relevant to the question of investor response to proration. Hinrichs' data provide an empirical measure of the response to preferential tax rates with increasing marginal tax rates. The preferential provision in question is precisely the percentage inclusion and alternative tax that would be eliminated under proration. When an asset is held for six months, the tax liability on appreciation is reduced by 50 percent. A comparable present value of tax deferral under full inclusion of gains would be attained only if the asset were held five years or more. One would expect investors to respond less readily to a tax advantage made uncertain by potential intervening price movements than they do to the present, almost immediately available, preferential rates. Thus Hinrichs' elasticity estimates constitute an overestimate of the possible deferment under full taxation.[13]

The New York Stock Exchange estimates of unlocking associated with a reduction in the percentage inclusion are of little direct help in estimating the increase in deferment associated with proration. Those estimates were based on direct hypothetical questions concerning tax changes. Since most investors (according to Barlow, et al.) are not responsive primarily to taxes on appreciated investments, the answers to such a hypothetical question cannot be regarded as useful evidence.

If assets were held for longer periods under a system of proration for capital gains, what further consequences could be expected? The choice between dividends and appreciation in the portfolio would be affected. An increase in the level of asset taxation relative to taxation of dividends would mean a reduced choice of appreciation by investors. Increased holding periods would mean a somewhat smaller increase in the present value of asset taxation than might be anticipated

[12] Harley H. Hinrichs, "An Empirical Measure of Investors' Responsiveness to Differentials in Capital Gains Tax Rates Among Income Groups," *National Tax Journal,* Vol. 16 (September 1963), pp. 224-29; *A New Look at the Capital Gains Tax Rate"* (New York Stock Exchange, October 1965).

[13] A technique analogous to that used in preparing Table 8-1 could be applied to give the present value of a reduction in taxes at six months in relation to the present value of the asset after taxes.

FIGURE 8-1. Effect of Proration on Portfolio Choice

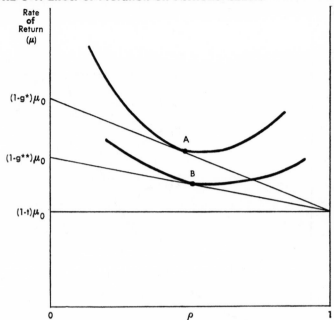

g^* Present value of the effective rate of capital gains taxation with preferential rates and presumptive realization (and a holding period N); the corresponding portfolio is A

g^{**} Present value of the effective rate of capital gains taxation with presumptive realization and proration of
gains (and a holding period $N^* > N$); the corresponding portfolio is B

p Payout ratio

from the change in legal rates applicable to realized gains.[14] The result would be a shift toward dividend payout. (See Figure 8-1.) That
shift in payout should increase new issues in the market and the general availability of capital (by the same argument that is used in
Chapter VII).

To the extent that asset sales are deferred, less extensive trading of
assets would occur. This would inhibit investors from maintaining a
desired income-liquidity-risk position as the character of assets shifted over time.

With the passage of time, the character of some investments would
change. Issues of new companies would evolve from high-risk, high-

[14] It is unlikely (but possible) that deferment of gains would increase enough to
offset the effect of a rate increase.

FIGURE 8-2. Dynamic Changes in the Risk and Rate of Return of a Given Portfolio

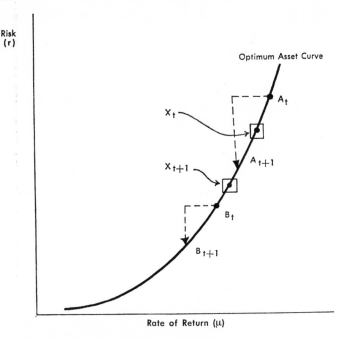

X_t represents desired portfolio at time t. Changes in the characteristics of particular securities (A and B) will cause a downward movement in the actual characteristics of the portfolio over time to a point such as X_{t+1}.

return investments into investments whose expected future return was both lower and more stable. In the extreme they might become worthless; in a more limited number of situations, securities with an initially low risk might become speculative and unstable with no greater prospects for earnings. As a result of such changes, investors would want a continual turnover in the securities in their portfolio to maintain a fixed income-risk position. Figure 8-2 illustrates the problem in a situation in which the speculative elements of the portfolio evolve into investments of average quality and return. To maintain an initial position X_t, based on a diversified portfolio of assets A_t and B_t, the investor would have to acquire new stocks with the characteristics of A_t. He would have to dispose of a part of the portfolio with low-risk, low-yield characteristics. This could be done by trading either B_{t+1} or A_{t+1}, or both. Investors in somewhat less extreme positions in the market might also have the same problem, and they would become ready buyers for the securities A_{t+1} and B_{t+1}.

A capital gains tax payable on realization could inhibit this process of turnover, but only to the extent that all securities that are candidates for sale have appreciated. If some undesired assets have little or no appreciation, they could be sold first to avoid realization of a concomitant tax liability.

The impact of proration on business taxation would be minimal. The analysis in Appendix D indicates that businesses could escape taxation on financial investments through the intercorporate dividend exclusion. Moreover, more than one-third of corporate gains are gains on business property or the special situations described earlier. (See Table 4-22.) Those types of gains would be greatly reduced by the narrowing of the area eligible for gains suggested in Chapter VI (pages 122-27).

Whatever the net outcome of all these reactions to proration, it is clear that the estimate of more than $3 billion in revenue yield from lifetime realizations (Table 4-30) is high. Some investors would be locked in by the tax increase.[15] (However, some of the appreciation on assets held by those investors would be captured by constructive realization at death.) Also, because some transactions would produce net gains on short-term sales of capital assets, the revenue from lifetime realizations would not disappear altogether.[16] Thus the net increase in revenue yields at existing rates would exceed the $2 billion anticipated from the additional taxation on gains presumed realized at death. A reduced rate progression could be financed from these additional yields. Any increased market turnover associated with (or in anticipation of) a reduction in legal bracket rates and provisions for taxation at death would offset some of the undesired deferment associated with the full inclusion of capital gains in taxa-

---

[15] The deferment of tax yields for capital gains taxation under proration is analogous to the deferment of yields associated with accelerated depreciation. No one can escape taxation indefinitely; however, as long as the amount of appreciated assets grows at a positive rate, the amount of deferred taxes in the aggregate will increase, so that the Treasury will never recoup its losses. See Robert Eisner, "Accelerated Amortization, Growth, and Net Profits," *Quarterly Journal of Economics,* Vol. 66 (November 1952), pp. 533-44.

[16] *Statistics of Income—1962, Individual Income Tax Returns* indicates that returns with net short-term gains were 6 percent of aggregate returns. The amount of such gains was about 2 percent of the amount of net gains reported. (U.S. Treasury Department, Internal Revenue Service, 1965.)

ble income. It is likely that the unlocking effect of presumed realization at death would far outweigh the additional lock-in caused by increased rates. However, the reader must judge the balance of these effects for himself.

Equity of Proration

Proration of capital gains is the first of the proposed reforms considered that clearly would have a major impact on the horizontal equity of the tax structure between investors in appreciating assets and investors in fixed-value assets. Previous revisions considered would affect principally the equity among investors in businesses with different products, with different degrees of associated management, and with varying degrees of familiarity with legal devices for tax avoidance. Proration would provide more uniform taxation between individuals with large net worth and those with limited net worth whose taxable incomes fall in the same bracket. Under the present law the rentier, widow, or retiree who makes $15,000 a year income from a portfolio has far more opportunity for favorable tax treatment than has the manager, professor, or civil servant whose income is largely from personal services. Proration of gains would be a major step in eliminating the inequities between these two groups. While the rentier would continue to have the advantage of tax deferral, he would be taxed at ordinary income rates on any income received, just as is his professional or managerial counterpart.

In addition, taxpayers with rapidly growing incomes from appreciating wealth would find their taxes increasing more substantially than under the present system. The tax system would become more effective as a device for limiting massive accumulations of wealth.

Averaging for All Income Sources

If the application of progressive tax rates to annual income streams produces an inequitable burden of taxation on individuals with highly fluctuating incomes, the income history of the taxpayer or his prospective income must be used to determine tax liability. (See Chapter III, pages 52-53.) A wide variety of devices could be used to bring this averaging about.

Income could be averaged to determine a rate to be applied to the entire taxable income realized during the year (as was done for a time in Australia), or the averaging could be used to spread the taxable base over time, or the accounting period could be extended to cover more than one year as the unit for assessment of the tax. Averaging could be either a periodic reassessment, possibly including the amendment of returns previously filed, or a continuing procedure. The average itself could be either a simple uniform average or one giving relatively less weight to periods in the more remote past. It could cover a relatively short period, or it might extend over longer periods up to the entire lifetime of the taxpayer. Without further elaboration on possible averaging schemes, some general features of full taxation of capital gains under a comprehensive system of averaging for all income sources will be discussed.[17]

Under a scheme of full inclusion and general averaging, incentives to convert highly fluctuating income into the form of capital gains would disappear. The importance of defining capital assets and delineating special rules for capital gains would become moot.

The integration of the ordinary income tax and the capital gains tax under one set of rates would eliminate hundreds of arbitrary distinctions that are now drawn in law and in regulations to distinguish income that may be taxed under preferential rates from the bulk of ordinary income. With an integrated structure there need no longer be concern over whether assets are held as stock in trade, whether assets are disposed of through installment sales, whether real estate has been significantly improved by the seller and for what purpose, whether bonds are sold at excessive discount, and so on.[18] Eliminating the distinction would do away with the costs of accounting and legal and management services that are currently engaged in channeling all manner of businesses into forms eligible for capital gains.

An integrated system of taxation would also eliminate the present distortion of investment in favor of areas in which income can be cloaked as capital gains—over-depreciated real estate, livestock, coal and iron ore royalties, timber, and interests in owner-controlled enterprises. Integrating the capital gains and income taxes thus

[17] Steger, *op. cit.*

[18] Stanley S. Surrey, "Definitional Problems in Capital Gains Taxation," in House Committee on Ways and Means, *Tax Revision Compendium* (1959), Vol. 2, pp. 1203-32; Peter Miller, "The 'Capital Asset' Concept: A Critique of Capital Gains Taxation," *Yale Law Journal*, Vol. 59 (April and May 1950), pp. 837-85 and 1057-86.

would eliminate some of the inefficiencies of the present system. Some of these advantages could be obtained by full inclusion of gains and proration, as was pointed out at the beginning of this chapter. However, a general averaging scheme would be the only sure way to eliminate the excessive compliance costs associated with the differentiation of capital gains from ordinary income in the law.

A second major advantage of general averaging is that it could be justified on different grounds than could limited proration of gains. Since full averaging of income may be considered a device for assessing tax liabilities according to the income history of an individual, it is of less significance that the averaging period bear any particular relationship to the period over which capital gains have accrued. The sporadic realization of capital gains is treated just as any irregular element in income. An averaging provision would ameliorate the impact of such realizations on tax liability.

Finally, a general averaging system could be more easily adapted to benefit cases of extreme inequity than could a system limited to capital gains and losses. The averaging permitted under the Revenue Act of 1964 is an extreme example of the limitation of averaging privileges to special circumstances.

Most general averaging schemes require that the taxpayer keep records on the taxable income that he has received in past years. Under a full averaging scheme, this burden would be extended to all taxpayers, whereas proration would not require any past income data and would affect only those taxpayers who receive occasional capital gains. The general averaging system would achieve greater equity by its universality, but at the expense of record-keeping problems.

Cumulative assessment and some forms of weighted averaging, notably the geometrical progression weighting, would require carrying forward only a relatively small amount of information from the tax return of the preceding year. For example, cumulative assessment requires data on adjusted total income, total taxes paid, and number of years filed. (See pages 185-86, below.) Thus the use of a voluntary averaging technique, or a geometrical series weighting, or cumulative assessment, could reduce this problem to minimal proportions.

To the extent that general averaging and proration result in similar effective tax rates, they would have a similar economic impact. Under both systems, tax deferral would be possible and would detract from the other beneficial economic and equity effects.

It is clear that it is only a short step from the proration proposal at the beginning of this chapter to general income averaging for capital gains and losses and all other income sources. The gain from taking this step would be largely one of administrative convenience, of ease of taxpayer compliance and reduction in compliance costs, and of combining consideration of the tax treatment of capital gains with the broader question of tax treatment of fluctuating income generally. The more general averaging plan would obviate the need for a capital assets definition and some of the arbitrary distinctions that such a definition would entail.

Reducing the Value of Deferring Tax Payments

As long as the taxpayer determines the timing of tax payment on appreciated assets, he can benefit from the postponement of tax liabilities in two ways: (1) He may defer tax payments to years in which he is taxable at low marginal rates; and (2) he may use the interest-free loan resulting from postponement of tax liability. The taxpayer thus controls for his own benefit resources corresponding to the reduced or deferred tax liability. Two methods may be used to reduce these benefits: Gains and losses may be made taxable on accrual; or tax liabilities may be determined by a scheme of cumulative averaging, with compensating interest adjustments.

Taxation on Accrual

Taxation of gains on accrual would require the taxpayer to inventory his assets with each return, value them, and add the change in value during the year to his adjusted gross income. This would keep tax payment in phase with changing asset values. Since changes in many security prices tend to lead cyclical movements in business conditions, the resulting automatic adjustments in tax liabilities would act as an automatic stabilizer on the economy.[19]

Taxing gains and losses on accrual would suffer from serious administrative difficulties. Preparing and evaluating an inventory of

---

[19] The conference participants agreed that accrual would present formidable valuation difficulties. Its application to listed securities and other areas where valuation is no problem might prove highly inequitable. The conferees voiced these opinions without indicating that they had considered the extensive revision of corporate income taxes that could be financed by accrual. (See Chap. X, pp. 214-16, and Chap. V.)

assets annually would be cumbersome and expensive, even for tax-payers with small and marketable holdings. Taxpayers with an equity in closely held enterprises might find valuation problems almost insuperable.

The valuation difficulties would probably favor assets that are hard to value, just as property assessment tends to favor properties with rare characteristics whose value is uncertain. Auditing property inventories would also prove difficult unless data processing techniques could be used to mechanize a comparison of taxpayers' reported valuations with market price data.

The taxation of gains on accrual might create hardships for tax-payers whose investments could not readily be liquidated and who could not meet cash tax payments from existing stocks of liquid assets or new loans.

Such compliance problems have led to the proposal that the taxation of capital gains on accrual be limited to periodic intervals of some arbitrary number of years. If taxpayers could anticipate the year of reporting, they could arrange for the necessary liquid balances and valuations at less cost than if reporting were required annually. To avoid dislocations in the capital markets, reporting years must be reasonably distributed among taxpayers over time. Otherwise, liquidations needed to make the tax payment might cause radical changes in market prices.[20] In addition, periodic accrual would have to be linked to some scheme of averaging to determine tax liabilities. Just as it is inequitable to subject the full amount of realized gains to progressive tax rates because they accrue over several years, it would be inequitable to subject a reported accrued gain to undue progression. Prorating accruals would suffice. A more comprehensive averaging scheme might be desirable to avoid undue influence on the amount of the total tax bill from the amount of ordinary income in the year of reporting.[21]

[20] Staggered dates would create some administrative problems. Taxpayers might regard themselves as unfairly assessed if the year of payment included an unusual peak in asset prices. Such problems would tend to be minimized by a long interval between assessments so that trend growth would dominate the amount of tax assessed. The staggered payment date is not widely used in taxation but has been applied to noncalendar-year taxpayers (who elect the starting date of their tax year) and to automobile license taxes, which are collected on the anniversary of purchase in some states.

[21] The Simons-Groves plan for recomputation of tax liability at periodic intervals (termed periodic averaging) would avoid this difficulty. Under the plan, taxpayers

The legal basis for any form of taxation of capital gains on accrual is more tenuous than that for constructive realization of gains at the time of transfer by gift or bequest. Both gift and bequest result from a decision by the taxpayer to convert appreciated gains or losses into a more desirable form—to enjoy the satisfaction that comes from voluntarily ceding property rights to a close friend or relative. While income in cash is not realized at the time of transfer, it is reasonable to recognize accrued gains at that time. The power to exercise property rights has passed to another person.

The periodic accrual of gains is not associated with any changes in the taxpayer's control over his assets, and so it requires that income be defined on an accrual basis for legal purposes.[22] Legal opinions on the taxability of accruing rights appear reasonably favorable to such a plan, in contrast to the earlier doctrine of *Eisner v. Macomber*.[23]

Cumulative Averaging

If the taxation of income on accrual poses difficult compliance and administrative problems, incentives to postpone the realization of capital gains could be reduced by cumulative income averaging, as proposed by Vickrey. Cumulative income averaging would reduce the value of deferring tax liabilities by crediting the taxpayer with the interest on the cumulative value of tax payments and computing tax liability on the basis of an adjusted cumulated total of income. The adjusted total income would include an imputed value of the interest that could have been earned on the amount paid in taxes. Thus taxpayers with equal earning resources would report the same total income regardless of the time when income was realized for tax purposes. Mathematically, the taxpayer would be subjected to the following:

---

could apply for a refund if the actual amount of taxes paid annually exceeded the hypothetical tax bill obtained by assuming income at the mean level for the entire period. To eliminate claims for trifling amounts, a variety of devices have been attached to this basic plan limiting refunds to instances where the recomputation made a substantial difference. See Vickrey, *op. cit.*, pp. 170-72.

[22] The tax treatment of earnings of domestically controlled foreign corporations represents the clearest precedent for this. A portion of the earnings of such foreign corporations are imputed to the shareholder even though they remain undistributed as dividends (Internal Revenue Code, Sections 951-72).

[23] Stanley S. Surrey, "The Supreme Court and the Federal Income Tax," *Illinois Law Review*, Vol. 35 (March 1941), p. 779.

(1) Adjusted total payments
$$T^* = (1 + r)T_{N-1}(Y_{N-1})$$

(2) Adjusted total income
$$Y_N = Y_{N-1} + rT_{N-1}(Y_{N-1}) + Y_n$$

(3) Tax due
$$t_n = T_N(Y_N) - T^*,$$

where r is the market rate of interest, Y_n is the current year's income, and $T_N(Y_N)$ is the tax function for the cumulative total of income. Where simple income averaging and constant tax rates are in effect for the entire N periods, $T_N(Y_N) = NT^A (Y_N/N)$, if $T^A (Y_N/N)$ is the annual tax liability applicable to an average income of Y_N/N.[24] The cumulative averaging system would eliminate the value of tax deferment, provided that the rate of interest credited to the tax-payer's cumulative tax payments and adjusted total income reflected the rate actually available on those investments that the taxpayer could obtain by deferring tax payments.

Vickrey argues that cumulative averaging is a flexible system, adaptable to changes in tax rates, sensitive to cyclical fluctuations in income, and capable of judging economic capacity on the basis of a variety of sophisticated measures of income more refined than those in use at present. Cumulative averaging would eliminate the need to distinguish capital gains from ordinary income to the extent that it is successful in determining the value of tax deferment to the taxpayer.

This system would have the advantage of keeping the taxpayer current in his tax payments. The timing of tax payments under cumulative averaging would be more appropriate to the size of the current year's income than under a moving average of income. When the current year's income fell sufficiently, refunds could result. A moving average might cause taxes associated with past high levels of income to accrue as liabilities in years of low income. Cumulative averaging would also avoid the bunching of tax payments at death that would result from a system of prospective averaging.

Cumulative assessment would not, to be sure, eliminate entirely all possible gains from tax anticipation or tax deferral for all taxpayers. The gains would merely be comparable to those that would be obtained from access to any other source of funds at the cost of the interest rate credited on the tax payments. While it might be

---

[24] See Vickrey, *op. cit.*, Appendix III, pp. 417-27.

FIGURE 8-3. Alternative Rates That Could Provide an Interest Adjustment for a Cumulative Averaging Scheme and Their Relationship to the Distribution of Yields on Investments

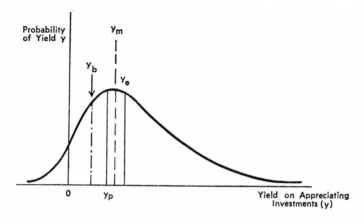

y_b Yield on government bonds

y_p Yield on prime commercial paper

y_m Mode

y_e Mean

superficially appealing to base the interest rate for the credit on tax payments on the yield of government bonds, probably a more appropriate rate would be that typically charged on prime commercial paper, or on brokers' loans, at least for those taxpayers with assets that could be manipulated to produce shifts in the time of payment of taxes. Investors who have access to investments that earn above the government's credited rate of interest would still find it in their interest to defer tax payments. Figure 8-3 illustrates the problem involved in setting a rate. Whatever rate is chosen would leave some investors in a situation in which tax deferral would be advantageous. However, some interest adjustment, such as the rate on commercial paper, would clearly reduce the extent to which it would be advantageous.[25] Using the mean rate of return to credit tax payments would provide a small subsidy to the majority of investments for

[25] Formulas similar to those used in calculating Table 8-1 give the value of tax deferral, except that the value accumulates according to $(1 + R)/(1 + B)$, where R is the return on a particular investment and B is the interest adjustment rate.

early realization. At the same time, most of the incentive to deferral would be eliminated.

The opportunity to defer taxes might not even be a significant source of additional credit, since the action taken would in many cases be apparent to banks and other sources of credit, and the existence of a deferred tax liability would tend to reduce correspondingly the taxpayer's ability to borrow from private sources. The major gain from tax deferral would then be merely the greater convenience, if any, of borrowing in this way from the government rather than from a bank.

To be sure, in some cases a taxpayer could borrow in this way from the government when he could not borrow from private sources on as favorable terms. This is most likely to be the case if the investment is risky. The government is in a better position to lend where the security, in effect, consists of tax refunds that would be due the taxpayer in the event of loss. A private lender might find it more difficult to establish such a lien or collect on it. But the advantages thus given to the taxpayers making such risky investments can be regarded as merely the result of an improved functioning of the loan market, rather than of discrimination inherent in the tax law. In any case the discrimination is in favor of risky investment and so would probably be deemed desirable rather than otherwise.

Since the deferral of tax could be interrupted at any time by realization of the gain, the interest rate credited should preferably be related to short-term rather than long-term rates. Furthermore, it should be an established policy to adjust the rate according to market conditions—perhaps yearly—although the principles on which the rate is determined should be fairly clearly established on a permanent basis.

A cumulative assessment system would require that the basic concept of annual income as a measure of taxable capacity be replaced by a multi-period concept, as indeed all averaging systems do to some extent. Computation would be easier for taxpayers under a cumulative averaging system than under a moving average or periodic average system, since only the adjusted total tax payment and the cumulative adjusted total income need be brought forward in computing the current year's tax. It would be easy for tax administrators to provide a certified stub with this information, along with the return forms for the next taxable year and the tax computation tables appropriate to the number of years of income history of the particular taxpayer.

The main difficulty with the cumulative averaging system lies in establishing the appropriate taxpaying units and determining the beginning and end of the averaging period. The chief problems occur at the time of marriage, separation, and entering or leaving a particular jurisdiction. One possibility would be to return to the practice of separate returns for husband and wife, each being taxed according to his own income history. But aside from the considerable appeal that the split-income method has for many on equity grounds, the use of separate returns as the norm would reintroduce the whole range of problems associated with interspousal transfers. Perhaps the more attractive alternative would be to keep the split-income method but to require at least a declaration of value of assets, with constructive realization of gains and losses, at the time of marriage or separation. It would be possible to adjust the tax schedules for the different averaging periods so that this interruption of the averaging period would not always be to the disadvantage of a taxpayer who faced these interruptions relatively near together in time, whether from a change in marital status or a change in residence. Nevertheless, it would not be possible to make the interruption a matter of indifference in all cases, and some restraints would have to be imposed on the values that could be declared for tax purposes for assets held at the time of a break in the averaging period. Disputes over valuations should be relatively minor, however.

It is difficult to know whether such a system would be politically acceptable. While the computations required would be simple enough for relatively unsophisticated taxpayers, the rationale of the procedure would be more difficult to explain, and somewhat complicated tax tables would be required. The system would make the income tax a reasonably neutral revenue instrument, free from undue influence on business and other decisions.[26]

Economic Effects of Devices To Reduce Deferral

Disincentives to the sale of assets under a system of full taxation of capital gains would result in some reduction in the depth of the asset

---

[26] There was general agreement at the conference that interest adjustment is appropriate in order to reduce incentives to postpone realizing capital gains. The cumulative averaging system was considered analytically correct but politically infeasible. See Chap. X, pp. 216-18.

market. (See the section on Proration of Capital Gains, above.) The reduction could be limited by presumptive realization of gains at death. The latter would terminate any lock-in and would require liquidation of part of the estate. Both periodic accrual and cumulative averaging could be used to offset a substantial part of the effect of deferment.

Periodic accrual would have the advantage of being entirely beyond the control of the taxpayer. If accrual were required every N years on a staggered basis, appreciation on approximately $1/N$th of all wealth would be realized for tax purposes quite independently of voluntary realizations.[27] Since asset prices, and stock prices in particular, are extremely sensitive to economic conditions, periodic accrual would increase the built-in flexibility of income tax yields. The tax due on assets that have appreciated very rapidly would be collected periodically.[28] Such assets are likely to be held by persons whose income has grown almost as rapidly. The result would be that rapidly growing incomes would be taxed more heavily than under the present system. Deferral would still be possible within the accrual period.

The increase in the tax would cause an increase in market turnover compared with that under the proration system discussed above. Investors whose accrued appreciation would be taxed in the current year could liquidate some appreciated investment to pay taxes. They could also trade investments to improve their portfolios, since no marginal tax cost would be incurred on the transaction.

If cumulative averaging were associated with an interest rate that adequately reflected the market rate of return, it would be even more effective than periodic accrual in eliminating the incentive to deferment. Under cumulative averaging each investor would decide for himself when trading of assets and payment of taxes were most appropriate. He would not be influenced by an administratively determined accrual period, and there would be no need to distinguish var-

---

[27] Staggered groups could be established by name or by social security number. Alternatively, taxes on appreciation could be levied according to the holding period of the asset. The latter approach would require annual returns and would entail greater compliance costs.

[28] See Harley H. Hinrichs, "Dynamic-Regressive Effects of the Treatment of Capital Gains on the American Tax System During 1957-1959," *Public Finance,* Vol. 19, No. 1 (1964), pp. 73-83.

ious investor groups in order to avoid the peculiar effects of the tax payment date.[29]

Ease of administration, simplicity, and flexibility in realizing gains and incurring the corresponding tax liability—all favor the cumulative averaging scheme over periodic accrual. Problems concerning the general desirability of cumulative averaging as the core of the tax structure are the major impediments to its use to limit the tax advantages of deferment.[30]

Effect of Capital Gains Tax Revision

The two tax devices discussed in the preceding section closely approximate an income tax based on an accretion definition of income. Capital gains would be fully taxed when realized. Either cumulative averaging of income with interest credits, or the combination of periodic accrual and general income averaging would remove incentives to lifetime deferment of asset sales; presumptive realization under either alternative would remove the tax advantage in postponing sales in anticipation of death.

Under either system income would receive roughly equal taxation, whether it were earned, derived from property, or associated with the sale of assets. Tax avoidance by a broad group of investors would become vastly more difficult. Existing inequities in tax treatment between persons with large net worth and those with little net worth in the same income brackets would be eliminated. At the same time inequities that now arise from the inconsistent treatment of short-term gains, long-term gains, and appreciation that escapes taxation at death would be eliminated. The nominal rate structure of the tax system would more nearly approximate effective vertical progression.

Implications for Tax Reform

Eliminating preferential rate treatment on capital gains would create a foundation on which other reforms of the tax structure could be based. If preferential treatment were not eliminated, tax reform in

[29] Periodic accrual would actually be a capital levy on appreciation over the accrual period, applied at the taxpayer's marginal income tax rate.

[30] Defining the taxpaying unit would also be a problem under any system of compulsory averaging. Periodic accrual would have the merit of being applicable in combination with proration, so that no general averaging system would be required.

other areas would frequently result in the creation of additional capital gains, taxable under present law at a maximum rate of 25 percent. The holding of tax-exempt securities, for example, would be replaced by the holding or sale of growth securities.[31] A change in percentage depletion or in the expensing of mineral exploration and development costs would also create only a token change in the tax system if capital gains were not taxed as ordinary income. The developer would simply sell property with known oil-production capabilities for capital gains; he would thereby capture the entire future earnings prospects of an income-producing property at capital gains rates.

Situations in which ingenuity, good management, creative use of resources, and exploitation of natural wealth create value that was not previously recognized in the market place show the paradox of the present preferential tax system. Sale of a copyright generating a stream of royalties must be looked on by the seller as constituting an assignment of income; it is therefore taxable in full. Good will created by good management may be sold at capital gains rates, although the current income of the business is fully taxed. Timber may be sold from the land to produce capital gains, regardless of the circumstances. This seemingly incompatible treatment of alternative forms of yield from productive effort arises from the difficulty of defining a meaningful area eligible for capital gains. If timber sold piecemeal from the land is to be taxed at ordinary income rates, why should the outright sale of the land and timber receive preferential treatment? If a person can capitalize the value that he has added to a business through good management and sell his interest, why should the discounted stream of income be taxed more favorably than it would be if he chose to retain the business? If one is an author, why should the value he creates be taxed differently than if he develops new plastics and sells the patent on them?

The foregoing examples show how preferential rate treatment of capital gains creates inequities and undermines the basic fabric of the tax structure. Retention of the present capital gains structure could be defended by citing the beneficial economic effects of preferential

---

[31] Barlow, Brazer, and Morgan discovered less motivation to hold tax-exempts among high-income investors than might have been expected from a priori inspection of marginal tax rates, precisely because capital gains are subjected to a ceiling rate of 25 percent (*op. cit.*).

taxation. In the earlier argument it was shown that, compared with the comprehensive taxation of gains under one of the alternatives sketched above, the present tax structure induces the following beneficial and adverse effects:

1. A reallocation of investment to areas favored by the special situations and treatment of owner-managed enterprises.

2. An increase in investor savings in preferentially taxed areas that is associated with two offsetting movements—a decline in saving for bequests and an increase in saving associated with increased yields available on appreciating assets.

3. A decline in aggregate risk-taking associated with the income effect of reduced taxation of income from investments and more limited loss offsets.

4. A decrease in lifetime turnover of assets associated with increased incentives to defer realization.[32]

5. A redistribution of tax on personal services from owner-managers to wage and salary earners and persons with little net worth in relation to their current income.

6. An increase in corporate retentions of earnings stimulated by the differential tax on earnings received as dividends and earnings that become translated into appreciation of stock prices.

The cumulative balance of these effects is unclear. A careful study of their interdependency and their combined consequences for the rate of growth remains to be undertaken. Until that analysis has been completed, caution must be used in drawing inferences about the optimal capital gains tax structure.

While the exact impact of preferential capital gains taxation is uncertain, the potential range of effects that might be expected ought to be placed in a more general context of public economic policy.

Over the past decade, economic stability at full employment and maximum economic growth have been the prime goals of policy makers. Their policy tools for seeking these goals have included budget policy and monetary policy, as well as specific policies concerning the tax structure. The capital gains tax is relevant to the goal, primarily because it stimulates growth.

---

[32] The present system creates lock-in; the proposed systems would reduce the incentive for lock-in.

Implications for Saving and Growth

While there are many complaints that the present capital gains tax locks-in the investor, those who defend the preferential tax contend that to tax appreciation at regular income tax rates would impede significantly the growth of the national product as well as its quality. The argument is seldom spelled out in full, but the claim that preferential taxes are needed to induce risk-taking and a healthy capital market is based on the following economic reasoning:[33]

The preferential taxation of capital gains reduces the effective tax rate on income saved in the form of gains on capital assets. On balance this subsidy favors saving in the form of assets eligible for the low tax rate. As a result, (1) more funds become available in the capital markets; (2) businesses respond to the increase in the supply of funds with increased outlays on real capital; (3) increased outlays raise the level of productive capacity and may increase the rate of development of new technology and its adoption; and (4) the economy benefits from increased growth. The links in the chain of argument will be examined one by one.

It was indicated above that preferential capital gains taxation probably increases the volume of saving, since it discriminates in favor of savers who accumulate assets eligible for the low tax rate.[34] Lifetime savings rise in response to increased yields, while target saving for bequests falls. Simultaneously, risk-taking is reduced; and the volume of new issues in the market falls (points 2 and 3 on page 193, above). What impact will an increased supply of funds have

---

[33] See also Walter J. Blum, "A Handy Summary of the Capital Gains Arguments," *Taxes,* Vol. 35 (April 1957), pp. 247-66; Jonathan A. Brown, "The Locked-in Problem," *Federal Tax Policy for Economic Growth and Stability,* U.S. Congress, Joint Committee on the Economic Report, 84 Cong. 1 sess. (November 1955), p. 376; Raymond L. Richman, "Reconsideration of the Capital Gains Tax—a Comment," *National Tax Journal,* Vol. 14 (December 1961), pp. 402-04.

[34] The tax has significant income as well as substitution effects. The taxes that investors avoid through the capital-gains loophole reduce *both* the average rate of taxation *and* the marginal rate applicable to capital gains. Households are sensitive to the difference. They adjust work effort, consumption, and saving in noneligible forms of investment in response to adjustments in their income. What clues are there to the outcome? Both Barlow *et al.* and Break suggest that for high-income groups the effective tax rate may have little to do with work effort (George F. Break, "Income Taxes and Incentives to Work," *American Economic Review,* Vol. 47 [September 1957], pp. 529-49; and Barlow, Brazer, and Morgan, *op. cit.*).

on business investment expenditures? An increased supply of funds will mean more offers to buy both new and existing securities, both new and existing real capital. The investor has no preference between the new issue of an old company and outstanding equities. What becomes of the additional supply of funds to the capital market thus depends on the business demand for new investment funds relative to the available supply.[35] If there is no demand for investment funds above and beyond the amounts that business can obtain from internal sources, such as depreciation and the retention of earnings, the entire increase in the supply of savings can be translated into an increase in the price and value of existing securities. If the available supply of funds exceeds the demand for new investments, prices rise but by less than in this extreme case. Conversely, if the demand for new investment funds exceeds available supplies, equity prices fall and divert a part of existing asset values into new investment uses. The supply of funds is critical to the level of investment only insofar as the demand is present.

It appears that the ultimate impact of additional savings generated by preferential capital gains taxation on investment can be evaluated only by a model of asset markets that includes investment demand. Despite the work of Jorgenson, Meyer, and Kuh, and many others, our knowledge of the investment function is very incomplete.[36] It is not known whether the availability of funds under conditions that will not precipitate declines in stock prices is an important element in investment demand. The anticipated rate of consumer spending and spending for the national product appear to be more important factors. When spending rates are high, plants operate near capacity. Demand for investments is created by physical needs as well as by the anticipated success of higher quality products and more productive techniques. At the same time, the high rate of spending generates investor optimism that contributes additional funds to the available supply. Business activity results in a high level of profits and correspondingly high retained earnings.

In the last decade, the need of corporations to finance new invest-

[35] Irwin Friend's study for the Securities and Exchange Commission demonstrates that new issues are purchased at substantially the same yields as existing issues (*Wall Street Journal*, Nov. 29, 1965, p. 1).

[36] Dale W. Jorgenson, "Capital Theory and Investment Behavior," *American Economic Review*, Vol. 53, No. 2 (May 1963), pp. 247-59; and John Meyer and Edwin Kuh, *The Investment Decision* (Harvard University Press, 1957).

ments through new issues of securities has not been strongly influenced by the volume of investment in new plant and equipment. In fact, in the recession troughs of 1958 and 1961, corporate business financed a higher proportion of new investment from new issues than in any other year but 1957. While these statistics do not disprove assertions that a preferential capital gains tax is desirable, they indicate that growth-producing investment is not necessarily highly sensitive to the volume of household savings seeking investment in the stock market.

While the exact effect of increased household savings on real investment is in doubt, the volume of internally retained earnings is certainly increased by preferential taxation of capital gains.[37] This latter effect increases investment to the extent that capital rationing is in effect. That is, some companies find that a reduced market demand for dividend payments improves their cash position to a point where the cost of desired investment projects can be covered by a combination of internal and external financing. In a high dividend payout market, the company would not be able to finance those investment projects without reducing the market value of its shares by failing to make dividend payments in proportion to their value at the beginning of the period. Higher payouts of dividends could create a broader market in new issues and reduce the capital rationing that exists under present preferential taxes.

To the extent that external financing is limited by *ad hoc* rules of banking institutions and transactions costs associated with the financing venture, external funds may be limited, unavailable, or rationed. Preferential capital gains taxation will circumvent such limitations to the extent that corporate savings rise. However, reduced demand for external funds may also limit the effectiveness and increase the transactions costs associated with any external financing. It is not clear what the net effect of these opposing influences might be.

To verify the third link in the argument that relates capital gains taxation to growth, more information must be collected on the relation between investment in plant and equipment and the increase in capacity gross national product. Available studies indicate no strong connection between investment in construction, machinery, and other producer durable goods and economic growth. Although there

[37] See John A. Brittain, *Corporate Dividend Policy* (Brookings Institution, 1966).

is certainly a link, its magnitude is still in doubt. Massell demonstrates that 90 percent of the growth in output per man-hour of labor from 1919 to 1955 can be accounted for by technological factors, information, organization, and similar factors. Ten percent is accounted for by increases in capital stock per worker. Denison estimates that it would take an increase in private investment of 1.4 percent of GNP to raise the rate of growth by even 0.1 percent.[38] He also states that reducing the lag between the discovery and adoption of new techniques by two and two-thirds years would improve the rate of growth by another 0.1 percent. If a greater availability of funds would induce more rapid adoption of new techniques, a corresponding stress on investment stimuli would be warranted.

On balance, the growth argument in favor of a preferential capital gains tax in the United States is not overwhelming; neither has it been completely refuted.[39] The alternative tax structures discussed in this chapter would be more equitable and less prone to the arbitrary and highly localized allocation effects of the present preferential capital gains tax. However, it may be that preferential capital gains taxation provides a form of political safety valve which permits steeply progressive tax rates to be legislated without hindering growth of the economy. This need for a preferential capital gains tax rests on political grounds and is beyond the realm of this study. The fact remains that such a choice entails certain equity and allocation costs that could be sufficiently large to warrant an alternative solution.

[38] Benton F. Massell, "Capital Formation and Technological Change in United States Manufacturing," *Review of Economics and Statistics,* Vol. 42 (May 1960), pp. 182-88. Edward F. Denison, *The Sources of Economic Growth in the United States and the Alternatives Before Us,* Supplementary Paper No. 13 (Committee for Economic Development, 1962).

Studies by Solow point to a somewhat greater contribution of investment to growth, but the results are not yet clear cut. Robert M. Solow, "Technical Progress, Capital Formation, and Economic Growth," *American Economic Review,* Vol. 52, No. 2 (May 1962), pp. 76-86. Some discussion of Solow's work and an alternative model by Eitan Berglas appear in Arnold Harberger, "Taxation, Resource Allocation, and Welfare," in *The Role of Direct and Indirect Taxes in the Federal Revenue System,* a Conference Report of the National Bureau of Economic Research and the Brookings Institution (Princeton University Press, 1964), pp. 66-68.

[39] An interesting discussion of related issues appears in *The Role of Direct and Indirect Taxes in the Federal Revenue System* (cited in note 38 above), especially in Harberger's article on allocation effects.

CHAPTER IX

Proposals To Reduce the Lock-in Effect

UNDER THE PRESENT LAW, owners can postpone capital gains taxes indefinitely by holding their assets and avoiding realization through sale or exchange. The disincentives to trading assets inherent in this system could be eliminated in any of three ways: The tax could be freed from the principle of realization, and a means could be developed to tax gains periodically as they accrued. (See Chapter VIII.) Alternatively, the capital gains tax could be modified so that tax liability would not be incurred when assets were sold or exchanged. Finally, the extent to which capital gains are taxed could be reduced to minimize the tax costs associated with realization. Several versions of these approaches have been developed.

Reduction of the Capital Gains Tax

Most prominent among the reduced-taxation proposals are those that call for an increase in the capital gains deduction. It has been suggested that the proportion of capital gains excluded from gross income be increased to 70 or 75 percent.[1] As the exclusion of capital

[1] Jonathan A. Brown, "The Locked-in Problem," in Joint Committee on the Economic Report, *Federal Tax Policy for Economic Growth and Stability*, 84 Cong.

gains from the tax base was increased, the income tax would approach a schedular tax levied largely on recurrent contractual payments of rent, interest, and salaries. Other forms of income could be converted into capital gains. The incentives to convert profits, dividend payments, and other returns to entrepreneurial activity into the form of capital gains would become progressively greater as the margin between capital gains and ordinary income taxation was widened. Taxpayers could and would take advantage of the difficulty of defining eligible transactions to convert their receipts into capital gains.

Countries that have applied a schedular tax to income that excludes capital gains have discovered that a large proportion of the income of high-income persons escapes taxation.[2]

The taxpayer compliance costs, legal fees, and management effort that would be required in ferreting out the opportunities for tax avoidance would be augmented by a greater exclusion of capital gains from income. Greater stress would be placed on the weak links in the present capital assets definition and the arbitrary devices used to separate ordinary income from capital gains. The administrative effort devoted to litigation and auditing capital gains deductions would have to be increased. Tax yields would be reduced by a continuing erosion of income presently taxed at ordinary rates.

The effects on the capital market of a greater exclusion of capital gains would be mixed. Increased trading and increased savings would be associated with a lower level of disincentives and more preferential treatment of income saved through appreciation. However, the increased rates of retention of corporate earnings stimulated by the preferential capital gains tax might increase capital rationing and reduce the availability of funds to fledgling enterprises. (See pages 150-55 and 174-80.)

The New York Stock Exchange and the Treasury Department both have estimated that enough trading of assets would be induced under a system of reduced inclusion to increase Treasury revenues permanently. Reduced inclusion thus could finance a limited reduc-

---

1 sess. (1955), pp. 367-81. Reduced inclusion *and* a reduced maximum alternative rate were recommended in the New York Stock Exchange's interview study reported in *A New Look at the Capital Gains Tax Rate* (New York Stock Exchange, October 1965).

[2] Richard M. Titmuss, *Income Distribution and Social Change; A Study in Criticism* (London: George Allen & Unwin, 1962).

tion in current tax rates. Any economic effects of this change in tax structure would be secondary in character. The Treasury has estimated that with the capital gains deduction increased to 70 percent, there would be a net revenue increase of approximately $600 million when the proposal was fully effective.[3] The New York Stock Exchange estimated that a $120 million increase in revenues would be associated with the sale of stocks if the deduction were increased to 60 percent and that the alternative tax would provide for a maximum rate of tax on capital gains of 20 percent. An increase in revenues of $320 million would result from sales of stock if the deduction were increased to 75 percent of capital gains and the alternative maximum rate were reduced to 12.5 percent. Since the gains on corporate stock comprised slightly less than half of all gains realized in 1959, one would expect an aggregate increase in revenues of perhaps twice as much. However, it is likely that the turnover of assets of other types would be less influenced by tax considerations. Real estate and business assets are less liquid and more likely to be held for current income.

A reduced percentage inclusion would have some positive economic effects—at an unpredictable cost of increased distortion of investment activity toward areas particularly favored by capital gains treatment, and of decreased equity in the tax structure.

Roll-over of Capital Gains

Several proposals to mitigate the lock-in effect of capital gains taxation call for the postponement of tax liability so long as the proceeds of an asset transaction are appropriately reinvested. This proposed modification of the income tax has been termed a "roll-over of capital gains."

Since roll-over is basically a principle for determining the timing of tax payments on capital gains, it could be incorporated into any one of many systems for taxing capital gains. Gains may be taxed at

[3] *President's 1963 Tax Message,* Hearings before the House Committee on Ways and Means, 88 Cong. 1 sess. (1963), Pt. 1, pp. 63 and 708. The immediate revenue loss would be $110 million on the present tax base for individuals; however, the increased turnover of assets would produce a $450 million increase; and induced changes associated with the increased level of economic activity stimulated by the tax cut proposed in 1963 would produce a $260 million increase.

FIGURE 9-1. Roll-over of Gains When Net Investment Accompanies Trading

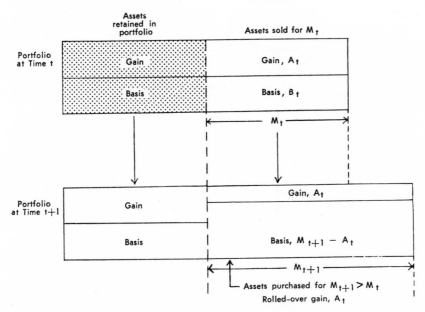

preferential or at ordinary income rates; losses may be recognized immediately, or they may be deferred so long as gains are not recognized. Whatever the corollary aspects of the tax structure, roll-over would increase the investor's ability to defer taxes on capital gains if he maintained a stock of assets that did not decrease. (See Figures 9-1 and 9-2.)

Reuben Clark has offered the following proposal for roll-over treatment:

1. If the amount of purchases of capital assets exceeded the amount of sales, any net gain on those sales would be deducted from the basis of the assets acquired. The deduction from basis would be prorated among the assets acquired in proportion to their acquisition cost.

2. If the amount of purchases of capital assets were less than the amount of sales, gains on the sales would be recognized to the extent of the net reduction in value of the capital assets. Any gain in excess of that difference would be deferred by reducing the basis of assets acquired, as in 1.

FIGURE 9-2. Roll-over of Gains When Net Disinvestment Occurs

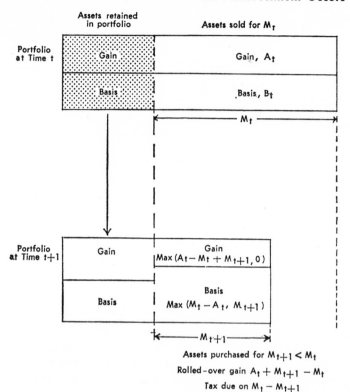

3. If sales of capital assets resulted in a net loss for the current tax year, the loss could be deducted from ordinary income as under present law.

In combination, these rules establish the mechanics of rollover.[4] Compliance with the proposal would require little more effort than

[4] Reuben Clark, "The Paradox of Capital Gains: Taxable Income That Ought Not To Be Currently Taxed," in House Committee on Ways and Means, *Tax Revision Compendium* (1959), Vol. 2, pp. 1243-56.
Mr. Clark supplied the following examples:

(1) *Realization of net gain with full reinvestment of proceeds*
Assume taxpayer A holds three assets at the beginning of a taxable year with cost basis in his hands of $200, $150 and $125, respectively. During the year he sells asset No. 1 for $235, retains asset No. 2, and sells asset No. 3 for $120. His net gain for the year is thus $30. Also, during the same year he purchases asset No. 4 for $300 and asset No. 5 for $150. Thus, his cost basis in the new assets is, without adjustment, $450. Since his total purchases for the year ($450) exceed

with present law. The taxpayer would have to allocate his gains to the basis of new property acquired during the year. He would also have to compare the value of purchases (not now required in reporting income) with the value of sales. The necessary accounting is required now when gains on sales of residences or nonrecognized exchange are reported for tax purposes.

Administrative Problems of Roll-over

Simplicity for the taxpayer does not mean corresponding ease of tax administration. The accounting required would be more difficult to police than under taxation on realization, since the market does not provide an automatic check on the amount of appreciation in any individual's portfolio. The price of an asset on the date of purchase is not generally the basis of property sold. Thus, tax administrators are not able to verify the basis of property sold by checking the published prices of securities. Verification requires that the taxpayer maintain a record of gains allocated in the year of purchase. This record would entail a complete tax history for any taxpayer who has done a lot of asset trading. Maintenance of a tax history could easily become an administrative nightmare for taxpayers and tax administrators alike. However, the Internal Revenue Service could maintain a file of the required data, just as the Social Security Administration now main-

---

his sales ($355), the full amount of his gain is considered to be reinvested, with nonrecognized gain of $30 being allocated proportionately to reduce the basis of the new assets. Thus, at the end of the year, A holds asset No. 2 with a cost basis of $150, asset No. 4 with a basis of $280, and asset No. 5 with a basis of $140.

(2) *Realization of net gain with partial reinvestment of proceeds*
    Assume, in example (1) above, that asset No. 4 costs $250 and asset No. 5 costs $100. In this event, total sales ($355) would exceed total purchases ($350) by $5 and, accordingly, gain in this amount would be recognized. The total basis of the new assets would be reduced by $25. At the end of the year, A thus holds asset No. 2 with a cost basis of $150, asset No. 4 with a basis of, to the nearest dollar, $232, and asset No. 5 with a basis of $93.

(3) *Realization of net loss with full reinvestment of proceeds*
    Assume, in example (1) above, that asset No. 1 is sold for $195 and asset No. 3 for $120. An ordinary loss of $10 is allowed for such year, with no adjustment being made in the cost basis of assets No. 4 and No. 5. Thus, at the end of the year, A holds asset No. 2 with a cost basis of $150, asset No. 4 with a basis of $300, and asset No. 5 with a basis of $150.

tains a partial wage history for every earner who has ever paid Social Security payroll taxes.

The treatment of losses under Clark's proposal appears to be anomalous.[5] Taxpayers would be permitted current loss offsets, yet could defer all gains. As a result, taxpayers could defer not only the taxes due on the average appreciation, but also the taxes on the average losses incurred in a diversified portfolio. To avoid the resulting deferral of tax payments, it would seem desirable to establish a way of limiting roll-over to the amount of gains in excess of realized losses. That could be accomplished by the capital loss reserve proposed in Chapter VI.

The incentives to avoid tax payment on gains could be reduced, but not eliminated, by an interest adjustment. The cumulative value of gains and losses rolled over could be used as the principal upon which the government would apply an interest charge, say at the rate charged on commercial paper. With this adjustment, an investor would be faced with three choices: (1) to hold the investment for later sale, (2) to sell and pay concomitant capital gains taxes, or (3) to sell, roll over gains, and pay interest adjustment now and capital gains taxes later.

Alternative 3 would not require the investor to liquidate a part of his investment to make tax payments at the time that trading appears profitable. He would have to recognize the value of tax deferral through the interest adjustment. Under this system there would be no interest adjustment for appreciation that is accruing on the portfolio. The interest adjustment would begin only when assets in the portfolio were sold. This alternative may be regarded as a hybrid of a complete system of interest adjustment (such as is possible with cumulative averaging) and the present system (in which no interest adjustment occurs, even when gains are not recognized and rolled over).[6]

In fact, there is considerable latitude within the present law to avoid recognition of gain, even when assets are traded or exchanged.

---

[5] He defends the treatment on the grounds that he advocates full taxation of capital gains. That appears to be a *non sequitur*. The rate of taxation does not prevent taxpayers from deferring income taxes by culling capital losses from their growing portfolios.

[6] There was considerable support for roll-over in the conference discussion. Discussants were prepared to accept roll-over if a satisfactory interest adjustment could be developed. The adjustment proposed here was developed in response to the conferees' interest. See Chap. X, pp. 219-20.

There is no quantitative data on the amount of such roll-overs (permitted under Sections 1031-34, 351, and others, of the Internal Revenue Code). Lawyers and investment counselors are quick to advise their clients on the benefits provided; and it is possible that roll-over is already being used on a substantial number of exchanges of businesses, real property, and corporate properties in the process of reorganization. A comprehensive roll-over system with an interest adjustment would rationalize the *ad hoc* system that has already developed. (See Chapter II, pages 13-17.)

A system providing for the roll-over of capital gains taxes clearly calls for presumptive realization of capital gains at death (if one is interested in preserving a modicum of income taxation) or a sufficient increase in estate taxation to offset the lifetime accumulation of assets that becomes possible under an expenditure tax system. If gains were not recognized at death, roll-over would mean zero taxation of capital gains of all investors whose assets were accumulated for bequest or inadvertently not consumed prior to death. An investor who maintained until his death a stock of assets that did not decrease would never be required to pay tax. Other investors would have to pay taxes on gains only to the extent that accumulated assets were sold to meet retirement consumption. Such consumption could be financed indirectly by loans against assets; in that case, capital gains taxes would not be paid in spite of liquidation of the taxpayer's net worth. The small amount of capital gains taxes that were paid would be paid principally by aged persons who were consuming their lifetime accumulation of wealth and by a few luckless individuals who were unable to maintain an inventory of assets.

Without presumptive realization, the proposed plan for capital gains roll-over would be similar to a schedular income tax that exempted capital gains altogether, regardless of the rate treatment of realized gains. The incentives to convert income into gains on capital assets might well be greater than under the present system with reduced rates on capital gains. Under roll-over any short-term investment could be used to produce gains that would permanently escape taxation. Under the present system with reduced rates, a nominal tax would be collected.

If presumptive realization were combined with roll-over, the tax advantage of capital gains over ordinary income would consist only of preferential rate treatment and a lifetime deferment of actual tax payment. Roll-over in combination with presumptive realization at preferential rates would mean a lower present value of tax payments than would the current system with presumptive realization added. The roll-over scheme would eliminate lifetime incentives to defer asset sales. It would do so at the cost of taxing gains realized by persons who were unable to maintain a beginning-of-the-year level of investment in capital assets. The burden of tax payment thus would fall more heavily on those who were likely to have suffered reverses in their business activities or who had especially great need for current consumption. Thus, a system of periodic accrual of gains would seem to provide more equitable tax treatment.

Clark and others who support roll-over suggest taxing gains at death at a rate determined by rates applicable to ordinary income and an averaging provision. This would mean a greater lifetime tax burden than under the present system. However, the increased revenues could be used to reduce tax rates generally, thus reducing some of the need to liquidate portfolios.

The Scope of Roll-over

The rate treatment of recognized gains, the definition of eligible assets, and the treatment of gains accumulated in a decedent's estate would continue to be the same perplexing problems that they are under the present law. Furthermore, roll-over would not be appropriate for corporate income taxation.

If roll-over were applied to sales of capital assets by corporations, gains could be deferred indefinitely. This possibility could be avoided by excluding corporations from the privileges of roll-over.[7] However, that solution would limit the favorable effects to changes in the portfolio behavior of individuals. Corporations would continue to experience whatever lock-in effect presently influences their portfolio behavior.

Whether roll-over should be applied to fiduciary taxpayers is not clear. Insofar as fiduciaries serve purposes other than tax avoidance and have a definite life span, roll-over appears appropriate. However, trusts established with a lifetime longer than that of the average investor could rapidly absorb a large part of all capital gains, with the prospect that gains could be carried forward for periods as long as, or longer than would be possible with carry-over of basis. When this

[7] Clark proposed both this exclusion and presumptive realization (*op. cit.*, p. 1255).

possibility is considered, along with the fact that use of fiduciaries to avoid taxation is increasing rapidly and that professional managers of fiduciaries are well aware of the possibilities of reducing tax liabilities through capital gains, how much roll-over should be granted fiduciaries becomes problematical. Perhaps roll-over ought to be denied such legal entities as a check against the other tax advantages which they make possible.[8]

If it were enacted, roll-over would have to be restricted to a narrower set of transactions than those included under the present capital asset definition, or the tax base could become seriously eroded.[9] Restricting roll-over treatment to transactions included under an investment asset definition would probably be more equitable, since tax avoidance would be restricted to investments with broad markets. The problems that would be entailed in narrowing the area eligible for preferred treatment are the same as those discussed in Chapter VI.

The roll-over proposal cannot be defended as an approach to expenditure taxation. Recognition of gain is not related to changes in net worth, but only to changes in assets held. In addition, the deferral of tax on gains provided by roll-over would not exempt saving (other than saving through asset appreciation) from taxation. Thus roll-over can be defended only as an *ad hoc* and limited solution for eliminating lifetime lock-in experienced by individuals.

Roll-over would probably create new administrative difficulties in the taxation of capital gains in return for some unlocking of individual portfolios. Presumptive realization and narrowing of the area eligible for preferred treatment would be necessary if undermining of the tax on ordinary income is to be avoided.

[8] The conferees indicated that fiduciaries were not concerned with lock-in of assets. Professional managers generally consider it advantageous to trade investments and realize capital gains regularly to avoid progression on fiduciary income. That is, the fiduciary can minimize taxes by realizing limited amounts of capital gains annually rather than accumulating a large gain that would be taxable at higher rates. (The fiduciary, of course, is taxed under the same schedule as individuals, and only the largest trusts are likely to produce enough income or capital gains to be affected by the alternative rate computation.)

For an elaboration of this view, see the conference summary, Chap. X, p. 219.

[9] Clark (*op. cit.,* p. 1253) favors eliminating the present favored treatment for timber and coal royalties and situations in which the assets sold represent mere "rights to receive future income." He also favors averaging and applying ordinary income rates to gains (pp. 1247, 1249).

Roll-over would result in a difference between the tax treatment of corporations and that of individuals that does not appear desirable and would fail to solve lock-in problems of the corporation. It thus appears a rather mixed offering which is appealing at first glance but presents some problems on closer examination, as do all the alternatives examined in this and previous chapters.

CHAPTER X

Conference Discussion and Conclusions

THIRTY-TWO ECONOMISTS, lawyers, and investment counselors convened in May 1966 to discuss problems associated with capital gains taxation and the various proposals that have been made for structural changes in the present system. The group consisted of experts well versed in various phases of the present law and its operation. Each participant contributed a rich personal experience in analyzing and using capital gains tax provisions in his professional life.

The conference made clear that fundamental questions of tax equity and the incentive effects of capital gains taxation are at issue in seeking an alternative to the present system. Technical expertise did not and cannot resolve debate over questions that have to do basically with the appropriate progression of the tax structure and the desirable level of estate and transfer taxation. Experts could agree that some possible alternatives are technically inferior to the present system and that it would be possible to redesign the present tax system, without altering existing *effective* tax rates, if an objective for change in the system could be established.

The conferees could not agree on what is the probable impact of the present tax structure on investment and economic growth. Disagreement among the conferees reflected varying opinions on the importance of this effect for the economy, on the magnitude of the effect on investment, and on the particular structural elements of the tax system that might induce or inhibit investment effects.

This conference summary thus reports areas of technical agreement and substantive disagreement. The relative numbers who expressed particular points of view do not imply that legislators, the educated public, or policy makers have similar feelings. Thus agreement among the conferees does not indicate overwhelming popular support or agreement among policy makers sufficient to produce changes in the procedures for taxing capital gains in this country. Some indications of the relative numbers adhering to particular views are supplied to give the flavor of the conference discussion, and not to suggest that opinions expressed in the group are in any sense representative.

Capital Gains and Taxpaying Ability

The conference began with a discussion of the basic question: Do capital gains represent taxpaying ability? Two views were expressed. The first was that income ought to be measured by the consumption and accretion of net worth enjoyed by a taxpayer during a given period. Proponents of this accretion definition of income regard capital gains as ordinary income. They argued that although capital gains are sometimes windfalls, they are more often deliberately sought.

The alternative view—that capital gains are *not* income—was argued on three principal grounds. (1) Empirical studies suggest that capital gains do not produce the same effect on consumption as does personal income as defined in the national accounts. To look on capital gains as income thus would mean modifying the convenient aggregative relationships that have characterized Keynesian economics. (2) Capital gains are excluded from the national accounts definition of personal income. If a taxable-income concept that includes capital gains were adopted, the tax base would aggregate to a dollar amount that is larger (or smaller) than personal income by the dollar amount of capital gains (losses). (3) The view was expressed that the tax burden should be divided according to real rather than nominal concepts. Nominal capital gains arising from inflation would not be included in the concept of taxable capacity; only those gains that were additions to real wealth would be taxed.

Economic Aspects of the Definition of Taxable Income

In the discussion that followed, many qualifications were suggested.

Since there are many measures of "income," each of which serves its own particular purpose, it is not relevant that the aggregate tax base (including the capital gains of all individuals) does not equal income under a national income concept; "national income" was never intended to be used as a basis for taxing individual incomes.

The Keynesian theory of consumption would not necessarily be altered if consumers made decisions on the basis of permanent income and capital gains currently consisted of large transient windfalls. Finally, there is a large class of capital gains and losses which cancel in the aggregate; for example, gains to an innovator in production techniques are offset by the losses suffered by his competitors, and so on. The question remains whether the former enhance the taxable capacity of the innovator and the latter reduce the taxable capacity of competitors, quite independently of any aggregative calculus of national income.

The questions raised by this discussion led the group to consider the global effects of taxation. Achieving equity in taxation would require first a determination of the combined incidence of wealth and income taxes. The total tax burden should be equitably apportioned in relation to some aggregate measures of taxpaying capacity that go beyond income. Since the conferees did not lay down any concrete guidelines for wealth taxation, this point of view was not developed.

Real Measures of Taxable Capacity

Of those who felt that capital gains are in fact income, a considerable number proposed that *real*, rather than nominal, income should measure taxpaying ability. Specifically, gains and losses on assets corresponding to general price movements and to secular shifts in market rates of interest, and perhaps even those corresponding to changes in the community's capitalization of potential earnings, should be excluded from the tax base. It was felt that in the postwar period recapitalization has occurred because investors have come to believe that major depressions can be avoided.

Some who proposed taxing all real income felt that any nominal capital gains not taxed as income could be assessed under a system independent of the income tax. A fixed excise on capital gains excluded from real income measures would accomplish this objective.

Some who proposed adjusting the definition of capital gains to exclude nominal gains corresponding to an aggregate concept of personal income felt that the present tax system provides a rough compromise. Income is generally taxed at high rates, but the tax rate on capital gains never exceeds 25 percent.

Gains could be viewed as a separate base, whose taxability is a matter for policy determination without reference to income taxation. Indeed, one conferee proposed the abolition of all capital gains taxation. He considered it unnecessary and undesirable in its economic effects.

Incentives and the Definition of Capital Gains

Recent research has shown that many people do not treat their capital gains as income,[1] suggesting that taxing capital gains may have different economic effects than taxing other income. One participant pointed out that a major difference between income and capital gains is that people control the timing of capital gains tax payments, but they do not have control over the timing of income tax payments. Others felt that since capital gains taxes reduce savings rather than consumption, it is desirable to give capital gains preferential tax treatment in order to maintain the flow into the investment stream of funds that are accumulated through saving. However, it was pointed out that this treats savings obtained through the reinvestment of earnings from equity assets differently from savings obtained by other means. The feeling of most participants was that if exemption of savings from taxation is desired, it would be better to deal with the problem generally, rather than exempt only savings from certain sources. Although there was no general consensus on the exact nature of capital gains as a basis for taxation, participants generally agreed that capital gains do represent taxpaying ability.[2]

---

[1] John J. Arena, "Postwar Stock Market Changes and Consumer Spending," *Review of Economics and Statistics,* Vol. 47 (November 1965), pp. 379-91.

[2] One participant said, "It seems to me that there is no a priori criterion for what constitutes a proper definition of income. It is entirely functional and depends on what you are going to use it for."

Use of Additional Revenue from Capital Gains Taxation

Few conferees advocated reducing the present rate of tax on capital gains. If this consensus were implemented, any change made in the capital gains tax would probably result in an increase in tax revenue. The following proposals for using the additional revenue from capital gains were mentioned at the conference: (1) increase the personal income tax exemption, (2) reduce all personal income tax rates, (3) reduce the corporation tax, (4) reduce the income tax so as to maintain the existing effective tax rate in each bracket, (5) reduce the estate tax, and (6) reduce top bracket income tax rates to a maximum of 40 or 50 percent.

There was very little discussion of these possible alternative revenue uses. The conferees seemed more inclined to discuss the various reform packages treated in the next section. However, there was some specific comment on the estate tax. First, there was general agreement, based on data such as those presented in Chapter IV, that constructive realization of capital gains at gift and bequest would yield revenue comparable in amount to the revenue yield of the present estate tax. The added revenue from the capital gains tax then could be used to reduce the estate tax rate if that were desired. Second, it was pointed out that constructive realization tied with a reduced estate tax would produce a gain in equity. Two persons with the same amount of gain, one of whom realizes before death and the other of whom does not, would be taxed equally under constructive realization; without constructive realization, the taxpayer who did not realize during his lifetime would pay less total tax.[3]

Considerable interest was kindled by a discussion on how much the corporate tax rate could be reduced if capital gains were taxed as they accrued. It was estimated that taxing accrued capital gains on publicly traded corporate stocks could finance a reduction in the corporate rate to 23 percent if the typical marginal rate of the corporate stockholder were 50 percent.[4] However, the discussants were unde-

---

[3] See also discussion of constructive realization in the section on Some Separable Issues, below.

[4] For a detailed analysis of the theory behind these calculations, see Martin J. Bailey, "Capital Gains and Income Taxation," in Arnold C. Harberger and Martin J. Bailey (eds.), *Taxation of Income from Capital* (Brookings Institution, 1968). The analysis is based on Bailey's estimate of the effective capital gains tax rate. The basic formula used is presented in this book as Equation (6.1).

cided whether such a change in tax structure would be desirable, even if the practical difficulties could be overcome.

There were two differing views about the use of additional revenue from changes in capital gains taxation if they should be made. One member said, "I would think that if there is revenue to be gained in this sort of revision, it ought to be applied in the same tax area rather than in the area of estate and gift taxes," although another said, "The question of what you do with the additional revenue . . . [from] constructive realization reminds me of my clients who feel if they have a loss on U.S. Steel, they have to buy other steel stocks; and I say, 'You have cash. See what is good to buy'. It seems to me that [from the point of view of] . . . the Treasury, we have this much to distribute in [revenue from] gains, and we should find the best way to do it, and it doesn't necessarily relate to capital gains."

General Revision of Capital Gains Taxation

During the discussion of the income concept and the structure of personal tax rates, the participants spoke of limited amendment of and general revision of the capital gains tax. The discussion of general revision centered around: (1) taxation of accrued gains, tied with a corporate rate reduction; (2) cumulative averaging, with interest adjustments; (3) prorating gains, and (4) roll-over. Underlying all of these is the idea that constructive realization of gains at gift or death would apply to all assets and that capital gains would not receive preferential rate treatment.[5]

Taxation of Capital Gains on Accrual

The accrual proposal discussed at the conference had two elements: (1) taxing gains on marketed assets, which are easily valued as they accrue, and (2) choice of either accrual or taxation of gain on realization for other assets. It was pointed out that exempting one form of investment from accrual would create an incentive to shift investment into that form. Serious misallocation of resources and ad-

---

[5] While roll-over need not necessarily tax 100 percent of the gains that are not reinvested, that is the proposal that was discussed at the conference.

verse growth effects might result. The lawyers and investment counselors present emphasized the valuation difficulties that might arise with accrual. They pointed out that since a closely held corporation can show almost any income it wants, it would be very difficult to obtain a valuation for tax purposes.[6]

Several possible solutions were suggested. The value of assets other than publicly traded corporate shares and bonds could be assessed by the owner with an accompanying (publicly announced) offer to sell the asset at, say, 20 percent above the valuation price. Another alternative would be to value closely held businesses and real property at intervals longer than one year if an appropriate interest adjustment were introduced to reduce the value of deferral to the taxpayer; this provision would be applied only to those assets on which there was no ready way to determine market value.[7]

Economists tended to emphasize the economic benefits of accrual taxation. Simplification of the tax law[8] and the complete elimination of lock-in were those most often cited. One difficulty with the proposal is that taxpayers might not have ready cash to pay the accrued tax. It was pointed out that some of the needed cash might be generated by increased dividend payout by corporations, especially if accrual were tied with a reduced corporate tax rate, as proposed. Unfortunately, there was not enough time at the conference for participants to give much thought to this latter point, which may account for some skeptical comments regarding the feasibility of the proposal.

One participant guessed that the current $300 billion to $500 billion in stock outstanding might fluctuate in value from year to year by as much as $100 billion. Perhaps one-third of that fluctuation would be reflected in revenue yield. Further, because gross national product and the level of the stock market are not always well correlated, revenue fluctuations under accrual might sometimes be stabilizing and at other times destabilizing, thus requiring frequent ad-

[6] In response to this, one discussant replied, "Still there are an awful lot of assets that can be valued annually, and I am not sure you should throw out the opportunity to do that just because others can't [be valued]."

[7] "It is quite apparent that if we moved to accrual and did not distinguish, therefore, capital assets from other types of assets, we could dispense with about half to two-thirds of the Internal Revenue Code, including all the reorganization provisions and a great deal of other material in there."

[8] One member observed that so much attention to the taxing of gains from property ought to be matched with equal concern for taxing human wealth; perhaps capital gains associated with education ought to be taxed.

justments of income tax rates in the interest of maintaining economic stability.

A possible way of making an orderly transition to an accrual system was also discussed. Taxing only gains occurring after accrual was enacted was considered as the most likely procedure. Gains that had accrued before that time would be taxed when the taxpayer disposed of the securities. In short, new gains accruing would be taxed on accrual, and past gains would be taxed on realization. It was observed that this transition rule would entail a complete inventory of asset values at the time when accrual became effective. This would be cumbersome and expensive for the same reasons that subsequent valuations would be difficult, as was pointed out above.

Cumulative Averaging

The discussion turned to an alternative to accrual: a cumulative averaging system, with built-in interest adjustments and 100 percent inclusion of capital gains in income. Great differences of opinion were expressed. Some regarded cumulative averaging as a logical way to solve the major problems in capital gains taxation. Electronic data processing would make accounting easy and exact.[9] Others maintained that cumulative averaging was not attractive politically or administratively. There seemed to be two main reasons for the latter position.

First, a cumulative averaging system would present the taxpayer with a book of tables from which he would find his tax. "These tables would simply be a great mystery. They would be handed down by somebody in the administration. The ordinary citizen would have no way of determining that he was being fairly treated . . . "

Second, the individual taxpayer would have a very hard time determining his exact marginal rate of taxation, which might affect his economic behavior. Proponents of averaging pointed out that taxpayers would still have a general idea of their marginal rates—which may be all the information that is available to them *ex ante* under the present system. The need to know one's marginal tax rates would be reduced since cumulative averaging would remove the incentive for taxpayers to take taxes into account when making decisions about the timing of capital asset sales.

[9] "I would just like to say that though I advocate accrual I also advocate this [cumulative averaging], and of the two I think this one is by far the more feasible; and I think it would accomplish virtually everything that accrual taxation would."

Using a single interest rate for an adjustment factor would be rather imperfect. Some people with a high prospective return on their investments would continue to gain from deferral by the difference between that return and the interest adjustment factor. But it was pointed out that there is no interest adjustment for deferral now; whatever positive rate was used for an interest adjustment factor, it would be better than the present situation. However, although it would be ideal to catch everyone at the margin, it would not be feasible to do so.[10]

The question of different time paths of income brought up the problem of how far back averaging should go. Some participants felt that as of some date in the past "by-gones should be by-gones," on both practical and equity grounds.[11] Others felt that the differing time paths of income in different occupations called for averaging over an entire lifetime. As a compromise it was suggested that arbitrary weights be given to the income of earlier years so as to include that income but not give it very much importance.[12]

Most members did not have strong views on the appropriate length of the averaging period. Some felt that it should be less than one's lifetime and that Vickrey's cumulative averaging scheme was too extreme on that point. Many felt that a five-year averaging system, with some interest adjustment, should suffice. This would assume constructive realization at gift and bequest and would permit recomputation of the tax once, and only once, every five years as if the income

[10] The possible treatment of secondary labor force participation under a cumulative averaging system also brought comments. Should a wife be allowed to average if she works until she has children and returns to the labor force when the children are old enough to go to school?

Another problem discussed was when to allow students and others with long training periods to start averaging. If they are allowed to average only after they have completed their training, they would be taxed more heavily than others with equal total lifetime incomes earned over a longer period of time. One suggestion to create more equitable tax treatment was to allow a person to start averaging as soon as he begins professional training. Another was to let everyone start averaging at the same age.

[11] "[I do not regard] the equities of a lifetime averaging system . . . as obvious. I think it is much less equitable than a short-period accounting system, one year or up to five years, or something like that. I see no reason why a tax on a gain in 1980 should be influenced by the tax we had in 1960."

[12] However, one member summed up the opposition to this compromise as follows: "To me, straining for some abstract point of perfection at the loss of comprehensibility [of the tables] is much too high a price to pay."

were received ratably over the five-year period. The date of inception would be voluntary.[13]

A disadvantage of the cumulative averaging proposal, cited at the conference, is that the timing of losses would still be controlled by the taxpayer. A taxpayer with both gains and losses could keep taking losses and offsetting them against current income, while the gains would be taxed in the distant future or at death.

Proration of Capital Gains

The next possible revision discussed was prorating gains. The package proposed was similar to that discussed in Chapter VIII and would moderate the effect of rate progression on realized capital gains. Prorating gains would be a way of avoiding a general averaging scheme with its need for data from past tax years. At the same time, prorating capital gains would reduce the tax consequences of the "bunching" of gains accrued over a long period of time.

One problem with a prorating device would be that prior to expected tax increases, taxpayers would get a premium by selling and prorating at the lower rate instead of waiting to sell in the following year, when the tax rates would be higher. It was suggested that this problem of timing in anticipation of tax changes could be avoided by applying the relevant marginal tax rate of each of the years to the prorated gain for that year. The conferees, however, were generally opposed to this on two grounds: First, the problem would not be great, especially if there were no great tax changes in the foreseeable future. Second, the added complications in the tax structure—especially for assets held for a long time—would be too high a price to pay for a minor refinement. The conferees felt that the best prorating device would be one that would reduce the progression on capital gains and that would be simple to use and administer. A brief discussion of the proration factor revealed no evidence contrary to that presented in Chapter IV. Simulation studies presented there suggest that it makes little difference whether the proration factor is three, five, or ten.

Most members of the conference supported the proration device, especially when it was presented with the present system as the alternative. A vocal minority thought that the tax system could be im-

---

[13] Essentially this is the Simons-Groves plan for averaging. See Chap VIII, notes 8 and 21.

proved still further by moving to a general averaging system, such as the proposed cumulative averaging system discussed above.

Roll-over of Capital Gains

The fourth alternative discussed was a package that would include roll-over for reinvested gains, the full taxation of remaining gains as ordinary income, constructive realization at gift and bequest (at capital gains rates), and limited income averaging. In addition, the conferees thought that it would be desirable to eliminate the benefit of tax deferral from continual roll-over through some interest adjustment.

Some felt that tax avoidance difficulties might arise if long-term trusts and fiduciaries were allowed to roll over gains corresponding to reinvested proceeds. A possible way around this problem would be to tax trusts and fiduciaries on an accrual basis. In addition, although this was not specifically discussed at the conference, corporations would probably not be allowed to roll over.[14]

The conference gave considerable support to the roll-over proposal. Many members felt that it would take away the offensive part of the present capital gains tax and that it would help to maintain and possibly increase the volume of savings in the investment stream.[15] Others felt that if roll-over were enacted, it would move the system in the direction of an expenditure tax. This same group felt that if expenditure taxation is desired, that form of tax should be adopted.[16]

A compromise system like the present one creates gross inequities. When the participants were presented with a choice between the current tax and the roll-over proposal with an interest adjustment, they seemed to prefer roll-over.

Losses constituted a major stumbling block to the roll-over pro-

[14] See Chap. IX for a more complete discussion of this point.

[15] Other conferees disagreed with the notion that roll-over would tend to increase savings. This disagreement highlights the great need for further empirical knowledge in this area.

[16] One participant remarked, "I don't see why a person who has a savings account which is never touched and gets interest which is reinvested in the savings account is in a fundamentally different position than [that of] someone who invests in the stock market and reinvests without taking out. . . . Hence, expenditure taxation is to be preferred over income and preferential capital gains taxation, which differentiate between the two situations described above. We are saying that consumption should be taxed but income that goes into savings, as long as it goes into savings and investment, should not be taxed."

posal. It was suggested that losses could either be recognized currently against ordinary income or else be used to adjust the remaining basis of the assets in the account after the losses were realized. Current recognition of losses was favored as necessary to stimulate risk-taking. However, if losses were recognized currently against ordinary income, it would be possible for a taxpayer to realize the losses and deduct them from ordinary income while rolling over gains. The taxpayer would thus get a deferment of liability far in excess of the average gain on assets. The conference could suggest no remedy for this problem during the brief discussion of roll-over.

Finally, it was emphasized that roll-over (like the proration proposal discussed above) would not solve the problem of determining which assets are capital assets. Roll-over would obviate the need for a holding period, with its accompanying notch effect on lock-in.

Some Separable Issues

Aside from the general revision schemes just reviewed, some separable issues were discussed extensively. The first and possibly the most important of these was constructive realization. Most of the participants felt that there was no justification for the present step-up of basis at death.

Constructive Realization vs. Carry-over of Basis

Only two or three conferees preferred carry-over of basis to constructive realization. Several arguments were made in favor of carry-over. Carry-over would create fewer liquidity problems than would constructive realization, since the timing of realization would be voluntary and would be accompanied by cash receipts in most cases. The deferral that would be possible under carry-over would limit the extent to which taxation would reduce the stock of savings rather than current income. Proponents of carry-over also expressed the view that any levy at death should be in the form of the estate tax, which is a tax purely on wealth, and not in the form of the capital gains tax, which contains aspects of an income tax.

The majority at the conference strongly preferred constructive realization to carry-over of basis. They argued that carry-over of basis would not solve, and might aggravate, lock-in problems. It would

also create great administrative difficulties. However, it would reduce present inequities in the taxation of incomes. Under carry-over
of basis, income would ultimately be subject to tax assessment regardless of its source. Lawyers and accountants at the conference objected to carry-over of basis because of allocation problems and the
information that would be required under such a system. Executors
of estates and fiduciaries would have to allocate both the current
value of an estate or trust and its basis to the various heirs. There
would be pressures to allocate higher basis items to the wealthier
heirs. The executor might have to trace ownership of an asset
through several persons or generations in order to determine its basis
over several past years.

Most, if not all, of the participants thought that transfers between
spouses should be excluded from constructive realization. Carry-over
of basis would apply to such transfers during the lifetime of the transferor or at his death. General sentiment also favored complete
exclusion from the estate tax of transfers to the spouse.[17] Whether
minor children should be given similar treatment was admitted to be
a difficult question and was unresolved at the conference.

The tax scheme envisaged by most of the conferees thus would
provide for constructive realization of gains on any assets passing to
individuals outside the marital unit, while ownership of assets of the
husband and wife would be viewed as if there were no legal distinction between the two individuals. There would not be a levy on capital gains resulting from any transfers between spouses, but accrued
capital gains would continue to be reflected in the potential liability
implied by the original basis of the asset.

Charitable contributions could be handled in several ways under a
system of constructive realization. Three alternatives were discussed:
(1) the present system of allowing full deduction of the value of the
asset from the value of the estate without constructive realization of
gains for income tax purposes, (2) a system of taxing gains constructively and at the same time allowing a full deduction, and (3) a system without constructive realization but with only the original basis

---

[17] One participant said: ". . . it seems to me one can argue that on the death of the
husband, the wife can't be said to be better off merely because property is now held
in her name instead of in joint tenancy or in the husband's name. Whereas, when
there is a transfer of property outside the husband-wife relationship, it seems just a
lot clearer that the recipient is better off than prior to the death of the decedent."

allowed as a deduction. Although no specific agreement was reached at the conference, there did seem to be a general feeling that continuing the present system would not cause any great problems. The conferees were concerned that little is known about the possible reduction in philanthropy that might result from a shift to the second or third proposals. Some past studies seem to indicate that the elasticity of amounts contributed with respect to the tax is less than one: tax treatment does not appear to affect community philanthropy and has only a modest impact on support of religious institutions. However, studies of philanthropic support of higher education suggest a high correlation between tax benefits and the volume of giving. Thus, the need for more information in this area is obvious.

The Transition to Constructive Realization

The practical difficulties that might be involved in constructive realization received considerable attention at the conference. Four proposals for the transition period were mentioned: (1) apply constructive realization to all gains measured from the original basis; (2) apply constructive realization to all gains accrued after some date in the past; (3) apply constructive realization only to gains accruing after enactment; and (4) apply constructive realization to all gains, as in (1), but provide that the resulting tax be reduced in inverse proportion to the time elapsed since enactment. For example, reduce the tax due on constructively realized gains by two-thirds in the year of enactment and one-third in the following year and apply the full tax in all following years. This would provide a period of 24 months in which investors could reorganize their portfolios without facing the full costs of constructive realization if they should die before their portfolios had been adjusted. Again, the conferees were divided on this subject. A few felt that the tax should not apply to all unrealized gains that have accrued up to the time of enactment because ". . . people have planned their estates, their portfolios, on the basis of the present step-up, and it would be unfortunate to change the rules on them . . . " Others felt that no real inequities would arise if the rules were changed. People anticipating a stepped-up basis at death, who refrained from taking advantage of some investment opportunity at some time in the past, couldn't have been considering an overwhelmingly attractive opportunity, or it would have justified paying the tax in order to take advantage of it. Thus, only a limited inequity would arise from going back to the original basis of an asset to calculate the gain constructively realized. The majority of conferees preferred this approach combined with a transition arrangement like that suggested in (4) above.

Three suggestions were offered to increase the administrative feasibility of constructive realization. A flat dollar exemption could be used to link the estate tax population with the population to whom constructive realization applied. Certain classes of assets could be excluded on which gains were unlikely or hard to evaluate, such as household furniture, jewelry, and other personal effects. Those items, which are presently excluded from the estate tax, and a small dollar exemption ($5,000-$15,000) would be a generally workable exclusion from constructive realization. A separate exemption for small businesses and farms could also be made, designed to facilitate transfers of those kinds of property. Administrative problems would arise in determining the basis of small gifts and of securities received as dividends or spin-offs many years previously, for which records are generally not kept. Some of these problems may be avoided by appropriate exclusions. On balance, the conferees agreed that constructive realization was feasible.

Treatment of Losses

There was agreement also on the treatment of losses, no support being expressed for the present law's asymmetric treatment of long-term gains and losses. The present provision for using long-term losses to fully offset short-term gains could be changed to allow only 50 percent of long-term losses to be used to offset short-term gains. Substantial support was expressed for this. There was also support for liberalizing the present limitation on losses that can be deducted from ordinary income. More liberal loss offsets are appropriate if they do not aggravate the deferral of gains or asymmetric treatment. Liberalizing loss offsets, it was pointed out, would not violate equity to any substantial degree and would promote risk-taking because the investor with a true net long-term loss is probably a small investor "for whom a loss offset is a little moderation of a really tough wallop." Further, "if you increased it [the limitation on loss offset] to $2,000 or $5,000, I don't think the public purse would be destroyed."

No one objected seriously to allowing a decedent to carry back losses indefinitely if constructive realization were enacted. However, the interesting suggestion was made that if losses could be deducted from the net value of the estate, then a rough reduction in tax liability could be achieved through the estate tax. The need to go back and amend past income tax returns would be eliminated.

The loss reserve proposal (see Chapter VI) also drew favorable comment from several participants at the conference. Under the proposal, net losses taken against ordinary income would be accumulated in a reserve; subsequent gains would be taxed as ordinary income to the extent of the net loss reserve; and the amount of the reserve would be reduced for each dollar of gain taxed as ordinary income. One participant observed that constructive realization would be needed if this were adopted. Otherwise a taxpayer with a positive loss reserve would be able to avoid taxation by giving away appreciated securities to a relative and having the relative realize gain on his behalf without a concomitant tax liability.

The Alternative Rate

Various views on the alternative rate applicable to capital gains were expressed. One group felt that it would be fairer and simpler to institute prorationing to take care of the bunching problem and eliminate the alternative tax. Others differed with this view because they felt that preferential treatment should be accorded to gains, not only because of the bunching of gains on realization, but also, and more importantly, because the flow of investment and the allocation of savings would be altered by eliminating preferential treatment. The alternative rate was not viewed as a major issue, and many conferees would be glad to see its role eliminated by structural changes in the tax which would reduce the ceiling statutory bracket rates on taxable income to 50 percent.

The Holding Period

The preferences of the participants ran from eliminating the holding period altogether to extending it on a graduated scale to, say, ten years.[18] Proponents of the graduated holding period contended that

---

[18] In order not to increase lock-in over that under the present system, the rate on assets held more than one year would be lower than the present capital gains tax rate. Even with this specification, however, some participants still felt that the graduated holding period would increase lock-in.

the longer the asset had been held, the more likely it would be that the gain would be incorporated into capital rather than identified as an income flow. In addition, extending the holding period would remove the present tax benefits to people who are converting income into capital gains. This might be the least offensive way of handling such problems. However, it was generally felt that the best solution would be a roll-over scheme, with ordinary income tax on gains that are not reinvested.[19]

A graduated holding period would create a cumbersome problem if constructive realization were also in effect. To avoid separate tax computations for assets held for different periods of time, it was proposed that the gains of decedents should be taxed at the lowest rate, regardless of how long they had been held.

Floor traders in the stock markets should not be allowed capital gains treatment on their profits. The holding period was seen as a somewhat imperfect technique for excluding such ordinary business profit from capital gains taxation.

Those who wished to eliminate the holding period altogether argued that anything that is defined as an investment qualifies as an investment, regardless of how long it is held. Thus, any preferential rate that is applied to capital gains should be applied regardless of the holding period.

Finally, it was noted that there would be no need for a holding period of any kind if the rate differential between capital gains and income were eliminated.

The Lock-in Problem

Although the problem of lock-in was discussed under the various reform alternatives, it also received attention as a separate issue. A consensus was reached at the conference that the zero rate of taxation at death due to step-up of basis is a major cause of lock-in. Conferees disagreed widely as to the force of the lock-in effect, though all agreed that it increases as an investor becomes very old. Investment counselors felt that lock-in effects are substantially reduced by professional investment counseling.

Fiduciaries are less likely to respond to lock-in incentives than are individuals. This is significant in view of the rapidly increasing role

[19] See above (pp. 219-20) for a more complete discussion of roll-over.

that fiduciaries have played in the management of wealthy taxpayers' finances in the last two decades. The fiduciary is unlikely to respond to lock-in incentives because (1) the executor or trust officer has a professional bias in favor of diversifying and avoiding large, closely held business interests; (2) he knows the level of taxation of gains and feels that tax costs may be a small price to pay for realizing current gains annually in order to avoid progressive rates on gains accrued over longer periods of time.[20]

One participant also noted that there may be a "push-out" effect to establish losses on stocks that have declined in order to save taxes.

Definition of Capital Gains

Definitional changes in the capital gains law were discussed briefly. One conference member favored defining "true capital gains" as those funds that are for investment and are maintained in the investment stream. Another felt that the definition should be narrowed if the present system is continued, but that it could be broadened under a cumulative averaging system, for example. Still another suggested that one could "try to delineate" those enterprises in which the owner conducts a substantial part of the business and exclude them from preferential treatment. Most members thought that this proposal was too harsh and that it would destroy the incentive for risk-taking.[21]

Conclusions

While only limited data are available on which to base policies affecting capital gains taxation, some tentative conclusions can be drawn from the foregoing analysis and summary. The need for research that would link financial quantities, tax structure, and real behavior in asset markets is clear, as is the need to understand better the consensus that defines the balance between income and wealth taxation and an appropriate degree of progression in rates.

[20] If fiduciaries do not have large incomes they are subjected to the rapidly increasing rates at the lower end of the tax-rate scale. Progression may therefore be substantial.

[21] One participant remarked, "It means the guy who works to create a value is going to be taxed more heavily than the guy who just happens to guess right in the stock market. There is something wrong with that."

Taxing gains on the sale of capital assets at preferential rates combines with many other provisions of the tax law to create an intricate and malleable framework for tax avoidance. Fifty years of experience have not been enough to develop a clear and uncontested distinction between transactions that generate gains taxable at preferential rates and those that are not so favored. The lines of demarcation between investment and speculation, between personal portfolio and business, between capitalized future income and property, cannot be rigorously drawn. Any system of preferential taxation of capital gains must face this fact. The existing basis is a shaky and *ad hoc* compromise among legislative enactments, judicial interpretations, and incentives for the taxpayer to minimize his tax. (See Chapter II.)

The basic concept underlying income taxation implies that taxes ought to be levied in full on capital gains as they accrue, but there is considerable disagreement with this point of view. Basically, the argument for preferential treatment of capital gains turns on the desirability of moderating rates on a type of income flow that tends to be saved. While there may be some justification for preferring expenditure taxation to income taxation, a preferential capital gains tax bears little relationship to an expenditure tax. (See Chapter III.)

Recent increases in the level of realized capital gains may reflect the increasing awareness by taxpayers of the possibilities for avoiding the impact of the ordinary rates. Increases also reflect a widening of the area eligible for preferential treatment, as well as the post-World War II increase in price-earnings ratios and in the capitalization of existing resources. A significant portion of the total amount of capital gains accrues to fiduciary and corporate taxpayers. Any alternative to the present system that is adopted must be adequate for individuals, fiduciaries, and corporate enterprises. (See Chapter IV.)

A large part of the appreciation that accrues on capital assets remains unrealized. Evidence suggests that at least half of the appreciation of corporate common stocks held by individuals is never taxed, since the assets are transferred by gift or bequest. Taxation of gains on assets in a decedent's estate would appear appropriate on equity grounds. In addition, this change in the tax structure would appear to have desirable effects on asset markets, saving, and investors' willingness to trade appreciated assets. (See Chapter VII and the section on Some Separable Issues in this chapter.)

Taxing capital gains at the same rates as ordinary income would obviate the need for a capital assets definition and would create even more incentives for deferring asset transactions than the present system does. These incentives could be eliminated by periodic taxation of accrued gains or a cumulative averaging system with interest adjustments. Accrual taxation or cumulative averaging probably would reduce aggregate savings, but would have other effects on the type of investment that might be desirable. On equity grounds either system would seem desirable, but there would be serious administrative problems under either system. The discussion of full taxation of capital gains revealed a lack of agreement on both the extent of the incentive effects and the desirability of a change in the present degree of progression in income and estate taxation. (See Chapter VIII and the section on General Revision of Capital Gains Taxation in this chapter.)

Roll-over of gains, with full taxation of gains at death, has been proposed as an alternative. It could result in a large burden of documentation on the taxpayer, and it would do nothing to change the effects of the capital gains tax structure on corporate decisions. However, the adoption of electronic data processing for tax administration and the existence of a substantial area for roll-over under the present law suggest that this proposal deserves more serious study than it has received. (See Chapter IX.) Moreover, the proposal seems to appeal both to those who feel that capital gains do not constitute income and to those who consider that consumption and increments to wealth are income.

Some changes in the taxation of capital gains would appear necessary as a prologue to revision of the tax rate structure and the tax base. With a maximum rate of 25 percent available on suitably designed asset sales, the statutory bracket rates on income have little relevance for many high-income taxpayers. Reducing exclusions from income or eliminating questionable deductions would have a limited impact on tax yields if the resulting increases in income could be converted into gains on capital assets. For example, taxing interest on tax-exempt securities would undoubtedly lead the owners of such assets to realize capital gains.

The enactment of some general, but distinctly limited, averaging provisions in the Revenue Act of 1964 may indicate a change in the sentiments of Congress. The use of averaging devices to reduce problems associated with the taxation of "lumpy" capital gains may thus become feasible. Such a change in tax policy would be a welcome relief from past Congressional use of preferential capital gains treatment as a convenient formula for the averaging of certain lumpy increments to income on an *ad hoc* basis.

Rising incomes, increasing wealth, and the desire of taxpayers to avoid taxes, have combined with a substantial extension of the area eligible for capital gains rates to produce a rapid growth in capital gains. The yield from the capital gains tax has grown approximately 10 percent a year since the end of World War II, while the overall yield of income taxes has grown at half that rate. Although the growth in capital gains may not continue at so rapid a pace, the existence of substantial unrealized gains and the obvious role that they play in financial investments suggest that the tax structure should be re-examined and its economic effects more precisely measured.

Conference Participants

Peter L. Bernstein
Bernstein-Macaulay, Inc.

Boris Bittker
Yale University

Walter J. Blum
University of Chicago

Gerard M. Brannon
U.S. Treasury Department

Harvey E. Brazer
University of Michigan

John A. Brittain
The Brookings Institution

Wynn Bussman
University of Wisconsin

Robert D. Calkins
The Brookings Institution

William M. Capron
The Brookings Institution

Samuel B. Chase, Jr.
The Brookings Institution

Reuben Clark
Attorney-at-Law

Martin David
University of Wisconsin

Richard Goode
International Monetary Fund

Arnold C. Harberger
University of Chicago

Michael E. Levy
National Industrial Conference
Board

Harry K. Mansfield
Ropes and Gray

W. Dutton Morehouse
Brown Brothers, Harriman
and Co.

Roger F. Murray
Teachers Insurance and Annuity
Association of America

Joseph A. Pechman
The Brookings Institution

Lawrence H. Seltzer
Wayne State University

Carl S. Shoup
Columbia University

Richard E. Slitor
U.S. Treasury Department

Dan Throop Smith
Harvard University

Conference Participants (*Continued*)

Lawrence M. Stone
  University of California
    (Berkeley)

Stanley S. Surrey
  U.S. Treasury Department

Theodore Tannenwald, Jr.
  Tax Court of the United
    States

Norman B. Ture
  National Bureau of Economic
    Research

William S. Vickrey
  Columbia University

Henry C. Wallich
  Yale University

Stan West
  New York Stock Exchange

Melvin I. White
  U.S. Treasury Department

Laurence N. Woodworth
  Joint Committee on Internal
    Revenue Taxation, U.S.
    Congress

Reporting Gains and Losses on the Sale of Property

A FACSIMILE OF THE Internal Revenue Service forms for reporting gains and losses appears in Figure A-1. The forms illustrate definitions and accounting for capital gains.

The present tax law may also be represented mathematically.

Let:

C_L = net long-term gains or losses,
C_S = net short-term gains or losses,
$\psi(Y)$ = tax rate function (for individuals),
Y = ordinary income.

An individual's tax liability is determined according to the following:

(A.1)

1. Long-term transactions yield a net gain ($C_L > 0$)

   a. Short-term transactions yield a net gain ($C_S \geq 0$):

   $$T_1(Y, C_L, C_S) = \text{min. } [\psi(0.5C_L + C_S + Y), \psi(C_S + Y) + 0.25C_L]$$

   b. Short-term losses are less than long-term gains

   $(-C_L < C_S < 0)$:

   $$T_1(Y, C_L, C_S) = \text{min. } [\psi(0.5[C_L + C_S] + Y), \psi(Y) + 0.25(C_L + C_S)]$$

   c. Short-term losses exceed long-term gains ($C_S \leq -C_L < 0$):

   $$T_1(Y, C_L, C_S) = \text{max. } [\psi(Y - 1,000), 0, \psi(C_L + C_S + Y)]$$

2. Long-term transactions yield a net loss ($C_L \leq 0$):

   $$T_1(Y, C_L, C_S) = \text{max. } [\psi(Y - 1,000), 0, \psi(C_L + C_S + Y)]$$

233

The definition and derivation of terms are given below.

A. C_L and C_S are defined as follows:

(A.2)
$$\begin{cases} C_L = C^*_{L-1} + A_{1L} + A_{2L}, \\ C_S = C^*_{S-1} + A_{1S}, \end{cases}$$

where:

$C^*_{L-1} \leq 0$ long-term net loss carry-forward from taxable year $T-1$,
$C^*_{S-1} \leq 0$ short-term net loss carry-forward from taxable year $T-1$,
A_{1L} = long-term gains or losses on capital assets,
A_{1S} = short-term gains or losses on capital assets,
A_{2L} = net long-term gain on Section 1231 property.

(If sales of Section 1231 property produce net long-term losses, those amounts are reflected in Y above.)

B. The short-term and long-term carry-forwards are defined as follows for individual taxpayers:

Let $D(Y)$ represent the amount of net capital loss deductible from income. $D(Y)$ is related to income:

$$\begin{aligned} D(Y) &= 1,000 & &\text{if } Y \geq 1,000; \\ &= Y & &\text{if } 1,000 > Y \geq 0; \\ &= 0 & &\text{if } 0 > Y. \end{aligned}$$

Then N, the nondeductible capital loss, is defined as:

$$N = C_L + C_S + D(Y).$$

Whenever $N < 0$, some loss carry-forward must be accounted for. Since deductible losses must first be taken against short-term losses before deductions can be made for long-term losses, the following rules define C^*_L and C^*_S:

(A.3)
$$\begin{cases} C^*_S = N, & C^*_L = 0 & \text{if } C_L \geq 0; \\ = 0, & = N & \text{if } C_S \geq 0; \\ = C_S + D(Y), & = C_L & \text{if } C_L < 0 \\ & & \quad \text{and } C_S \leq -D(Y); \\ = 0, & = N & \text{if } C_L < 0 \\ & & \quad \text{and } -D(Y) < C_S < 0. \end{cases}$$

Whenever $N \geq 0$, $C^*_L = C^*_S = 0$.

C. A_{1L} is the algebraic sum of gains and losses on capital assets held for more than six months.

A_{1S} is the algebraic sum of all gains and losses on other sales of capital assets.

D. A_{2L} is computed from three categories as follows:

$$(A.4) \quad \begin{cases} A_{2L} = \Sigma M + \Sigma R + \Sigma P & \text{if } \Sigma M + \Sigma R + \Sigma P > 0, \\ \quad\;\; = 0 & \text{if } \Sigma M + \Sigma R + \Sigma P \leq 0. \end{cases}$$

M = net gains or losses on machinery and equipment, Section 1245 property.

R = net gains or losses on real estate, Section 1250 property.

P = net gains or losses on Section 1231 property that is not 1245 or 1250 property.

(If $\Sigma M + \Sigma R + \Sigma P \leq 0$, the amount is included in Y.)

E. M, the gain or loss on Section 1245 property, is computed for each transaction as follows:

For all assets sold during the year, let:

B_1 = cost basis less accrued depreciation charges,

D_1 = depreciation charged for tax purposes in taxable years beginning after December 31, 1961,

Q_1 = sales proceeds.

$$(A.5) \quad \begin{cases} M = Q_1 - (B_1 + D_1) & \text{if } Q_1 - B_1 - D_1 > 0, \\ \quad = 0 & \text{if } D_1 \geq Q_1 - B_1 > 0, \\ \quad = Q_1 - B_1 & \text{if } Q_1 - B_1 \leq 0. \end{cases}$$

(If $D_1 \geq Q_1 - B_1 > 0$, the difference $Q_1 - B_1$ is included in Y; if $Q_1 - B_1 > D_1$, D_1 is included in Y.)

F. R, the net gain or loss from the sale of depreciable real estate, is computed for each transaction as follows:

B_2 = cost basis less accrued depreciation charges,

ΔD = excess of depreciation actually claimed under accelerated methods and straight-line depreciation,

Q_2 = sales proceeds,

D_2 = depreciation charged for tax purposes since December 31, 1963,

H = number of months the property has been held.

If $H \leq 12$ or $Q_2 - B_2 < 0$, R is defined in a fashion analogous to M, replacing

$$B_1, D_1, Q_1, \text{ by } B_2, D_2, Q_2.$$

(A.6)
$$\begin{cases} \text{If } H > 12, Q_2 - B_2 > \Delta D, \\[1em] \quad R = Q_2 - (B_2 + \Delta D) \\[1em] \qquad\qquad (\Delta D \text{ is included in } Y) \ 12 < H \leq 20 \\[1em] \quad = Q_2 - \left(B_2 + \Delta D \left[\dfrac{120 - H}{100}\right]\right) \\[1em] \qquad \left(\dfrac{H - 20}{100} \Delta D \text{ is included in } Y\right) 20 < H \leq 120 \\[1em] \quad = Q_2 - B_2 \quad H > 120. \\[1em] \text{If } H > 12, 0 < Q_2 - B_2 < \Delta D, \\[1em] \quad R = 0 \text{ if } 12 < H \leq 20 \\[1em] \qquad\qquad (\text{The difference } Q_2 - B_2 \text{ is included in } Y.) \\[1em] \quad = \text{max.}\left(0, Q_2 - B_2 - \Delta D \left[\dfrac{120 - H}{100}\right]\right) 20 < H \leq 120 \\[1em] \qquad \left(\text{max.}\left[Q_2 - B_2, \dfrac{H - 20}{100} \Delta D\right] \text{ is included in } Y\right) \\[1em] \quad = Q_2 - B_2 \quad H > 120. \end{cases}$$

The corporate income tax is similar to the individual income tax. No capital gains deduction from gross income is permitted, and net capital losses are not allowed to offset current income:

(A.7)
$$\begin{cases} T_2(Y, C_L, C_S) = \text{min.} (\phi[Y + C_S] + 0.25 C_L, \phi[Y + C_S + C_L]), \\[0.5em] \qquad\qquad\qquad\qquad \text{when } C_L > 0, C_S > 0, \\[0.5em] \qquad = \text{min.} (\phi[Y] + 0.25[C_L + C_S], \phi[Y + C_L + C_S]), \\[0.5em] \qquad\qquad\qquad\qquad \text{when } -C_L < C_S < 0, \\[0.5em] \qquad = \phi(Y), \qquad\qquad\qquad \text{when } C_S + C_L \leq 0, \\[0.5em] \qquad = \phi(Y + C_S + C_L), \quad \text{when } 0 < -C_L < C_S, \end{cases}$$

where ϕ is the corporation tax rate function.

If $C_L + C_S \leq 0$ in any given year, the deficit may be used to offset any positive net (short-term or long-term) gain in the five successive years. The formula $T_2 (Y, C_L, C_S)$ applies to the net of those two amounts.

GURE A-1. Internal Revenue Service Form 1040, Schedule D.

SCHEDULE D (Form 1040)	GAINS AND LOSSES FROM SALES OR EXCHANGES OF PROPERTY	1965

U.S. Treasury Department—Internal Revenue Service

Attach this schedule to your income tax return, Form 1040

ame and address as shown on page 1 of Form 1040

Part I—CAPITAL ASSETS

Short-term capital gains and losses—assets held not more than 6 months

a. Kind of property and how acquired (if necessary, attach statement of descriptive details not shown below)	b. Date acquired (mo., day, yr.)	c. Date sold (mo., day, yr.)	d. Gross sales price	e. Depreciation allowed (or allowable) since acquisition (attach schedule)	f. Cost or other basis, cost of subsequent improvements (if not purchased, attach explanation) and expense of sale	g. Gain or loss (d plus e less f)

2. Enter your share of net short-term gain (or loss) from partnerships and fiduciaries................................

3. Enter unused short-term capital loss carryover from preceding taxable years (attach statement)..................

4. Net short-term gain (or loss) from lines 1, 2, and 3................................

Long-term capital gains and losses—assets held more than 6 months

5. Enter gain from Part II, line 3................................

		Total long-term gross sales price..				

6. Enter the full amount of your share of net long-term gain (or loss) from partnerships and fiduciaries................................

7. Enter unused long-term capital loss carryover from preceding taxable years (attach statement)................................

8. Capital gain dividends................................

9. Net long-term gain (or loss) from lines 5, 6, 7, and 8................................

0. Combine the amounts shown on lines 4 and 9, and enter the net gain (or loss) here................................

1. If line 10 shows a GAIN—Enter 50% of line 9 or 50% of line 10, whichever is smaller. (Enter zero if there is a loss or no entry on line 9.) **(See reverse side for computation of alternative tax)**................................

2. Subtract line 11 from line 10. Enter here and in Part IV, line 1, on reverse side................................

3. If line 10 shows a LOSS—Enter here and in Part IV, line 1, the **smallest** of the following: (a) the amount on line 10; (b) the amount on page 1, line 11b, Form 1040, computed without regard to capital gains and losses; or (c) $1,000..

Part II—GAIN FROM DISPOSITION OF DEPRECIABLE PROPERTY UNDER SECTIONS 1245 AND 1250—assets held more than 6 months

Where double headings appear, use the first heading for section 1245 and the second heading for section 1250.

D

a. Kind of property and how acquired (if necessary, attach statement of descriptive details not shown below)	b. Date acquired (mo., day, yr.)	c. Date sold (mo., day, yr.)	d. Gross sales price	e. Cost or other basis, cost of subsequent improvements (if not purchased, attach explanation) and expense of sale

f. Depreciation allowed (or allowable) since acquisition (attach schedule)		g. Adjusted basis (e less sum of f-1 and f-2)	h. Total gain (d less g)	i. Ordinary gain (lesser of f-2 or h) ----OR---- (see instructions)	j. Other gain (h less i)
f-1. Prior to January 1, 1962 ----OR---- Prior to January 1, 1964	f-2. After December 31, 1961 ----OR---- After December 31, 1963				

2. Total ordinary gain.   Enter here and in Part IV, line 2, on reverse side.............

3. Total other gain. Enter here and in Part I, line 5; however, if the gains do not exceed the losses when this amount is combined with other gains and losses from section 1231 property enter the total of column j in Part III, line 1..

16—78871-1

FIGURE A-1- Continued

Schedule D (Form 1040) 1965   Page

Part III—PROPERTY OTHER THAN CAPITAL ASSETS

a. Kind of property and how acquired (if necessary, attach statement of descriptive details not shown below)	b. Date acquired (mo., day, yr.)	c. Date sold (mo., day, yr.)	d. Gross sales price	e. Depreciation allowed (or allowable) since acquisition (attach schedule)	f. Cost or other basis, cost of subsequent improvements (if not purchased, attach explanation) and expense of sale	g. Gain or loss (d plus e less f)
1. Enter gain from Part II, line 3						
. . . .						
2. Enter your share of non-capital gain (or loss) from partnerships and fiduciaries						
3. Net gain (or loss) from lines 1 and 2. Enter here and in Part IV, line 3 . . . . •						

Part IV—TOTAL GAINS OR LOSSES FROM SALE OR EXCHANGE OF PROPERTY

1. Net gain (or loss) from Part I, line 12 or 13	
2. Total ordinary gain from Part II, line 2	
3. Net gain (or loss) from Part III, line 3	
4. Total net gain (or loss), combine lines 1, 2, and 3. Enter here and on page 2, Part II, line 6, Form 1040	

COMPUTATION OF ALTERNATIVE TAX

It will usually be to your advantage to use the alternative tax if the net long-term capital gain exceeds the net short-term capital loss, or if the is a net long-term capital gain only, and you are filing (a) a separate return with taxable income exceeding $26,000, or (b) a joint return, or as surviving husband or wife, with taxable income exceeding $52,000, or (c) as a head of household with taxable income exceeding $38,00

1. Enter the amount from page 1, line 11d, Form 1040	
2. Enter amount from Part I, line 11, on reverse side	
3. Subtract line 2 from line 1	
4. Enter tax on amount on line 3 (use applicable tax rate schedule on page 11 of Form 1040 instructions)	
5. Enter 50% of line 2	
6. Alternative tax (add lines 4 and 5). If smaller than the tax figured on the amount on page 1, line 11d, Form 1040, enter this alternative tax on page 2, line 12, Form 1040 and write "Alternative" to left of entry	

INSTRUCTIONS—(References are to the Internal Revenue Code)

GAINS AND LOSSES FROM SALES OR EXCHANGES OF PROPERTY.—Report details in appropriate part or parts.

In column (a) of Parts I, II, and III, use the following symbols to indicate how the property was acquired: "A" for purchase on the open market; "B" for exercise of stock option or through employee stock purchase plan; "C" for inheritance or gift; "D" for exchange involving carryover of prior asset basis; and "E" for other.

"Capital assets" defined.—The term "capital assets" means property held by the taxpayer (whether or not connected with his trade or business) but does NOT include—

(a) stock in trade or other property of a kind properly includible in his inventory if on hand at the close of the taxable year;
(b) property held by the taxpayer primarily for sale to customers in the ordinary course of his trade or business;
(c) property used in the trade or business of a character which is subject to the allowance for depreciation provided in section 167;
(d) real property used in the trade or business of the taxpayer;
(e) certain government obligations issued on or after March 1, 1941, at a discount, payable without interest and maturing at a fixed date not exceeding one year from date of issue;
(f) certain copyrights, literary, musical, or artistic compositions, etc.; or
(g) accounts and notes receivable acquired in the ordinary course of trade or business for services rendered or from the sale of property referred to in (a) or (b) above.

Special rules apply to dealers in securities for determining capital gain or ordinary loss on the sale or exchange of securities. Certain real property subdivided for sale may be treated as capital assets. Sections 1236 and 1237.

If the total distributions to which an employee is entitled under an employees' pension, bonus, or profit-sharing trust plan, which is exempt from tax under section 501(a), are paid to the employee in one taxable year, on account of the employee's separation from service, the aggregate amount of such distribution, to the extent it exceeds the amounts contributed by the employee, shall be treated as a long-term capital gain. (See section 402(a).)

Gain on sale of depreciable property between husband and wife or between a shareholder and a "controlled corporation" shall be treated as ordinary gain.

Gains and losses from transactions described in section 1231 (see below) shall be treated as gains and losses from the sale or exchange of capital assets held for more than 6 months if the total of these gains exceeds the total of these losses. If the total of these

gains does not exceed the total of these losses, such gains and loss shall not be treated as gains and losses from the sale or exchang of capital assets. Thus, in the event of a net gain, all these tran actions should be entered in Part I of Schedule D. In the event net loss, all these transactions should be entered in Part III Schedule D, or in other applicable schedules on Form 1040.

Section 1231 deals with gains and losses arising from—

(a) sale, exchange, or involuntary conversion, of land (includir in certain cases unharvested crops sold with the land) and de preciable property if they are used in the trade or business an held for more than 6 months,
(b) sale, exchange, or involuntary conversion of livestock held f draft, breeding, or dairy purposes (but not including poultr and held for 1 year or more.
(c) the cutting of timber or the disposal of timber, coal, or domest iron ore, to which section 631 applies, and
(d) the involuntary conversion of capital assets held more than months.

See sections 1231 and 631 for specific conditions applicable.

Gains from section 1245 or 1250 property held more than months (Part II).—(*Report any gain from such propert held for 6 months or less in Part III.*) Except as provide below section 1245 property means depreciable (a) personal proper (other than livestock) including intangible personal propert (b) tangible real property (except for buildings and their structure components) if used as an integral part of manufacturing, produ tion, or extraction, or of furnishing transportation, communicatior electrical energy, gas, water, or sewage disposal services, or use as a research or storage facility in connection with these activitie and (c) elevators or escalators.

Except as provided below section 1250 property means depreciab real property (other than section 1245 property).

See sections 1245(b) and 1250(d) for exceptions and limita tions involving; (a) disposition by gift; (b) transfers at deat (c) certain tax-free transactions; (d) like kind exchanges, invc untary conversions; (e) sales or exchanges to effectuate FCC pc icies and exchanges to comply with S.E.C. orders; (f) property di tributed by a partnership to a partner; and (g) disposition principal residence (section 1250 only).

Column f of Part II.—In computing depreciation allowed c allowable for elevators or escalators, enter in column f-1 depreci tion prior to July 1, 1963, and in column f-2 depreciation afte June 30, 1963.

(Instructions continued on reverse side of duplicate

16—78871-1

FIGURE A-1. Continued

Column i of Part II, section 1250 property only.—If held for more than 6 months, but not more than 1 year, enter the smaller of (1) column h, or (2) column f-2.

If held for more than 1 year, enter the result of multiplying the smaller of (1) column h, or

(2) column f-2 less the amount of depreciation computed for the same period using the straight line method, by the percentage obtained by subtracting from 100%, one percentage point for each full month held in excess of 20 months.

Where substantial improvements have been made within the preceding 10 years, see section 1250(f).

Basis.—In determining gain or loss use cost, except as specially provided. The basis of property acquired by gift after December 31, 1920, is the cost or other basis to the donor in the event of gain, but, in the event of loss, it is the lower of either such donor's basis or the fair market value on date of gift. If a gift tax was paid with respect to property received by gift, see section 1015(d). Generally, the basis of property acquired by inheritance is the fair market value at the date of death. For special cases involving property acquired from a decedent, see section 1014.

Installment sales.—If you sold personal property for more than $1,000 or real property regardless of amount, you may be eligible to report any gain under the installment plan if (1) there is no payment in the year of sale, or (2) the payments in the year of sale do not exceed 30 percent of the selling price. The election must be made in the year of sale even though no payment was received in that year. See section 453.

· For treatment of a portion of payments as "unstated interest" on deferred payment sales, see section 483.

Sale of personal residence.—Tax on a portion or all of the gain from the sale of your principal residence may be deferred if:

(a) within 1 year after (or before) the sale, you purchase another residence and use it as your principal residence; or

(b) within 1 year after (or before) the sale, you begin construction of a new residence and use it as your principal residence not later than 18 months after the sale.

If you sold property for $20,000 or less on or after your 65th birthday which was owned and used by you as your principal residence for at least 5 of the last 8 years any gain on the sale need not be included in income. If the property was sold for more than $20,000 part of the gain must be taken into income.

Contact your nearest Internal Revenue Service office for full details or to obtain Form 2119 which may be used to report the sale or exchange or to figure your new basis.

Nonbusiness debts.—If a debt, such as a personal loan, becomes totally worthless within the taxable year, the loss resulting therefrom shall be considered a loss from the sale or exchange, during the taxable year, of a capital asset held for not more than 6 months. Enter such loss in column (g) and describe in column (a), Part I. This does not apply to: (a) a debt evidenced by a corporate security with interest coupons or in registered form and (b) a debt acquired in your trade or business.

Limitation on allowable capital losses.—If line 10 Part I, shows a net loss, the loss shall be allowed as a deduction, only to the extent of the smaller of (1) line 11b (or line 9 if tax table is used), page 1, Form 1040 computed without capital gains (losses), or (2) $1,000. The excess of such allowable loss over the lesser of items (1) and (2) above is called "capital loss carryover." Any such carryover loss may be carried forward indefinitely. Capital losses retain their character as either short-term or long-term when carried over to the succeeding year. To the extent the net capital losses are deducted from ordinary income, the net short-term capital loss must be considered as deducted first.

Losses in transactions between certain persons.—No deduction is allowable for losses from sales or exchanges of property directly or indirectly between (a) members of a family, (b) a corporation and an individual (or a fiduciary) owning more than 50 percent of the corporation's stock (liquidations excepted), (c) a grantor and fiduciary of any trust, (d) a fiduciary and a beneficiary of the same trust, (e) a fiduciary and a fiduciary or beneficiary of another trust created by the same grantor, or (f) an individual and a tax-exempt organization controlled by the individual or his family. Partners and partnerships see section 707(b).

Long-term capital gains from regulated investment companies.—Include in income as a long-term capital gain the amount you are notified on Form 2439 which constitutes your share of the undistributed capital gains of a regulated investment company. You are entitled to a credit of 25 percent of this amount which should be included with the amount claimed on line 17a, page 1, Form 1040. The remaining 75 percent should be added to the basis of your stock.

Losses on small business stock.—If you had a loss on section 1244 stock which would (but for that section) be treated as a loss from the sale or exchange of a capital asset, it shall be treated as a loss from the sale or exchange of an asset which is not a capital asset to the extent provided in that section.

16—78871-1

NOTES

Part I, line 11: This entry is the capital gains deduction.

Part II, line 1(i): This entry "recaptures gains" corresponding to excessive depreciation deductions and causes such gains to be taxed as ordinary income (Sections 1245 and 1250).

Part II, line 3: This is the point at which Section 1231 assets are accorded asymmetric treatment—capital gains treatment if net gain, ordinary income treatment if net loss.

Computation of Alternative Tax

Line 1: This entry is taxable income including capital gains less the capital gains deduction.

Line 2: This entry is the amount of net long-term gains less short-term loss included in income.

Line 3: This entry constitutes taxable income net of gains subject to the alternative tax.

APPENDIX B

Problems in the Interpretation of
Tax Data on Capital Gains

LITTLE IS KNOWN ABOUT what precipitates realizations of capital gains, and knowledge of the transactions themselves is further restricted by the tax accounting structure through which statistics on capital gains have been collected. Basic data on capital gains are collected by tabulating the items shown on the taxpayer's return. (See the form in Appendix A.) For individuals, data are given on (1) net gain or loss on all capital asset transactions included in income for tax purposes, (2) net capital loss carry-forward from prior years, and (3) the net of gains and losses shown on both short-term and long-term capital asset transactions. For fiduciaries, only (1) is available. For corporations, data are available only on net long-term gains less short-term losses (if any) and on asset sales to which the provisions of Section 1231 apply. Because of differences in data availability, it is impossible to compare the capital asset transactions of different classes of taxpayers.

As a result of the data collection process, the amount of gain on individual tax returns with net gain on sales of capital assets included in income may be either more or less than half of the net proceeds realized from the sale of assets during the current year. (See Table B-1.) One hundred percent of short-term capital gains is included in income; only 50 percent of long-term capital gains in excess of short-term losses is included. Thus the proportion of net gains included in income tends to be more than 50 percent. Gains reported on returns with net gains are the net

240

of some gains and a few losses and do not reflect the total transactions in the market. Net losses are understated, since their use as an offset to income for tax purposes is legally restricted. They reflect the difference between a few gains and larger losses. Furthermore, only those gains or losses that are legally eligible for capital asset treatment are reported in the tables here. Net gain arising from sales of assets that were not considered capital assets accounted for $2.1 billion of net gain for individuals and $17.2 billion for corporations during the period 1938-63. The data thus refer to only a part, albeit the largest part, of portfolio activity.

TABLE B-1. Relation of Net Gain Included in Income to Net Gain Reported on Returns with Net Gain, and Percentage of Loss Not Deductible in Current Period for Returns with Net Loss, 1952–64

Year	Net gain included in income (after loss carry-over) as a percentage of total net gain reported on returns with net gain	Percentage of loss not deductible in the current period for returns with net loss
1952	51.6	70.0
1953	51.3	72.1
1954	52.1	68.7
1955	51.9	68.8
1956	51.5	65.9
1957	50.9	68.4
1958	51.7	72.5
1959	51.7	72.0
1960	51.1	71.1
1961	51.8	70.9
1962	50.7	72.2
1963	51.2	74.5
1964	51.1	76.0

Source: U.S. Treasury Department, Internal Revenue Service *Statistics of Income—Individual Income Tax Returns* (1952–64).

APPENDIX C

Estimating Unrealized Gains on Privately Held Corporate Shares

THE TAX-EXEMPT SECTOR includes such nonprofit institutions as educational, religious, and charitable organizations, nontaxable pension funds, and certain beneficial trust funds. Holdings of securities listed on the New York Stock Exchange are reported in its *Fact Book*. Those estimates[1] were converted into all stockholdings by applying the indices of value of shares traded on the New York Stock Exchange to the value of all shares traded on regional and other national exchanges. The ratios are reported in the *Report of Special Study of Securities Markets of the Securities and Exchange Commission.*[2]

The estimated shareholdings of nontaxable institutions reported in the *Fact Book* go back only as far as 1949. Holdings by nontaxable institutions of stocks listed on the New York Stock Exchange were about 11.5 percent of all NYSE-listed stocks at the end of 1965. This estimate compares with 11.4 percent at the end of 1964, 7.5 percent at year-end 1956, and 4.8 percent at year-end 1949.[3] The values prior to 1949 back to 1940 are linearly extrapolated.

The basic data for realized gains can be found in either *Statistics of Income* or Seltzer's study.[4] Since these basic data exclude nontaxable

---

[1] *New York Stock Exchange Fact Book,* 1956 to 1966 issues.

[2] H.Doc. 95, 88 Cong. 1 sess. (1963), Pt. 2, p. 838.

[3] *NYSE Fact Book* (1966), p. 21.

[4] Lawrence H. Seltzer, *The Nature and Tax Treatment of Capital Gains and Losses* (National Bureau of Economic Research, 1951), p. 367, and "The Individual Income

242

fiduciaries prior to 1952, approximately 1 percent, or $542 million, was added to the grand totals to adjust gains in those years.[5]

Capital gains realized in each year from 1922 to 1963 were deflated to exclude gains and losses on assets other than corporate shares. Data obtained in *Statistics of Income—1959, Report on Sales of Capital Assets Reported on Individual Income Tax Returns* showed that 48.5 percent of net long-term capital gains can be attributed to corporate stocks (including rights) and distribution from investment companies. All years were deflated by that percentage on the assumption that the ratio of gains on corporate shares to total gains was the same in every year as it was in 1959. The estimated gains on all corporate shareholdings were then further deflated by the ratio of the value of listed shares to the value of all shareholdings to produce the estimates shown in Column (8) of Table C-1.

Table C-1 shows the data that were used to obtain the accrued gains estimated in Table 4-24, Columns (2) and (3).

Adjustments for Unreporting of Gains and Losses

Historical data indicate that realized net capital gains exceeded realized net capital losses only moderately during the period 1922-63. The figure reported in *Statistics of Income* excludes capital gains and losses realized by individuals who were not required to file returns for income tax purposes and by those who neglected to report isolated transactions. Because individuals reporting net incomes under $5,000 generally accounted for a more than negligible proportion of aggregate net capital gains and losses, it seems probable that those who were not required to file returns also realized gains and losses that may add up to a significant amount.[6]

Even though the exact total of the unreported capital gains and losses cannot be ascertained, a rough estimate can be made from various sources. The Treasury Department reported estimated dividend income of individuals not accounted for on the tax returns for 1959.[7] The dividend-reporting gap in 1959 amounted to $950 million, of which $110 million is attributable to nontaxable filers and $840 million to those who were taxable.

Tax," in *The Uses of Economic Research, Forty-Third Annual Report,* National Bureau of Economic Research (May 1963), Table IV. 11, p. 89.

[5] Martin J. Bailey, "Capital Gains and Income Taxation," in Arnold C. Harberger and Martin J. Bailey (eds.), *Taxation of Income from Capital* (Brookings Institution, 1968).

[6] Seltzer, *The Nature and Tax Treatment of Capital Gains and Losses,* pp. 111-12.

[7] *Revenue Act of 1962,* Hearings before the Senate Committee on Finance, 87 Cong. 2 sess. (1962), Pt. 1, p. 148.

TABLE C-1. Accrued Gains in Corporate Shares, 1922–63

(Amounts in billions of dollars, except stock price averages in column (5), which are in dollars)

Year	Year-end value of listed shares owned by				Stock price averages[e]	Gains accrued on Col. (4)[f]	Gains reported on individual and fiduciary returns	
	All holders[a] (1)	Taxable corpora- tions[b] (2)	Tax-exempt corpora- tions[c] (3)	House- holds[d] (4)	(5)	(6)	Total[g] (7)	Prorated to Col. (4)[h] (8)
1921	26.250	6.132	n.a.	20.118	$32.43			
1922	28.274	6.605	n.a.	21.669	39.25	4.23	0.23	0.04
1923	28.094	5.863	n.a.	22.231	38.62	− 0.35	0.19	0.03
1924	33.840	7.137	n.a.	26.703	46.07	4.29	1.02	0.18
1925	43.111	9.760	n.a.	33.351	55.73	5.60	2.00	0.41
1926	47.970	12.151	n.a.	35.819	58.25	1.51	1.87	0.38
1927	62.170	16.046	n.a.	46.124	74.17	9.79	2.36	0.48
1928	84.348	22.825	n.a.	61.523	98.87	15.36	4.56	0.93
1929	79.886	24.309	n.a.	55.577	86.00	− 8.01	2.93	0.59
1930	60.519	19.009	n.a.	41.510	65.90	−12.99	−1.38	−0.28
1931	32.956	10.549	n.a.	22.407	40.82	−15.80	−2.75	−0.55
1932	28.109	9.113	n.a.	18.996	21.05	−10.85	−2.71	−0.54
1933	40.858	13.406	n.a.	27.452	26.78	5.17	−1.42	−0.29
1934	41.894	19.116	n.a.	22.778	29.74	3.03	−0.64	−0.14
1935	57.251	29.043	n.a.	38.358	32.44	2.07	−0.09	−0.02
1936	73.022	26.492	n.a.	46.530	45.41	15.34	0.60	0.14
1937	47.401	16.917	n.a.	30.484	44.04	− 1.41	−0.11	−0.03
1938	57.916	20.693	n.a.	37.223	33.25	− 7.47	−0.35	−0.09
1939	56.668	18.797	n.a.	37.871	35.72	2.77	−0.27	−0.08
1940	50.471	16.751	0.197	33.523	33.84	1.99	−0.44	−0.12
1941	43.064	14.362	0.383	28.319	30.50	− 3.31	−0.91	−0.25
1942	46.593	11.168	0.652	34.773	26.66	− 3.57	−0.38	−0.11
1943	57.083	13.295	1.090	42.698	35.36	11.35	1.07	0.30
1944	66.402	15.664	1.609	49.129	38.12	3.33	1.62	0.45
1945	88.130	20.552	2.582	64.996	46.02	10.18	4.37	1.21
1946	81.856	18.704	2.816	60.336	51.34	7.51	6.67	1.85
1947	81.325	18.298	3.204	59.823	46.46	− 5.74	4.44	1.23
1948	79.629	18.617	3.543	57.469	47.46	1.29	4.45	1.23
1949	90.393	20.420	4.486	65.487	46.68	− 0.94	3.19	0.88
1950	111.014	23.635	6.715	80.664	56.23	13.40	6.19	1.70
1951	129.108	27.164	8.811	93.133	66.98	15.42	6.40	1.75
1952	141.474	29.526	11.159	110.789	71.73	6.60	5.29	1.44
1953	137.143	28.238	13.265	95.640	72.81	1.67	4.34	1.18
1954	197.143	38.601	15.483	143.059	89.04	21.32	7.48	2.02
1955	238.734	45.168	17.713	175.853	117.36	45.51	10.56	2.82
1956	253.970	47.086	19.930	186.954	130.55	19.77	10.14	2.73
1957	224.278	40.325	17.179	166.774	125.46	− 7.29	7.77	2.07
1958	312.616	59.147	25.068	228.401	132.02	8.72	9.64	2.53
1959	338.513	61.440	30.769	206.304	163.47	54.41	13.91	3.55
1960	335.117	60.120	37.907	237.090	155.46	−10.11	11.71	2.97
1961	426.199	77.398	45.292	303.509	185.66	46.07	16.55	4.22
1962	373.888	69.655	44.250	259.983	177.87	−12.75	12.37	3.15
1963	444.668	75.682	55.094	313.892	202.32	35.75	14.46	3.69
Total 1922–63						272.86	166.93	43.65

Note: See footnotes on page 245.

On the basis of this information, Hinrichs estimated that nonreporting of capital gains amounted to approximately one-third of realized capital gains.[8] Based on this estimate, realized gains were inflated by 30 percent to provide an alternative estimate of unrealized gains and step-up in basis in Table 4-24.

[8] Harley H. Hinrichs, "Unreporting of Capital Gains on Tax Returns or How To Succeed in Gainsmanship Without Actually Paying Taxes," *National Tax Journal*, Vol. 17 (June 1964), pp. 158-63. See also a criticism of Hinrichs' estimate by Stan West and James W. Riley, "How To Succeed in Figuremanship Without Having All the Figures," *National Tax Journal*, Vol. 18 (March 1965), pp. 78-90, and a reply by Hinrichs in the same issue, " 'Altruism on Wall Street or Who's Afraid of the IRS?' A Reply to West and Riley," *ibid.*, pp. 91-96.

---

n.a. Not available.

[a] The year-end aggregate value of all stocks listed on the New York Stock Exchange, as reported in the NYSE *Fact Book*, was adjusted by applying the index reported in the Securities and Exchange Commission study (*Report of Special Study of Securities Markets of the Securities and Exchange Commission* [1963], Pt. I, Table I-1, p. 27) of the market value of shares available for trading on all stock exchanges (14 registered and 4 exempted) in the United States. The value of unlisted shares was excluded due to the lack of reliable estimates. Since indices for selected years given in the SEC study are for 1940 (83.0), 1945 (83.7), 1950 (84.5), 1955 (87.0), 1956 (86.3), 1957 (87.2), 1958 (88.5), 1959 (90.9), 1960 (91.6), 1961 (91.0), and 1962 (92.5), linear interpolation and extrapolation were used to derive conversion ratios for years not given in the SEC study.

[b] Since there are no published data available on intercorporate shareholdings, a rough estimate was made as follows: From historical tables of corporate income tax returns, a ratio of dividends received from domestic corporations to distributions to stockholders other than in own stock was computed for each year. By multiplying this ratio by the year-end aggregate value of the listed shares (Col. 1) for each year, the aggregate value of intercorporate listed shareholdings of that year was estimated.

[c] Estimates of the aggregate values of shares held by nontaxable institutions for selected years, reported in NYSE *Fact Books* (1960, 1962, 1964–66), were inflated to arrive at the total market value of all exchanges. The adjustment ratios used are given in the SEC study (81 percent of noninsured pension fund holdings are traded on the NYSE[f] 78 percent of college endowments[f] 87 percent of foundations[f] and 82 percent of common trust funds'. SEC [*op. cit.*, Pt. 2, p. 838]). For this purpose, "nontaxable institution" was defined to include noninsured pension funds, nonprofit institutions (colleges and foundations), and common trust funds. The values of these shareholdings for selected years from 1949 to 1965 are available in the *Fact Book*. Linear interpolation and extrapolation were used for years not given in the *Fact Book*. The ratios given in the SEC study were applied uniformly throughout the period under the restrictive and arbitrary assumption that the relative distribution of nontaxable shareholdings over the various exchanges remained constant.

[d] Col. (1) minus the sum of Cols. (2) and (3).

[e] Weighted composite market price per share as reported in Moody's *Industrial Manual*.

[f] The method used in deriving accrued gains is: current year accrued capital gain $C_t = V_{t-1}[(P_t/P_{t-1})-1]$, where V_{t-1} equals the previous year-end value of the stock market (Col. 4) and P_t equals the current year-end stock price index (Col. 5). There are two defects in this method. First, it understates capital gains slightly because it omits gains on new issues during the current year. Second, since the total accrued gains are derived by aggregating accruals over the whole period, the method puts relatively greater weight on the later years, especially because of the stock market boom of the 1950's.

[g] The basic data for this series are in *Statistics of Income—Individual Income Tax Returns* or in Lawrence H. Seltzer, *The Nature and Tax Treatment of Capital Gains and Losses* (National Bureau of Economic Research, 1951), p. 367, and "The Individual Income Tax," National Bureau of Economic Research, *The Uses of Economic Research, Forty-Third Annual Report* (May 1963), p. 89. Seltzer's data do not include nontaxable fiduciaries. On the basis of information on nontaxable fiduciaries contained in *Statistics of Income—Fiduciary, Gift, and Estate Tax Returns* for the years 1952, 1954, 1956, 1958, and 1960, approximately 1 percent is added to the grand totals for all years prior to 1952 to adjust for the exclusion of nontaxable fiduciaries in these years. For the years for which fiduciary capital gains are missing linear interpolation has been used.

[h] Estimated under the assumption that the propensities to realize capital gains and to report these gains are identical for listed and unlisted shares, and that realized capital gains on corporate shares account for approximately 48.5 percent of all realized capital gains.

Estimates of Step-up in Basis

Step-up in basis was estimated from the following formulas:

$$\text{(C.1)} \qquad\qquad S_t = \sum_{k=t_0}^{t} s_k,$$

where s_t is the step-up in basis in year t, and S_t is the cumulative total of all step-up from year t_0 to year t.

$$\text{(C.2)} \qquad\qquad s_t = m_t \left(U_t + a_t - \frac{g_t}{2} \right),$$

where m is the mortality rate applicable to shareholders in year t, a_t is the accruing gain on shares, g_t is the gain reported in Column (8) of Table C-1, and U_t is the cumulative unrealized gain from prior years.

The appropriate share of *total* capital gains to be allocated to corporate shares is assumed to be g_t. However, if death or sales of stock are uniformly distributed through the year, decedents will realize only half as much gain or loss as the stockholding population as a whole. Hence, gain realized by decedents is $m_t g_t/2$. Their accrued and unrealized gains are assumed to be proportionate to those of the entire shareholding population; hence, Equation (C.2).

Once step-up has been calculated, cumulative unrealized gains can be determined by the equation

$$\text{(C.3)} \qquad\qquad U_t = U_{t-1} - s_t + a_t - g_t.$$

The ratios shown in Table 4-25 are ratios of S_t/U_t.

Effects of Capital Gains Taxation on Business Investment Decisions

IN ITS REGULAR OPERATIONS, the business firm seeks to create a net return, gather the information needed to expand available opportunities for profit, and possibly enhance some other values. A balance among the possible values that the firm seeks to enlarge is achieved by implicit or explicit rules defining priorities or the relative utility of alternative goals. One way to meet the desired goal of increasing net return is to reduce the costs of doing business. Taxes are an important cost. In minimizing its tax bill (or maximizing its net return) a business is influenced by the preferential capital gains tax in much the same way a household is in making its investments. Since a business may be entitled to treat as capital gains the proceeds from the sale of certain business and investment assets, it is affected *directly* by the law.

Corporate business decisions are also affected *indirectly* by capital gains taxation. The business acts as the agent of its owners in transmitting the proceeds of a profitable market operation to the owners for disposition. When the business is an unincorporated enterprise or a partnership, no distinction is made between the owner and the business as his agent; the tax law assigns all net returns and the value inherent in the ongoing activity of the business to the owner or owners. The effects of capital gains treatment are the same for households that own an unincorporated business as for those that do not, except that gains may nominally accrue to the business rather than to the individual.[1]

---

[1] However, the opportunities for converting income payments into capital gains for tax purposes by the judicious sale of assets are vastly greater for the household that makes investments in an enterprise in which it owns a controlling interest.

247

The existence of incorporated businesses radically changes this situation. Both the corporate body and the owners are subject to income taxes; both the corporate income tax and the individual income tax provide for capital gains treatment of certain types of income. The tax on net returns to business activities may be minimized by directly reducing taxable business income, by reducing the tax paid by the owners, or by some combination of these two. When corporate decisions lead to a reduction in the tax of the owners because of increased capital gains for the individual owner, the effect will be referred to here as an *indirect* effect of capital gains on the business unit. The extreme of such indirect effects can be observed in certain cases of merger and liquidation where the decisions of the business are motivated entirely by the provisions of the tax law, in particular by the effects of the capital gains tax.

The *direct* effects of capital gains taxation are discussed below. Choices among investments are compared by computing the discounted value of alternative investments.

The direct impact of the capital gains tax on business activity is on the allocation of funds for investment. The allocation among four major classes of assets and the tax consequences of each are considered. The major types of assets discussed are: (1) depreciable producer durable goods, (2) expensible investments, (3) investments yielding statutory gains, and (4) financial assets of other enterprises. The first includes expenditures on all the physical tools required to produce particular goods or services; the second, expenditures on research and development, on improving the organization of the business, and also on the purchase of livestock and on mineral exploration (mentioned on pages 125-27); the third includes coal and iron ore royalty payments and the sale of timber, while the fourth includes investments in stocks and bonds of other enterprises and in government securities.[2]

In the case of investments in durable goods there are special rules that govern the amortization of inital outlays as a depreciation deduction. Depreciation may be deducted according to any one of a variety of formulas over the lifetime of the investment. Any discrepancy between the initial investment, net of estimates of depreciation recorded in the books of account, and the actual decline in market value gives rise to an income (or loss) adjustment for the year in which the asset is sold. Receipts in excess of original cost are always treated as capital gains. On real proper-

[2] The physical tools of production may be further subdivided into personal and real property, which are accorded different treatment under the tax law. (See Chap. II.) Both investment tax credits and capital gains taxes are handled in different ways for the two property categories.

ty, receipts in excess of the initial investment less an amount for adjusted depreciation are currently treated as capital gains.[3]

Expenditures on expensible investments are immediately deductible from current income. They thus give rise to an immediate tax benefit and generate capital gains if the asset is sold prior to exhaustion.

Corporations have an additional investment choice. They may invest in the financial assets of other corporate enterprises,[4] and this may give rise either to future income payments through intercorporate dividends or to appreciation in the value of the financial assets held by the owning corporation. Eighty-five percent of dividends received by the owning corporation are deductible from income, while capital gains are taxable at 25 percent under the alternative tax provisions.[5] Investment in bonds may give rise to capital gains at the time of sale, but interest income is fully taxable.

Investments in the present period that yield identical streams of future receipts (G_k) for a period of N years are thus subjected to three different tax treatments depending on their physical and legal character. If no tax were levied, the present value of all three investments would be:

$$(D.1) \qquad V_1 = \sum_{k=1}^{\mu} \frac{G_k}{(1+\rho)^k} - C,$$

where ρ is the market rate of discount. If depreciation allowed for tax purposes reflects the actual decline in value, terminal gains on the investment can be ignored. The present value, net of cost, of investment in depreciable property is then given by the equation:

$$(D.2) \qquad V_2 = -C + \sum_{k=1}^{N} \frac{(G_k - D_k)(1 - t) + D_k}{(1+\rho)^k},$$

where D_k is the depreciation allowed for tax purposes on an investment of C dollars, k periods after acquisition, and ρ is the market interest rate.

The conversion of capital income into capital gains through an excessive

---

[3] See Chap. II and Appendix A for a discussion of Sections 1245 and 1250. For a summary of the present regulations on depreciation, see: U.S. Treasury Department, Internal Revenue Service, *Depreciation: Guidelines and Rules*. Publication No. 456 (1962; revised 1964), and the *Supplement* published as *Revenue Procedure 65-13, Internal Revenue Bulletin 1965-1* (January-June 1965), pp. 759-825.

[4] Investments of this type by unincorporated enterprises are not distinguishable from similar investments by individuals. Hence, they will be considered along with the general effect of capital gains taxation on individual portfolios.

[5] Actually the law does not permit corporations to deduct half of the capital gains from income prior to computation of the tax liability. Only an alternate tax computation is permitted. See Appendix A.

reduction of basis and the later sale of an asset at capital gains rates would have a present value:

$$(D.3) \qquad V_2^* = V_2 - g\frac{\sum\limits_{k=1}^{\tilde{N}} E_k}{(1 + \rho)^{\tilde{N}}} + t\sum\limits_{k=1}^{\tilde{N}}\frac{E_k}{(1 + \rho)^k},$$

where g is the capital gains rate and E_k is the excess deduction permitted by rapid write-off of the investment. The asset is sold after the first $\tilde{N} < N$ periods of use.[6] The optimum tax advantage obtains by holding for a period long enough to claim a maximum

$$\sum\limits_{k=1}^{\tilde{N}} E_k/(1 + \rho)^k.$$

There is such a point, since E_k becomes negative for a sufficiently large $\tilde{N}$. It is assumed that the market value of the asset at this time of sale is its value in the hands of the user after $\tilde{N}$ periods, that is:

$$(D.4) \qquad \sum\limits_{k=\tilde{N}}^{N}\frac{(G_k - D_k)(1 - t) + D_k}{(1 + \rho)^k}.$$

Thus, the owner may realize this amount by continuing to hold the asset if he chooses. By selling now, however, he obtains tax benefits equal to the difference between the present value of the capital gains liability owed on the excessive reduction in basis and the present value of the reduction in ordinary income liability associated with those deductions.

The present value of an investment in expensible goods or software can be represented by a similar formula:

$$(D.5) \qquad V_3 = \left[-C + \sum\limits_{k=1}^{N}\frac{G_k}{(1 + \rho)^k}\right](1 - t) = V_1(1 - t).$$

The formula assumes that the asset is held by the original owner until it is exhausted and valueless.[7] If it can be sold prior to exhaustion, the present value will be:

$$(D.6) \qquad V_3^* = V_1(1 - t) - \sum\limits_{k=\tilde{N}}^{N}\frac{G_k(1 - t)}{(1 + \rho)^k} + \frac{(1 - g)E_{\tilde{N}}}{(1 + \rho)^{\tilde{N}}},$$

where $E_{\tilde{N}}$ represents the market value on the date of sale. The sale of

[6] This possibility has been circumscribed for real estate. The tax avoidance possibilities have not been eliminated for assets held ten years or more (Section 1250 under the Revenue Act of 1964). For examples of the problem, see the Hearings cited in note 13 to Chap. VI, p. 124.

[7] Expensing of capital outlays frequently occurs in connection with major repairs of durable items of equipment. Such expenditures cannot easily be differentiated from large maintenance expenditures.

oil-producing properties immediately after production begins implies that
$E_{\tilde{N}} = E_1$ and:

(D.7) $\qquad V_3^* = - C(1 - t) + (1 - g)E_1/(1 + \rho)$.

The market value E_1 differs from the present value of receipts expected
from the property only insofar as taxes must be paid by the new owner.
He must depreciate his investment according to Equation D.2. Since the
asset can always be held to maturity by the present owner, $V_3^* > V_3$, or
no sale would be consummated. Hence:

(D.8) $\qquad V_1(1 - g) > V_3^* > V_1(1 - t) = V_3$.

As is well known, the rate of return on an expensible investment is
independent of the tax rate and of the durability of the investment.[8]

Investments yielding statutory gains may be similar to that illustrated
in Equation D.8 . Raising livestock, for example, involves expensible costs
over a period of years that produce capital gains when breeding stocks are
sold. The operation of small woodlots is another example, since a large
part of the cost of maintaining the forest stand may be written off as a current expense.

If the firm is incorporated and acquires financial assets of another enterprise as an investment, the situation is more complex. But the same an-
alytic framework can be used to suggest the differentials in favor of those
equities that produce capital gains for the purchasing company. There are
three types of equities: In *Case 1* the investment produces a stream of taxable income; in *Case 2* it produces a regular stream of intercorporate dividends; and in *Case 3* it produces no dividends, but results in a steady
rate of appreciation. A situation will be considered in which the corporation wishes to determine the present value after taxes of the stream of
receipts obtained from these equities when they are held for a period of N
years. It is thus assumed that the firm has a definite planning horizon of
that many years; it wants to reconsider its investment mix after N years.[9]

[8] Vernon Smith points out that expensing and depreciation by the annuity method
is the only way to avoid distorting investment decisions. See Vernon L. Smith, *Depreciation and Investment Theory*, Stanford Institute for Mathematical Studies in
the Social Sciences, Technical Report No. 165 (Dec. 28, 1961). This can be seen
by setting $V = 0$ and solving for ρ. Richard A. Musgrave discusses the effect of
depreciation policy on rate of return in *The Theory of Public Finance* (McGraw-
Hill, 1959), pp. 336-46.

[9] It is quite relevant to compare decisions over such a planning horizon with the
fixed life investments whose present value is computed above. Any time discrepancy
between that fixed life and the planning horizon can be eliminated by considering
these investments to be a series of physical assets or soft goods. The investment
plan under consideration then becomes a combination of an immediate expenditure
coupled with future expenditures that replace the immediate investment with sec-
ond-generation and third-generation investments, so that the investments are available for the entire planning period of N years. Equations D.2 to D.5 are unaffected.

Any transaction costs associated with a future shift to another investment should be fully recovered by the time the planning horizon is reached. That is, tax liabilities associated with an exchange, as well as those associated with the current stream of income, should be taken into account.

Case 1. If the equity yields interest income, the stream of receipts (G_k) must be defined similarly to the stream derived from a capital investment. However, the flow of funds from such an investment would actually consist of a stream of interest terminated by recovery of the initial investment at the end of the holding period. Conceptually that income stream is equivalent to the interest stream plus an annuity whose amount after N years equals the initial investment.

Therefore, the present value of that investment may be written as:

$$\text{(D.9)} \qquad V_4 = - C + \sum_{k=1}^{N} \frac{(G_k^* - A_k)(1 - t) + A_k}{(1 + \rho)^k},$$

where A_k is the annuity whose amount at the market rate of interest, ρ is C. When the method of depreciation used on physical assets is the annuity method, Equation D.2 is identical to Equation D.9.

Case 2. If the investment produces intercorporate dividends, the situation is identical, except that 85 percent of the dividends are deductible from income and some other corporation has already paid its own corporate tax liability on the original flow of receipts prior to the payment of dividends. The tax liability for the investing firm becomes:

$$\text{(D.10)} \qquad V_5 = - C + \sum_{k=1}^{N} \frac{(G_k^* - A_k)(0.15[1 - t] + 0.85) + A_k}{(1 + \rho)^k}.$$

Case 3. Finally, if the investment produces only future appreciation, the actual flow of receipts to the investing corporation consists of a single lump-sum terminal payment. Conceptually that terminal payment is equivalent to a stream of annual payments for the life of the investment. A portion of each annual payment reflects the annuity payment whose amount is the original investment; the remainder reflects the accruing increments in value producing the final appreciation. The present value of an investment in appreciating securities becomes:

$$\text{(D.11)} \qquad V_6 = - C + \left[\sum_{k=1}^{N} \frac{G_k - A_k}{(1 + \rho)^k} \right] \left[1 - \frac{t_g}{(1 + \rho)^N} \right] + \sum_{k=1}^{N} \frac{A_k}{(1 + \rho)^k},$$

where G_k^* is the equivalent annual income, t_g the tax rate on capital gains upon realization, and A_k an annuity whose amount at interest rate ρ is C.

In fact, the present values of investments in financial assets (Equations D.9-D.11) are not directly comparable to the present values of direct investments (Equations D.1-D.5). Any firm considering the present value of returns on a particular activity must in fact consider that returns from that activity are taxable to other corporations if investments are made by buying financial assets. The streams G_k^* shown in Equations D.9-D.11 are therefore smaller than the streams of receipts shown in Equations D.2-D.5. All present values can be reduced to a common basis by considering the net return to the investing corporation from an identical stream of receipts produced by direct investment under alternative ownership arrangements. It is assumed that the corporation making the direct investment retains funds equal to its initial investment in D.9 and D.10 and that the appreciation in D.11 results from reinvestment in earnings opportunities of the same kind as the original direct investment.

Then the firm that pays out the entire amount of its income in the form of interest produces an income flow to the investing company of:

$$G_k^* - A_k = G_k - D_k$$

in terms of the original flow of receipts from the direct investment. If payments are made to the investing corporation as dividends, the original flow is taxable to the corporation making the direct investment at a rate t^*, and the flow to the investing corporation becomes:

$$G_k^* - A_k = (G_k - D_k)(1 - t^*).$$

Finally, reinvestment results in accruing value to the investing corporation of:

$$G_k^* - A_k = (G_k - D_k)(1 - t^*)\frac{V^*}{C^*},$$

if the proceeds of the direct investment are taxable at a rate t^* and the direct investor has access to investment opportunities whose present value equals V^*/C^* per dollar invested. Rewritten in terms of the net return to the investing corporation, Equations D.9-D.11 become:

(D.12) $\quad V_4' = -C + \sum_{k=1}^{N} \dfrac{(G_k - D_k)(1 - t) + A_k}{(1 + \rho)^k}$

(D.13) $\quad V_5' = -C + \sum_{k=1}^{N} \dfrac{(G_k - D_k)(1 - t^*)[0.15(1 - t) + 0.85] + A_k}{(1 + \rho)^k}$

(D.14)
$$V_6' = -C + \left[\frac{V^*}{C^*}\sum_{k=1}^{N} \frac{(G_k - D_k)(1 - t^*)}{(1 + \rho)^k}\right]\left[1 - \frac{t_g}{(1 - \rho)^N}\right]$$
$$+ \sum_{k=1}^{N} \frac{A_k}{(1 + \rho)^k}.$$

The following conclusions can be drawn from these equations[10]:

1. Investment in expensible items is advantageous to investment in depreciable property ($V_3 > V_2$).

2. Selling tradable investments can be more advantageous than holding to maturity an investment acquired ($V_3^* \geq V_3$, $V_2^* \geq V_2$). (The timing of such sales is important, since the market available may be rather thin.)

3. For companies in the same tax bracket, direct investment in physical assets is preferable to investment in the same asset through debentures that assign all of the income to the investing corporation ($V_2 > V_4'$). (Of course, such an extreme commitment of income could not be obtained in any actual situation.) The advantage of direct investment lies in the fact that allowable depreciation methods permit recovery of the initial cost tax-free at a rate faster than the terminal recovery permitted for any financial investment.

4. If the tax rates of the investing corporation and of the corporation making the direct investment are the same ($t = t^*$), then debentures are preferable to dividend-paying assets; if, in addition, opportunities for appreciation are available only at the market rate ρ, debentures will be preferable to accumulation-yielding financial paper ($V_4' > V_5' > V_6'$). This is because income from direct investment is subjected to a second round of taxation either to the extent that intercorporate dividends are taxed, or to the extent that capital gains are taxed.

5. Finally, under the assumptions above concerning the amount of appreciation and tax rates of the two corporations, dividend-paying securities will have a higher present value to investing corporations than will investments in appreciating securities in most cases (V_5' usually $> V_6'$). This is because capital gains taxes at rates of 22 to 25 percent, unless they are highly discounted for a long period into the future, will exceed the effective 3 to 7 percent rate of tax on dividends implied by the 85 percent intercorporate dividend deduction.

Assuming that the case illustrated by debentures is unrealistic, corporations interested in maximizing their own net worth would be expected to concentrate on expensible investments and direct investment opportunities. Financial investments would be used only if opportunities were available for investing in companies with lower marginal tax rates, if financial investment would have indirect effects on the costs of the investing company, or if the investing company had reason to think it was investing in an enterprise with a rate of return substantially in excess of the present market. In the latter case, which is unimportant in a competitive market,

---

[10] For the derivation of these results, see the note following this Appendix.

the investing company would be trading some increase in taxation for the limited legal liability associated with equity but not with direct investment. Otherwise it should follow the direct investment avenue.

On balance, there does not appear to be any strong *direct* motivation for the corporation to avail itself of opportunities that yield capital gains. It is not particularly advantageous to its own investment portfolio to do so.

For the unincorporated enterprise and the corporation alike, substantial tax avoidance can be achieved by gearing production to areas of statutory gains, investing in expensible equipment, and selling depreciable real estate. In practice, each of these possibilities can be expected to have adverse allocation effects. Moreover, the imperfections that actually exist in markets for real capital goods and the barriers to entry in certain areas of production will limit the number of businesses that can actually make use of such tax avoidance possibilities.

Note to Appendix D

The results on page 254 may be derived as follows:

1. Expensible versus depreciable investment

$$V_3 - V_2 = \sum_{k=1}^{N} \frac{G_k}{(1+\rho)^k}(1-t) - \sum_{k=1}^{N} \frac{(G_k - D_k)(1-t) + D_k}{(1+\rho)^k}$$
$$- C[1-t] + C$$
$$= Ct - \sum_{k=1}^{N} \frac{D_k t}{(1+\rho)^k} = + \left(C - \sum_{k=1}^{N} \frac{D_k}{(1+\rho)^k} \right) t$$

but $\sum_{k=1}^{N} D_k = C$, and $\rho > 0$, so that $\sum_{k=1}^{N} \frac{D_k}{(1+\rho)^k} < C$.

Hence, $V_3 - V_2 > 0$.

2. (See Equations D.3 and D.8.)

3. Direct investment versus indirect investment in debentures

$$V_2 - V_4' = \left[\sum_{k=1}^{N} \frac{D_k}{(1+\rho)^k} - \sum_{k=1}^{N} \frac{A_k}{(1+\rho)^k} \right] t$$
$$= \left[\sum_{k=1}^{N} \frac{D_k}{(1+\rho)^k} - \frac{C}{(1+\rho)^N} \right] t,$$

since the definition of A_k is that annuity whose amount is C. Let $D_k = C/N$. This reflects straight-line depreciation, the present value of which is less than that obtainable under accelerated methods.

$$V_2 - V_4' = \frac{C_t}{(1+\rho)^N}\left[\frac{1}{N}\sum_{k=0}^{N-1}(1+\rho)^k - 1\right]$$

Clearly if $\rho > 0$, $V_2 - V_4' > 0$, since each factor of $1/N$ is multiplied by a fraction greater than unity.

4a. Indirect investment in debentures versus dividend-paying securities

When $t = t^*$,

$$V_4' - V_5' = \sum_{k=1}^{N}\frac{(G_k - D_k)(1 - t)(1 - 0.15[1 - t] - 0.85)}{(1+\rho)^k}$$

$$= \sum_{k=1}^{N}\frac{0.15(G_k - D_k)(1 - t)t}{(1+\rho)^k}$$

$$> 0, \text{ if } t > 0.$$

4b. Indirect investment in debentures versus appreciating securities

When $t = t^*$ and $V^*/C^* = 1$,

$$V_4' - V_6' = \left[\sum_{k=1}^{N}\frac{(G_k - D_k)(1 - t) + A_k}{(1+\rho)^k}\right] -$$

$$\left[\sum_{k=1}^{N}\frac{(G_k - D_k)(1 - t)}{(1+\rho)^k}\right]\left[1 - \frac{t_g}{(1+\rho)^N}\right] -$$

$$\left[\sum_{k=1}^{N}\frac{A_k}{(1+\rho)^k}\right]$$

$$= \frac{t_g(V_2 + C)}{(1+\rho)^N} > 0, \text{ if } V_2 + C > 0.$$

5. Indirect investment in dividend-paying versus appreciating securities

When $t = t^*$ and $V^*/C^* = 1$,

$$V_5' - V_6' =$$

$$\sum_{k=1}^{N}\frac{(G_k - D_k)(1 - t)\left([0.15(1 - t) + 0.85] - \left[1 - \frac{t_g}{(1+\rho)^N}\right]\right)}{(1+\rho)^k},$$

and $\left([0.15(1 - t) + 0.85] - \left[1 - \dfrac{t_g}{(1 + \rho)^N} \right] \right) \sum\limits_{k=1}^{N} \dfrac{G_k - D_k}{(1 + \rho)^k} \gtrless 0,$

when $\quad\quad\quad [0.15(1 - t) + 0.85] \gtrless \left[1 - \dfrac{t_g}{(1 + \rho)^N} \right].$

For corporations subject to the normal rate, $t = t_g = 0.22$, and the above becomes

$$0.15(0.78) + 0.85 = 0.97 \gtrless 1 - \frac{0.22}{(1 + \rho)^N}.$$

For corporations subject to surtax and the alternative tax, $t = 0.48$, $g = 0.25$, and thus:

$$(0.15)(0.52) + 0.85 = 0.93 \gtrless 1 - \frac{0.25}{(1 + \rho)^N}.$$

APPENDIX E

Bibliography

Ando, Albert, and Franco Modigliani, "The 'Life Cycle' Hypothesis of Saving: Aggregate Implications and Tests," *American Economic Review,* Vol. 53, March 1963. pp. 55-84.

Bailey, Martin J., "Capital Gains and Income Taxation," in Arnold C. Harberger and Martin J. Bailey, eds., *Taxation of Income From Capital.* Washington: Brookings Institution, 1968.

Bangs, Robert, "The Dilemma of the Cut-Rate Tax: Reflections on the History of the Federal Income Tax Treatment of Capital Gains and Losses," *Taxes,* Vol. 31, January 1953. pp. 31-41.

Barlow, Robin, Harvey E. Brazer, and James N. Morgan, "A Survey of Investment Management and Working Behavior Among High-Income Individuals," *American Economic Review,* Vol. 55, May 1965. pp. 252-64.

————. *Economic Behavior of the Affluent.* Washington: Brookings Institution, 1966.

Benewitz, Maurice C., "Theoretical Effect of Income Averaging for Tax Purposes on Investment Incentives," *National Tax Journal,* Vol. 6, June 1953. pp. 194-96.

Blum, Walter J., "A Handy Summary of the Capital Gains Arguments," *Taxes,* Vol. 35, April 1957. pp. 247-66.

————. "Taxation of Capital Gains in the Light of Recent Economic Developments—Some Observations," *National Tax Journal,* Vol. 18, December 1965. pp. 430-36.

Bravman, M. Francis, "Equalization of Tax on All Individuals with the

258

Same Aggregate Income over Same Number of Years," *Columbia Law Review,* Vol. 50, January 1950. pp. 1-28.

Brazer, Harvey E., *A Program for Federal Tax Revision,* Michigan Pamphlets No. 28. Ann Arbor: University of Michigan, Institute of Public Administration, 1960.

Break, George F., "Income Taxes and Incentives to Work: An Empirical Study," *American Economic Review,* Vol. 47, September 1957. pp. 529-49.

————. "On the Deductibility of Capital Losses Under the Income Tax," *Journal of Finance,* Vol. 7, May 1952. pp. 214-29.

Brittain, John A., "The Tax Structure and Corporate Dividend Policy," *American Economic Review,* Vol. 54, May 1964. pp. 272-87.

————. *Corporate Dividend Policy.* Washington: Brookings Institution, 1966.

Brown, E. Cary, "Analysis of Consumption Taxes in Terms of the Theory of Income Determination," *American Economic Review,* Vol. 40, March 1950. pp. 74-89.

Brown, Jonathan A., "The Locked-In Problem," *Federal Tax Policy for Economic Growth and Stability.* Papers submitted by panelists appearing before the Subcommittee on Tax Policy, November 9, 1955. Joint Committee on the Economic Report, 84 Cong. 1 sess. Washington: Government Printing Office, 1955. pp. 367-81.

Butters, J. Keith, and John V. Lintner, *Effect of Federal Taxes on Growing Enterprises.* Boston: Harvard University, Graduate School of Business Administration, Bureau of Research, 1945.

Cain, G. F., "The Labor Force Participation of Married Women." Unpublished doctoral dissertation, University of Chicago, 1964.

Clark, Reuben, "The Paradox of Capital Gains: Taxable Income That Ought Not To Be Currently Taxed," *Tax Revision Compendium,* submitted to the House Committee on Ways and Means in connection with panel discussions beginning November 16, 1959, Vol. 2. Washington: Government Printing Office, 1959. pp. 1243-56.

Cloe, Carl W., "Capital Gains and the Changing Price Level," *National Tax Journal,* Vol. 5, September 1952. pp. 207-17.

Colm, Gerhard, and Fritz Lehmann, *Economic Conséquences of Recent American Tax Policy.* New York: New School for Social Research, 1938.

Denison, Edward F., *The Sources of Economic Growth in the United States and the Alternatives Before Us.* Supplementary Paper No. 13. New York: Committee for Economic Development, 1962.

Director, Aaron, "Capital Gains and High Rates of Progressive Taxation," National Tax Association, *Proceedings of the Forty-Sixth An-*

nual Conference on Taxation, 1953. Sacramento, 1954, pp. 144-50.

Domar, Evsey D., and Richard A. Musgrave, "Proportional Income Taxation and Risk-Taking," American Economic Association, *Readings in the Economics of Taxation.* Homewood, Illinois: Richard D. Irwin, Inc., 1959. pp. 493-524.

Dosser, Douglas, "Tax Incidence and Growth," *Economic Journal,* Vol. 71, September 1961. pp. 572-91.

Eisner, Robert, "Accelerated Amortization, Growth, and Net Profits," *Quarterly Journal of Economics,* Vol. 66, November 1952. pp. 533-44.

———. "An Appraisal of Proposals for Tax Differentials Affecting Investment," *Income Tax Differentials.* Princeton: Tax Institute, Inc., November 1957.

Eustace, J. S., and C. S. Lyon, "Assignment of Income: Fruit and Tree as Irrigated by the P. G. Lake Case," *Tax Law Review,* Vol. 17, 1962. pp. 293-430.

Farrar, Donald E., *The Investment Decision Under Uncertainty.* Englewood Cliffs, New Jersey: Prentice-Hall, 1962.

Gale, John F., "Land Sellers' Awareness of the Tax on Capital Gains: Great Plains Land Market, 1957," *Agricultural Finance Review,* Vol. 23, April 1962. pp. 9-14.

Gemmill, Robert F., "The Effect of the Capital Gains Tax on Asset Prices," *National Tax Journal,* Vol. 9, December 1956. pp. 289-301. "Note" by Charles C. Holt, *National Tax Journal,* Vol. 10, June 1957. pp. 186-87.

Goldsmith, Raymond W., and Robert E. Lipsey, *Studies in the National Balance Sheet of the United States,* Vol. I. Princeton: Princeton University Press for the National Bureau of Economic Research, 1963.

Goode, Richard, *The Individual Income Tax.* Washington: Brookings Institution, 1964.

———. *The Corporation Income Tax.* New York: John Wiley and Sons, 1951.

Griswold, Erwin Nathaniel, *Cases and Materials on Federal Taxation.* Brooklyn: The Foundation Press, 1960.

Groves, Harold M., "Taxation of Capital Gains," *Tax Revision Compendium,* submitted to the House Committee on Ways and Means in connection with panel discussions beginning November 16, 1959, Vol. 2. Washington: Government Printing Office, 1959. pp. 1193-1201.

Gurin, Gerald, J. Veroff, and S. Feld, *Americans View Their Mental Health.* New York: Basic Books, 1960.

Guthrie, Harold W., "Intergeneration Transfers of Wealth and the Theory of Saving," *Journal of Business,* University of Chicago Press, Vol. 36, January 1963. pp. 97-108.

Harberger, Arnold C., "The Taxation of Mineral Industries," *Federal Tax Policy for Economic Growth and Stability.* Papers submitted by panelists appearing before the Subcommittee on Tax Policy, November 9, 1955. Joint Committee on the Economic Report, 84 Cong. 1 sess. Washington: Government Printing Office, 1955. pp. 439-49.

————. "Taxation, Resource Allocation, and Welfare," in *The Role of Direct and Indirect Taxes in the Federal Revenue System,* a Conference Report of the National Bureau of Economic Research and the Brookings Institution. Princeton: Princeton University Press, 1964. pp. 25-70.

Head, J. G., "The Case for a Capital Gains Tax," *Public Finance,* Vol. 18, Nos. 3-4, 1963. pp. 220-49.

Heller, Walter W., "Investors' Decisions, Equity, and the Capital Gains Tax," *Federal Tax Policy for Economic Growth and Stability.* Papers submitted by panelists appearing before the Subcommittee on Tax Policy, November 9, 1955. Joint Committee on the Economic Report, 84 Cong. 1 sess. Washington: Government Printing Office, 1955. pp. 381-94.

Hinrichs, Harley H., "An Empirical Measure of Investors' Responsiveness to Differentials in Capital Gains Tax Rates Among Income Groups," *National Tax Journal,* Vol. 16, September 1963. pp. 224-29.

————. "Dynamic-Regressive Effects of the Treatment of Capital Gains on the American Tax System During 1957-1959," *Public Finance,* Vol. 19, No. 1, 1964. pp. 73-83.

————. "Unreporting of Capital Gains on Tax Returns or How to Succeed in Gainsmanship Without Actually Paying Taxes," *National Tax Journal,* Vol. 17, June 1964. pp. 158-63.

————. " 'Altruism on Wall Street or Who's Afraid of the IRS?' A Reply to West and Riley," *National Tax Journal,* Vol. 18, March 1965. pp. 91-96. [See West and Riley.]

Holt, Charles C., "Averaging of Income for Tax Purposes: Equity and Fiscal-Policy Considerations," *National Tax Journal,* Vol. 2, December 1949. pp. 349-61.

Holt, Charles C., and John P. Shelton, "The Lock-In Effect of the Capital Gains Tax," *National Tax Journal,* Vol. 15, December 1962. pp. 337-52.

————. "The Implications of the Capital Gains Tax for Investment Decisions," *Journal of Finance,* Vol. 16, December 1961. pp. 559-80.

Illersic, Alfred Roman, *The Taxation of Capital Gains.* London: Staples Press, 1962.

Jantscher, Gerald R., *Trusts and Estate Taxation.* Washington: Brookings Institution, 1967.

Jorgenson, Dale W., "Capital Theory and Investment Behavior," *American Economic Review,* Vol. 53, May 1963. pp. 247-59.

Kaldor, Nicholas, *An Expenditure Tax.* London: George Allen and Unwin, 1955.

Katona, George, *The Powerful Consumer.* New York: McGraw-Hill, 1960.

Katona, George, Charles A. Lininger, and Richard F. Kosobud, *1962 Survey of Consumer Finances.* Ann Arbor: University of Michigan, Institute for Social Research, Survey Research Center, 1963.

Klem, Charles, "The Stock Exchange Point of View on Capital Gains Taxation," National Tax Association, *Proceedings of the Forty-Sixth Annual Conference on Taxation,* 1953. Sacramento: 1954. pp. 138-44.

Krutilla, John V., and Otto E. Eckstein, *Multiple Purpose River Development.* Baltimore: Johns Hopkins Press, 1958.

Levy, Michael E., *Fiscal Policy, Cycles and Growth.* Studies in Business Economics, No. 81. New York: National Industrial Conference Board, 1963.

Lewis, Wilfred, Jr., *Federal Fiscal Policy in the Postwar Recessions.* Washington: Brookings Institution, 1962.

Likert, Rensis, *New Patterns of Management.* New York: McGraw-Hill, 1961.

Lintner, John, "Dividends, Earnings, Leverage, Stock Prices and the Supply of Capital to Corporations," *Review of Economics and Statistics,* Vol. 44, August 1962. pp. 243-69.

Markowitz, Harry M., *Portfolio Selection.* New York: John Wiley and Sons, 1959.

Massell, Benton F., "Capital Formation and Technological Change in United States Manufacturing," *Review of Economics and Statistics,* Vol. 42, May 1960. pp. 182-88.

Mayer, Thomas, "The Empirical Significance of the Real Balance Effect," *Quarterly Journal of Economics,* Vol. 73, May 1959. pp. 275-91.

McClung, Nelson, "The Distribution of Capital Gain on Corporate Shares by Holding Time," *Review of Economics and Statistics,* Vol. 48, February 1966. pp. 40-50.

Meyer, John R., and Edwin Kuh, *The Investment Decision.* Cambridge: Harvard University Press, 1957.

Miller, Merton H., and Franco Modigliani, "Dividend Policy, Growth, and the Valuation of Shares," *Journal of Business,* Vol. 34, October 1961. pp. 411-33.

Miller, Peter, "The 'Capital Asset' Concept: A Critique of Capital Gains Taxation: I," *Yale Law Journal,* Vol. 59, April 1950. pp. 837-85.

———. "The 'Capital Asset' Concept: A Critique of Capital Gains Taxation: II," *Yale Law Journal,* Vol. 59, May 1950. pp. 1057-86.

————. "Capital Gains Taxation of the Fruits of Personal Effort: Before and Under the 1954 Code," *Yale Law Journal,* Vol. 64, November 1954. pp. 1-83.

Miller, Roger F., and Harold W. Watts, "A Model of Household Investment in Financial Assets," in *Determinants of Investment Behavior.* National Bureau of Economic Research, Conference Series 18. New York: Columbia University Press, 1967.

Mincer, Jacob, "Labor Force Participation of Married Women: A Study of Labor Supply," in National Bureau Committee for Economic Research, *Aspects of Labor Economics, A Conference of the Universities.* Princeton: Princeton University Press, 1962.

Modigliani, Franco, and Richard Brumberg, "Utility Analysis and the Consumption Function: an Interpretation of Cross-Section Data," *Post-Keynesian Economics,* Kenneth K. Kurihara, ed., New Brunswick: Rutgers University Press, 1954.

Morag, Amotz, *On Taxes and Inflation.* New York: Random House, 1965.

Musgrave, Richard A., *The Theory of Public Finance.* New York: McGraw-Hill, 1959.

National Association of Manufacturers, *A Tax Program for Economic Growth.* New York: National Association of Manufacturers, 1955.

New York Stock Exchange, Department of Research and Statistics, "On the Effects of Reducing the Capital Gains Tax Rate: Its Impact on Locked-In Capital and Federal Revenues." (Summary of a survey of investors by Louis Harris and Associates, Inc., New York.)

Pechman, Joseph A., "A Practical Averaging Proposal," *National Tax Journal,* Vol. 7, September 1954. pp. 261-63.

————. "Individual Income Tax Provisions of the Revenue Act of 1964," *Journal of Finance,* Vol. 20, May 1965. pp. 247-72 (Brookings Institution Reprint 96).

————. *Federal Tax Policy.* Washington: Brookings Institution, 1966.

Perry, J. Harvey, "Capital Gains: The British Point of View," *Canadian Tax Journal,* Vol. 1, November-December 1953. pp. 548-61.

Petrie, J. R., "Capital Gains in Canada," Canadian Tax Foundation, *Tax Bulletin,* Vol. 2, September 1952. pp. 264-70.

Pierce, Melville, "What Are the Capital Gains?," *Canadian Chartered Accountant Tax Review,* September 1953. pp. 117-23.

Projector, Dorothy S., "Consumer Asset Preferences," *American Economic Review,* Vol. 55, May 1965. pp. 227-51.

Richman, Raymond L., "Reconsideration of the Capital Gains Tax—A Comment," *National Tax Journal,* Vol. 14, December 1961. pp. 402-04.

Samuelson, Paul A., "The Pure Theory of Public Expenditure," *Review of Economics and Statistics,* Vol. 36, November 1954. pp. 387-89.

Schouton, D. B. J., "Theory and Practice of Capital Levies in the Netherlands," *Oxford Institute of Statistics Bulletin,* Vol. 10, April 1948. pp. 117-22.

Seltzer, Lawrence H., "Capital Gains and the Income Tax," *American Economic Review,* Vol. 40, May 1950. pp. 371-78.

———. "Evolution of the Special Legal Status of Capital Gains Under the Income Tax," *National Tax Journal,* Vol. 3, March 1950. pp. 18-35.

———. "Should Capital Gains Be Taxed? . . . The American Approach," *Report of the Proceedings of the Thirteenth Annual Tax Conference, Convened by the Canadian Tax Foundation.* Toronto: The Foundation, 1960.

———. with the assistance of Selma F. Goldsmith and M. Slade Kendrick, *The Nature and Tax Treatment of Capital Gains and Losses.* New York: National Bureau of Economic Research, 1951.

Shoup, Carl S., *Federal Estate and Gift Taxes.* Washington: Brookings Institution, 1966.

Silverstein, Leonard L., "The Capital Asset Definition," *Tax Revision Compendium,* submitted to the House Committee on Ways and Means in connection with panel discussions beginning November 16, 1959, Vol. 2. Washington: Government Printing Office, 1959. pp. 1285-99.

Simons, Henry C., *Personal Income Taxation.* Chicago: University of Chicago Press, 1938.

———. *Federal Tax Reform.* Chicago: University of Chicago Press, 1950.

Slitor, Richard E., "Problems of Definition Under the Capital Gains Tax," *National Tax Journal,* Vol. 10, March 1957. pp. 26-37.

Smith, Dan Throop, "Tax Treatment of Capital Gains," *Tax Revision Compendium,* submitted to the House Committee on Ways and Means in connection with panel discussions beginning November 16, 1959, Vol. 2. Washington: Government Printing Office, 1959. pp. 1233-41.

———. *Federal Tax Reform: The Issues and a Program.* New York: McGraw-Hill, 1961.

Smith, Vernon L., *Depreciation and Investment Theory,* Stanford Institute for Mathematical Studies in the Social Sciences, Technical Report No. 165. Stanford: Stanford University Press, December 28, 1961.

Somers, Harold M., "An Economic Analysis of the Capital Gains Tax," *National Tax Journal,* Vol. 1, September 1948. pp. 226-32.

———. "Estate Taxes and Business Mergers: The Effects of Estate Taxes on Business Structure and Practices in the United States," *Journal of Finance,* Vol. 13, May 1958. pp. 201-10.

————. "Reconsideration of the Capital Gains Tax," *National Tax Journal,* Vol. 13, December 1960. pp. 289-309.

————. "The Capital Gains Tax: Some Misunderstandings," *Commercial and Financial Chronicle,* Vol. 189, December 10, 1959.

Sprinkel, Beryl W., and B. Kenneth West, "Effects of Capital Gains Taxes on Investment Decisions," *Journal of Business,* Vol. 35, April 1962. pp. 122-34.

Stanley, Joyce, and Richard Kilcullen, *The Federal Income Tax: A Guide to the Law.* New York: The Tax Club Press, 1955.

Steger, Wilbur A., "Averaging Income for Tax Purposes: A Statistical Study," *National Tax Journal,* Vol. 9, June 1956. pp. 97-114.

————. "Averaging of Income for Income Tax Purposes." Doctoral thesis, Harvard University, 1956.

————. "Economic Consequences of Substantial Changes in the Method of Taxing Capital Gains and Losses," *Tax Revision Compendium,* submitted to the House Committee on Ways and Means in connection with panel discussions beginning November 16, 1959, Vol. 2. Washington: Government Printing Office, 1959. pp. 1261-83.

————. "Simulation and Tax Analysis: A Research Proposal," *National Tax Journal,* Vol. 14, September 1961. pp. 286-301.

————. "Statement," *Income Tax Revision.* Panel discussions before the Committee on Ways and Means, House of Representatives, 86 Cong. 1 sess. Washington: Government Printing Office, 1960.

————. "The Taxation of Unrealized Capital Gains and Losses: A Statistical Study," *National Tax Journal,* Vol. 10, September 1957. pp. 266-81.

Steiner, Peter O., "The Non-Neutrality of Corporate Income Taxation—With and Without Depletion," *National Tax Journal,* Vol. 16, September 1963. pp. 238-51.

Stockfisch, Jacob A., "A Study of California's Tax Treatment of Manufacturing Industries." Report submitted to State of California. Sacramento: California Economic Development Agency, 1961.

Suits, Daniel B., "The Determinants of Consumer Expenditure: A Review of Present Knowledge," *Impacts of Monetary Policy,* Commission on Money and Credit. Englewood Cliffs, New Jersey: Prentice-Hall, 1963.

Surrey, Stanley S., "Definitional Problems in Capital Gains Taxation," *Tax Revision Compendium,* submitted to the House Committee on Ways and Means in connection with panel discussions beginning November 16, 1959, Vol. 2. Washington: Government Printing Office, 1959. pp. 1203-32.

————. "The Supreme Court and the Federal Income Tax: Some Implications of the Recent Decisions," *Illinois Law Review,* Vol. 35, March 1941. pp. 779 ff.

Titmuss, Richard M., *Income Distribution and Social Change: A Study in Criticism.* London: George Allen & Unwin, 1962.

Tobin, James, "Liquidity Preference as Behavior Towards Risk," *Review of Economic Studies,* Vol. 25(2), February 1958. pp. 65-86.

Tudor, Owen, "Exemption of Capital Gains From the Capital Gains Tax," *Taxes,* Vol. 35, February 1957. p. 101.

————. "The Equitable Justification for the Capital Gains Tax: Existing Dissatisfaction with [it] and the Alternatives," *Taxes,* Vol. 34, September 1956. pp. 643-46.

Turvey, Ralph, "Equity and a Capital Gains Tax," *Oxford Economic Papers,* Vol. 12, June 1960. pp. 181-92.

————. "A Tax System Without Company Taxation," *Canadian Tax Journal,* Vol. 11, September-October 1963. pp. 409-19.

Twentieth Century Fund, *Facing the Tax Problem.* New York: The Fund, 1937.

Uhr, Carl G., "Implications of 'New Proposals for Capital Gains Taxation,' " *Taxes,* Vol. 35, April 1957. pp. 267-72.

U. K. Royal Commission on the Taxation of Profits and Income, *Final Report,* Cmd. 9474, June 1955.

U. S. Congress. House of Representatives. Committee on Ways and Means. *Income Tax Revision.* Panel discussions. 86 Cong. 1 sess. Washington: Government Printing Office, 1960.

————. *President's 1963 Tax Message,* Hearings, Part 1. 88 Cong. 1 sess. Washington: Government Printing Office, 1963.

————. Subcommittee on Internal Revenue Taxation. *List of Substantive Unintended Benefits and Hardships and Additional Problems for the Technical Amendments Bill of 1957.* Washington: Government Printing Office, 1956.

U. S. Congress. Joint Economic Committee. *The Federal Tax System: Facts and Problems, 1964.* 88 Cong. 2 sess. Washington: Government Printing Office, 1964.

U. S. Treasury Department. Internal Revenue Service. *Depreciation: Guidelines and Rules,* Publication No. 456. Washington: Government Printing Office, 1962; revised 1964.

————. *Statistics of Income, Corporation Income Tax Returns,* and *Individual Income Tax Returns,* various issues. Washington: Government Printing Office.

————. *Statistics of Income—1962, Supplemental Report, Sales of Capital Assets Reported on Individual Income Tax Returns,* Publication No. 458. Washington: Government Printing Office, 1966.

————. *Statistics of Income—1959, Supplemental Report, Sales of Capital Assets Reported on Individual Income Tax Returns,* Publication No. 458. Washington: Government Printing Office, 1962.

U. S. Treasury Department. Tax Advisory Staff of the Secretary. *Federal Income Tax Treatment of Capital Gains and Losses.* Washington: Government Printing Office, 1951.

Vandermeulen, Alice John, "Capital Gains: Two Tests for the Taxpayer and a Proposal for the President," *National Tax Journal,* Vol. 16, December 1963. pp. 397-404.

Vickrey, William S., *Agenda for Progressive Taxation.* New York: Ronald Press, 1947.

Wallich, Henry C., "Taxation of Capital Gains in the Light of Recent Economic Developments," *National Tax Journal,* Vol. 18, June 1965. pp. 133-50.

Watts, Harold W., "An Objective Permanent Income Concept for the Household." Unpublished Cowles Foundation Discussion Paper, No. 99. New Haven: The Cowles Foundation, November 23, 1960.

Wells, Anita, "Legislative History of Treatment of Capital Gains Under the Federal Income Tax, 1913-1948," *National Tax Journal,* Vol. 2, March 1949. pp. 12-32.

West, Stan, and James W. Riley, "How to Succeed in Figuremanship Without Having All the Figures," *National Tax Journal,* Vol. 18, March 1965. pp. 78-90.

Woods, J. B., "Taxation of Extraordinary Income," *Taxes,* Vol. 33, May 1955. pp. 353-69.

Yaari, Menahem E., "Lifetime Consumer Allocation Under Certainty and Uncertainty," U. S. Navy Department, Office of Naval Research, Technical Report No. 120. Washington: August 1, 1962.

————. "On the Consumer's Lifetime Allocation Process," *International Economic Review,* Vol. 5, No. 3, 1964.

————. "Uncertain Lifetime, Life Insurance, and the Theory of the Consumer," *Review of Economic Studies,* Vol. 32, April 1965. pp. 137-50.

————. "On the Existence of an Optimal Plan in a Continuous-Time Allocation Process," *Econometrica,* Vol. 32, October 1964. pp. 576-90.

Index

sales, 75, 99; proposed change in, 128-40, 143, 163, 224-25; as basis for prorating, 167, 171, 173, 176; effect of proration on, 175-77; and accrual taxation, 190*n*; under roll-over, 220

Holt, Charles C., 8*n*, 131*n*, 133, 146*n*

Hotchpotch problem, 30

Household goods, losses on, 13*n*

Households: stock ownership by, 67; unrealized gains of, 93-97; savings of, 154

Incentives to hold assets, 137, 158-59, 164, 175, 177, 206; effect of proration on, 104; effect of tax treatment of capital gains on, 106, 111, 147, 163; to invest, 115; to sell, 149, 157, 159, 171, 174, 179; effect of roll-over on, 206; effect of capital gains definition on, 212-14

Income, adjusted gross, definition of, 19*n*; as a measure of taxable capacity, 44, 210; and underreporting of gains, 69; allotted to holding period, 78-79; and size of gain or loss, 78-79, 81; of taxpayers reporting gains, 81, 89; of corporations, capital gains in relation to, 87-88; gains as a proportion of, 83-84; current, *vs.* enlargement of portfolio, 152-54

Income, definition of (*see also* Income, measurement of), 5-6, 45*n*, 47-51, 58, 210; accretion concept, 6, 49-51, 109, 111, 113, 115, 191, 210; factor income, 47; Hicks' *ex ante,* 50; Friedman's transitory, 50*n*; in national accounts, 210-11; taxable-income concept, 210-12

Income, future, assignment of. *See* Recurrent income flows

Income, measurement of (*see also* Income, definition of), 51-53, 58; frequency of assessment, 51-52

Income, ordinary (*see also* Business profits; Recurrent income flows; Services, return to): tax treatment of, 19*n*, 25, 39, 153, 191, 207*n*, 227-28; and royalties, 24, 41-42; *vs.* capital

gains (*see also* Recognition of gain or loss), 25-28, 37, 40-42, 54, 57-58, 63, 111, 114, 116, 141, 164, 167, 170-71, 181, 186, 192-93, 99, 205, 210, 212, 228; progressive taxation of, 37-39, 53-54, 59, 112-13, 165, 170, 172, 173*n*, 218, 226

Income redistribution: and the tax structure, 45, 51-52, 56; effect of changes in capital gains tax on, 62

Income-splitting, 104*n*

Income tax, 47, 213; *vs.* capital gains, 3, 4, 65; as basis of tax system, 51; progression in, 52, 111, 113-14, 118, 164, 167*n*, 184, 197, 209, 218; marginal and average rates of, and capital gains, 84, 227; deductions and marginal rates, 84-86, 117; coverage of, 113; *vs.* transfer tax, 162-63; integrated with capital gains tax, 181-82

Income, taxable: and capital gains, 5-6, 50, 194*n*, 210, 212; timing and measurement of, 9, 48-49, 51-53; definition of, 19*n*, 49-51; accrual *vs.* realization, 52

Individuals: capital gains of, 35-36, 62, 63-69, 73*n*, 81-86, 94, 95, 97, 106-7, 227; net losses of, 36; taxation of, 43, 45, 51

Inflation, and increments to capital, 37, 47, 210-11

Installment payments, *vs.* rent, 25*n*

Installment sales of assets. 41-42. 73. 127. 181

Interest adjustment: under roll-over, 204, 219; under cumulative averaging, 185-88, 190, 204, 214, 216-17, 228

Interest income, of gains recipients, 81

Interest rate: fluctuations in, 47; secular shifts in, 211

Intergenerational equity, and the tax structure, 44

Internal Revenue Code, 1954, 5, 10, 12-13, 15, 17-18, 18*n*, 20, 22, 24, 24*n*, 25*n*, 26*n*, 27, 29, 93, 155*n*

Internal Revenue Service, Form 1040, Schedule D, 234-36

Interspousal transfers, 162, 189